The Portland GuideBook

Linda Lampman & Julie Sterling

The Writing Works, Inc.
Mercer Island, Washington

Library of Congress Cataloging in Publication Data

Lampman, Linda, 1936-
    The Portland guidebook.

    Includes index.
    1. Portland, Or.—Description—Guide-books.
I. Sterling, Julie, 1929-   joint author.
II. Title.
F884.P8L35   917.95'45   76-21789
ISBN 0-916076-02-4

Published by The Writing Works, Inc.
            7438 S. E. 40th Street
            Mercer Island, Washington 98040
Library of Congress Catalog Card Number: 76-21789
International Standard Book Number: 0-916076-02-4
Manufactured in the United States

For Don and for Jack—
but especially for Portland.
Her name will always mean home.

Follow the Accents

⟮ Throughout the book this symbol appears following names or places which are covered elsewhere in the book as well. Refer to the Index for page numbers.

Photo and Illustration Credits

Cover: James Torson—23, 94, 110, 206
Photos: Portland Chamber of Commerce—viii, 6, 12, 86, 93, 151, 164, 169, 180, 203
David Falconer—152
U. S. Forest Service—136
Sketches: John Reed—115, 165
Maps: Jack Pierce—Inside Front & Back Covers, 30, 102, 107, 170, 177
Tri-Met—90

Acknowledgments

This guide would not have been compiled without the cooperation of the businesses and agencies mentioned in its various sections. We wish to express our special thanks to them for helping make this the most comprehensive book of this nature available on Portland.

Thanks also to Doug Baker, Ed Goetzl, Tom McAllister, Bill Mulflur, and Andy Rocchia of the *Oregon Journal* and to Bill and Jane Hilliard, Ted Mahar, and John Wendeborn of *The Oregonian* for assistance in their special fields; to Tri-Met for its Fareless Square maps; to the Portland Chamber of Commerce for excellent resource material; to Gail Meredith of the Bureau of Parks and Recreation for strict attention to infinite detail; to Bob Cramer, master of minutiae; and to T.E. Hogg, sports consultant.

About the Authors

Linda Lampman McIsaac and Julie Courteol Sterling met when both joined *The Oregonian* staff within two weeks in 1960.

Linda comes by her writing talents from her mother, Evelyn Sibley Lampman, author of 40 books for young people. Her grandfather was Ben Hur Lampman, poet laureate of Oregon. At *The Oregonian* she was a general assignment reporter. She is the mother of two boys, part-time veterinarian to her farm animals, and public school volunteer in West Linn. Before *The Oregonian* Linda worked in public relations for the Georgia-Pacific Corp. She has also done PR assignments for the Oregon Historical Society. She is married to Jack L. McIsaac, an executive of the Pacific Power and Light Co.

Julie was also a reporter, first covering police and political news for *The Evanston Review* and then clubs for *The Oregonian.* Along with researching and writing *The Portland GuideBook*, she promotes good public education in Portland as a full-time volunteer. She has three children and is married to Donald J. Sterling, Jr., editor of the *Oregon Journal.*

The authors continue their collaboration as children's book review editors for *The Sunday Oregonian.*

CONTENTS

Sightseeing 1
  Viewpoints 3
  Some Parks and Gardens 5
  Museums and Other VIPs 12
  Guided Tours 29
Restaurants 41
Entertainment 51
  Theater 51
  Music 53
  After Dark 55
  Electronics 58
Shopping 59
  Antiques 59
  Books 60
  Bakeries 61
  Cooking Supplies 62
  Crafts 63
  Gift Shops 65
  Gourmet Shops 66
  Imports 67
  Men's Specialty Shops 68
  Nurseries 68
  Toys 70
  Women's Apparel 71
  Shopping Centers and Special Spots 71
  Thrifty Places to Shop 74
  Back Road Bargains 80
Transportation 87
Places to Stay 95
Walking Tours 101

Park Blocks-PSU-Portland Center   101
Old Town   105
Sports and Recreation   111
Spectator Sports   111
Bicycling   114
Boating   118
Fishing   123
Golf   127
Hiking   132
Jogging and Track   140
Skiing   142
Tennis   150
Parks   153
Art   155
Art in Public Places   157
Getting Away From It All   163
Oregon Coast   163
Mt. Hood   168
Willamette Valley   173
Covered Bridges   177
Bits and Oddments   181
Annual Events   181
Name Dropping   185
Children   189
Senior Citizens   194
Schools   195
Publications   197
Weather   198
Historic Landmarks   199
Telephone Numbers   207
Index   211

PREFACE

NATIVE PORTLANDER Jim Torson, who was commissioned to do the cover art for *The Portland GuideBook*, also provided the inside drawings of downtown Portland scenes and Old Town buildings from his portfolio. Jim served in the U.S. Marine Corps' combat art program before becoming a graphic artist in Portland about five years ago. His courtroom drawings have been seen on KATU (Channel 2).

John Reed, the gentle soul whose pen and ink drawings reflect his views of Portland in this book, has taken the time to smell the flowers.

A renaissance man whose day includes laughter, Reed is a successful lobbyist for a large Oregon-based firm. But, his dream is to sail his own crab boat out of Lincoln City. "I don't think there are many crabs out of Lincoln City, but that is fine since they scare me anyway," he admits.

His sketches can be seen at Zillah, Wash., at "The Picket Fence," where he has converted his father's turn of the century pharmacy into a gift shop and antique store. The little town, 20 miles south of Yakima, is happy to welcome its native son home again, if only for weekends.

Photographer David Falconer uses his camera as Carl Sandburg used his pen, to capture the many moments which bring America alive.

From sunrise over Mt. Hood to a single tear on the sticky face of a tired six year old, no detail escapes the sensitive Falconer eye.

Portland is Dave Falconer's home town, and although he spent a week at the White House as a personal guest of President Gerald Ford, he remains a hometown boy. Some of his best shots have been captured on his way to and from work when he spots a moment too good to allow time to steal. His camera has caught and held the essence of the city for all of us, who from time to time forget to look up, look down, or even see at all.

SIGHTSEEING

Places To Visit—Things To See

A FAVORITE PORTLAND JOKE tells of the man living on the west side of the Willamette River who is saving his money so that he can bring his mother over from the east side.

Even if he does, she probably won't like it because east siders love their friendly and spacious neighborhoods just as much as west siders admire their glittering downtown and the array of homes which climb the west hills like stairsteps.

Eleven bridges tie Portland's more populous east side to her more affluent west side like shoelaces; still, the city is an east side-west side town.

Unlike Gaul's three parts, Portland street addresses are divided into five parts: southwest, northwest, southeast, northeast, and north. The river divides east from west; Burnside Street divides NE from SE and NW from SW; and Williams Avenue, on the east side of the river, divides N from NE. Unless you watch directional designations you may find yourself on the right street but on the wrong side of the river.

Portland's bridges, from north to south, are St. Johns (a suspension bridge and Portland's most beautiful), Five Point One (a railroad bridge 5.1 miles north of Union Station), Fremont (the newest), Broadway, Steel, Burnside, Morrison, Hawthorne, Marquam, Ross Island, and Sellwood.

Major suburban areas ringing Portland are Beaverton and Lake Oswego (SW) and Gresham, Milwaukie, and Oregon City (SE).

Dunthorpe, an unincorporated area between Portland and Lake Oswego, generally rates as the most exclusive place to live. Its fine homes are so well hidden behind

1

lush Pacific Northwest greenery you barely see much of them. In its presewer days Dunthorpe was known as the "land of septic tanks and social pretentions."

Portland is a major seaport but that is not the reason for its name. It might have been named Boston. In 1845 two early settlers, Francis W. Pettygrove from Maine and A.L. Lovejoy from Boston, flipped a penny for the right to name their townsite. Pettygrove won and chose the name of the largest city in his home state.

Either name was appropriate because sea captains from New England figured prominently in the early settlement of the pioneer trading center. Portland still reflects a conservative view attributed by many to those founding New Englanders who recognized the value of the site near the Willamette's confluence with the Columbia River as a fresh-water haven for traders.

Today, Portland attracts large freighters through her network of bridges almost to the heart of downtown that's 110 miles from the Pacific Ocean.

Portland is the hub of Oregon's far-flung timber and agricultural interests. Ranchers in cowboy boots come from east of the mountains to buy and sell. Portland is also the cultural center of the state, although Salem, 47 miles to the south, is Oregon's capital.

Portland's metropolitan population in 1974 totaled 1,071,500, with the city accounting for 372,200. The city is located mainly in Multnomah County but its metropolitan area includes Clackamas and Washington Counties to the south and west and Clark County, Wash., across the Columbia River to the north.

Because of persistant rain in western Oregon, Oregonians are known as webfoots.

A tongue-in-cheek campaign to keep people from moving to the state by spreading the word about the rain has only heightened interest in Oregon. Ex-Gov. Tom McCall was chief promoter. (You can see him, by the way, as a news commentator on Portland television—KATU, Channel 2.)

The rain didn't matter when surveyors for a "Quality of Life" study of 243 communities in the U.S. ranked Portland at the top among large cities. Survey categories included health and education, environment, and political, social, and economic conditions.

What most outsiders don't know is that eastern Oregon is as dry as western Oregon is wet.

Viewpoints

To get a general impression of Portland, try different viewpoints on its many hills for a varied perspective of the city.

Northwest

Pittock Acres Park—3229 NW Pittock Dr. Pittock Acres Park and its Pittock Mansion overlook the geography of Portland from 1000 feet up. In view are four snow-capped Cascade mountain peaks—Hood, Adams, St. Helens and Rainier—as well as Portland's port and industrial districts, downtown business center and residential neighborhoods to the east and southwest. Pittock Acres is part of a 5,000-acre 6-park system extending nine miles across Portland's west hills. Part of this system, maintained by the city's park bureau, is Forest Park, said to be the largest wilderness-type park within any city's limits in the U.S. It is laced with hiking trails and dotted with picnic sites.

To get there: By car, travel west on West Burnside to NW Barnes; turn right to NW Irving; turn right on Irving to park entrance; turn right again and follow signs. By bus—no close service.

Southwest

Washington Park—Among the many vistas and views in Washington Park, the outlook to the east from the International Rose Test Garden is the most sensational. Mountains provide the backdrop for riotous color when roses are at the peak of their bloom—June and September.

To get there: Travel west on W. Burnside past 23rd to the Zoo-Rose Garden marker. At Tichner, turn left; turn right on Kingston and follow signs. The parking area for the Rose Gardens is east of the tennis courts. By bus, take #53 from downtown to 23rd and Burnside. Transfer to the #76 bus, which stops next to Henry Thiele's Restaurant. Get off at Kingston and Fairview and walk down Kingston a block and a half into Washington Park.

Council Crest Park—Highest viewpoint within the city is Council Crest Park, nearly 38 acres of hilltop 1,073 feet above Portland Heights, one of the city's most handsome residential neighborhoods. To the southwest, notice the burgeoning suburban neighborhoods of the Tualatin Valley.

To get there: Travel south on SW Broadway to Broadway Drive which winds uphill to a spider intersection which includes SW Greenway; turn left on Greenway and follow the signs to the Council Crest viewpoint at the foot of the radio transmission towers on the hilltop. By bus, take #51 to Council Crest.

Southeast

Mt. Tabor Park—Mt. Tabor, east of SE 60th between Yamhill and Division, is believed to be the only extinct volcano inside a city's limits within the continental United States. An outdoor amphitheater occupies the north end of the crater. (If you use the rest room there, don't miss the architecture.)

To get there: From downtown, cross the Morrison Bridge to SE Belmont; continue east to SE 69th; turn right. Follow a winding road to the park. By bus, board #21 going east on SW Yamhill at 10th, Park, or 6th, downtown. Get off at east end of Mt. Tabor Park near SE 69th.

Willamette National Cemetery and Mt. Scott—A sweeping view of downtown, the Willamette and Columbia Rivers, and mountains to the north and east is your reward for driving to Willamette National Cemetery, which straddles the Multnomah-Clackamas County line southeast of the city. The cemetery, which some call the Arlington of the west, includes an amphitheater where Memorial Day services are held annually. Nearby are Mt. Scott (elevation 1,083 feet) and Top O' Scott Golf Course.

To get there: Take U.S. 30—I-80N east to NE 82nd; travel south on 82nd to SE Flavel; turn left (east) and follow signs to cemetery. By bus, no service.

Northeast

Rocky Butte (Joseph Wood Hill Park)—The stone viewing platform on top of this Portland hill is a familiar

landmark along the route to the airport. Another landmark is a flashing airplane beacon. Since radar obsoleted
the beacon as a navigational aid, it serves no purpose
other than as a reminder of the pre-jet era in flying.

To get there: Drive east on I-80N to the SE 82nd exit;
turn right (north) on 82nd; at Fremont, turn right (east),
past the gates of Judson Baptist College, and follow Fremont to the park. By bus, take #40, get off at Fremont and
walk 8 blocks to park.

North

Mocks Crest—Look down on an excellent view of
Portland's busy Willamette River harbor, the Port of
Portland's dry docks, and the industrial area on Swan
Island.

To get there: Take I-5 north to Portland Blvd. exit;
turn left (west) on Portland Blvd.; turn right on N.
Willamette and follow it to the viewpoint just east of the
University of Portland campus. By bus, take #1 and get
off at the east end of the University's campus.

Some Parks and Gardens

Washington Park—One of Portland's oldest, it is 145
acres of views, walks, and winding roads and includes the
International Rose Test Gardens, Japanese Garden, Zoo
Railway station, tennis courts, statuary, play equipment,
picnic facilities, and groves of tall Douglas firs. Wear
walking shoes to tour the park.

The Park Place entrance (end of Park Place near Vista)
is marked by a formal garden and the Lewis and Clark
column erected for the Lewis and Clark Exposition of
1905.

Not far up the one-way road which begins at the formal
garden, you'll see atop a jagged rock one of Portland's
most moving pieces of sculpture, a bronze statue of
Sacajawea, the Indian guide for Lewis and Clark, dis-
coverers of the transcontinental route to Oregon. While on
the trail, Sacajawea had the baby seen slung on her back.
His father was an expedition interpreter.

Immediately after passing Sacajawea, take a fork to the
right up a confusing spiral road that takes you (don't give

up) past another piece of fine old Lewis and Clark-inspired statuary, "The Coming of the White Man," which depicts the reaction of two natives to the arrival of Lewis and Clark. Travel down the spiral to a five-point intersection. Take the marked road to the Rose Gardens; parking is provided at the south end. Other parking is accessible only to travelers approaching the gardens from Kingston.

June and September are the best times to view the hundreds of varieties of roses, all labeled. You'll find new ideas for your rose garden or inspiration to plant a new rose garden.

Stroll down through the three terraces of roses to Queen's Walk where plaques set in the walk name Portland Rose Festival Queens as far back as 1907. An ex-

cerpt from another plaque sums it up: "One is nearer God's heart in a garden than anywhere else on earth."

Adjoining the garden to the south is a Shakespeare Garden planted with flower and shrubs mentioned in the bard's plays. To the north is a sunken garden theater where music and theater productions are staged by the Portland Bureau of Parks and Recreation in summer. Call for a brochure on the summer schedule (248-4315). These attractions are free and so popular that parking can be difficult. Take a shuttle bus from Henry Thiele's Restaurant at NW 23rd and W. Burnside. The buses leave every 15 minutes on concert nights. You may also park at the zoo and ride the Zoo Railway to the park.

West of the Rose Garden beyond the tennis courts, the *Japanese Garden* features five traditional garden forms. Admission is $1.50 for adults; 75 cents for students under 18; children under 6, free. Special rates for organized groups.

The garden is open during the summer, spring, and fall months but closed from the end of Oct. until April 1. Spring and fall schedule: Sat. and Sun., noon-6 p.m.; Tues.-Fri., 10 a.m.-4 p.m. Summer schedule: Tues.-Sat., 10 a.m.-6 p.m.; Sun., 10 a.m.-8 p.m. The garden is closed Mondays except on national holidays when it is open from 10 a.m.-6 p.m. Shuttlebus service from the parking facilities to the garden is provided on weekends during the spring and fall and every day in the summer.

Annual memberships in the Japanese Garden Society of Oregon, which has developed the garden, are $10 for families and $5 for senior citizens and students.

Washington Park is the only station stop for the Portland Zoo Railway. During the summer months passengers may board the zoo trains at the Washington Park terminal. Ticket price of $2.50 for adults and $1.25 for youth includes zoo admission (Portland residents, $1.75 and 75 cents). Below the terminal is an attractive covered picnic area.

To get there: Take SW Jefferson west from downtown; turn right (north) on SW 18th to Salmon; turn left (west) and continue up the hill, jogging right and then left (west) to Park Place which leads to the entrance. By bus, take #53 from downtown; get off at 23rd and Burnside. Transfer to #76; get off at Kingston and Fairview, and walk down Kingston a block and a half into Washington Park.

For the intrepid in small cars, try a one-way scenic approach to Washington Park on an unmarked road to the left off W. Burnside, just west of the shopping center at 23rd.

Hoyt Arboretum—400 SW Fairview Blvd. (228-1223). Pick up a self-guided tour brochure at the office before you begin your visit to this wooded showplace, which boasts one of the nation's largest collections of conifers, many of them labeled. Through the 214 acres are seven miles of trails but don't panic; the self-guided tour is only a mile long.

To get there: Take W. Burnside west; pass SW 23rd and turn south at Tichner; climb hill to Kingston and turn right; turn right on Fairview and continue to the Arboretum. By bus, take #62 to the Zoo-OMSI-Forestry Center complex. Cross to the north side of the Western Forestry Center. A trail marker indicates the path to the arboretum.

Pittock Wildlife Sanctuary and Audubon House—53rd Drive & Cornell Road (292-6855). Maintained by the Oregon Audubon Society, this 25-acre wilderness area is accessible by trail from the Pittock Mansion. A natural setting for bird and animal life, the sanctuary protects raccoons and occasional large animals plus more than 100 different birds. The Audubon House, which is open to the public certain days (phone for specifics) displays exhibits. No admission charge.

Across Cornell Road from the Sanctuary is *Macleay Park*, part of the wilderness network which includes Forest Park. Macleay is only one of the legacies left Portland by one of its most colorful founding fathers, Donald Macleay. This imaginative and innovative Scot was a shipper by trade. Macleay gave the 107 acres of forested land for Macleay Park with the provision that "no wheeled vehicles" be allowed—ever. A good system of trails—15 miles of them—is contained within the boundaries of Macleay and Forest Park.

To get there: Take W. Burnside west to SW 23rd; turn right on 23rd and travel north to Lovejoy (the streets climb the alphabet on this route so Lovejoy follows Kearney); turn left (west) and continue to Cornell Rd. Follow Cornell to 53rd Drive. Bus #53 puts you near Forest Park Headquarters and within hiking distance (4.6 miles) of the sanctuary and Macleay. Get off near NW

29th & Thurman and take steps down from the east end of the Thurman St. viaduct.

South Park Blocks—One block east of SW 10th, this strip of green extends from Salmon for six blocks south to and through the Portland State University (PSU) campus all the way to the freeway.

Anchored at the north end by the prestigious Arlington Club, a private men's club, and at the south by PSU, the South Park Blocks (not to be confused with the North Park Blocks on the other side of Burnside) provide an interlude in the downtown scene.

The South Park Blocks have changed dramatically since Portland State University spilled out of the vacated high school where it began and into many buildings both old and new in the surrounding area. Streets that formerly crossed the Park Blocks at their south end were closed to form a stage for the campus with pleasing effects. Viewed from the hills above, Portland State and the South Park Blocks exhibit an old-world university atmosphere in the busy downtown scene.

A walk in the Park Blocks with its roses, statuary, museums, churches, and university is well worth the time. Downtown office workers brown-bag-it amidst the roses during the summer and fall months.

To get there: Ride Tri-Met free in Fareless Square or walk from your downtown location.

American Rhododendron Society Test Garden— SE 28th near SE Woodstock. During April or May, no visitor to Portland or resident would dare miss a visit to these opulent gardens filled with fat rhododendrons and their relative, the delicate azalea. Catch the azaleas at their peak in April; in May, the rhododendrons. The colony of ducks inhabiting the lake adds a touch of magic. More than 2,000 rhododendron plants are maintained by the American Rhododendron Society's Portland Chapter. New residents visit the garden to choose their favorites before shopping at a nursery. This visit can be combined with a walk on the Reed College campus (a classic) just across SE 28th.

To get there: From downtown, travel south to the Ross Island Bridge, cross it, and get on McLoughlin Blvd. going south. At the Bybee underpass, turn east to 28th. Turn left on 28th and continue to the garden. By bus, take #28 (Union Manor) to SE 32nd and Woodstock.

Walk four blocks west (ahead) on Woodstock to Eastmoreland Park and entrance to garden.

Westmoreland Park—SE 22nd & Bybee, across McLoughlin Blvd. from the Rhododendron Garden. For spur-of-the-moment summer recreation the park, site of Portland's first municipal airport in 1920, now serves as a popular "port" for model plane flying and yachting, fly casting, bowling on the green, bocci ball, softball, and baseball. The fly casting pool is lighted.

To get there: Follow directions to Rhododendron Garden, turning west at Bybee instead of east. By bus take #28 (Union Manor) and get off on Bybee near the park.

Laurelhurst Park—SE 39th & Oak. An outing designed to cure the "I-can't-stand-the-kids-another-minute" syndrome, winter or summer, is to Laurelhurst Park to feed the ducks. This 33-acre park includes a lake and many playground and recreation facilities. It is part of one of Portland's fine old east side neighborhoods.

To get there: Cross the Burnside Bridge, going east, and follow E. Burnside to SE 39th; drive south one block. By bus, take #20.

The Grotto—Off the rush of Sandy Blvd. traffic at 8804 NE Skidmore (254-7371), are 58 acres of peaceful solitude run by the Order of Servants to Mary (Servites). Known as the Grotto, this shrine to all mothers includes chapel, wild-flower-lined stations of the cross, and the magnificent grotto itself which is the scene for outdoor masses offered Sundays at noon from May through September. An elevator on the lower levels carries visitors to the heights where the monastery and gardens are located.

To get there: By bus, board #14 east from any downtown location to Grotto entrance.

Kelley Point Park—In extreme North Portland, at the point where the Columbia River and the Willamette Rivers join is Kelley Point Park, a creation of the Port of Portland, now maintained by the city. It is named for Hall J. Kelley, a New Englander who made an unsuccessful attempt to colonize the "point" in the 1830s. View passing ocean-going ships here while enjoying the park's vast meadow, many beaches, wooded areas, and good swimming. This is a very popular park on hot summer weekends.

To get there: Take I-5N to North Marine Drive exit; travel west to Suttle Road, and follow signs for 4 miles to park. No bus service.

Outside of Portland to the south, but close enough to be considered city retreats are:

Tryon Creek State Park—Between Lewis and Clark College and Lake Oswego (Nature Center, 636-4550). Tryon, the state's first metropolitan state park, is a tribute to the determination of two Lake Oswego women who led a campaign to save the area from residential development. Its 600 acres of wilderness offer natural quiet for hikers, cyclists, horseback riders (no horses for rent), and nature lovers. The first park in Oregon to employ a full-time naturalist, Tryon's nature center is open daily, except Mon. and Tues.; be sure to try its unusual drinking fountain. Tours are conducted at 1 and 3 p.m. on weekends and by request during the week. Phone for up-to-date information. Tryon Creek, home of much wildlife, even beaver, is part of the park scene.

To get there: Take SW Macadam south toward Lake Oswego to Riverside Drive; travel on Riverside to SW Terwilliger at the north edge of Lake Oswego; turn right to park on your left. By bus, take #38 from downtown on SW 5th. Get off where the bus leaves Terwilliger and forks onto Boones Ferry Road. Follow the bike path about 1½ miles to the Nature Center. Bus service on weekday peak hours only. Or take #39, also from SW 5th, and get off at Iron Mountain Road. Walk one block to Terwilliger, then north about a mile to the Nature Center.

Camassia Natural Area—West Linn. Of interest to geologists and naturalists, this area is an excellent record of the Missoula flood at the end of the Ice Age—a flood so vast that it extended all the way from Montana to Oregon. The 22½-acre area is preserved by the Nature Conservancy (228-9561). Call for directions.

Clackamette Park, just off SE McLoughlin, under the bridge at Oregon City. This well-marked park offers picnicking facilities, boat launching, and a beach for swimming. It is located at the confluence of the Willamette and Clackamas Rivers—thus the name.

To get there: Follow SE McLoughlin south to Oregon City (via the Ross Island Bridge if you're downtown). By bus, take #33 or #34 from downtown.

Museums and Other VIPs
(Very Important Places)

Three of our VIPs cluster around a single large parking lot on a west hills site which once was the county poor farm and is now known as the ***Zoo-OMSI-Forestry Center complex***.

On the hill immediately north of the complex is the Hoyt Arboretum.¶ At the west edge of the parking lot is the Hoyt Pitch and Putt Golf Course.¶

To get to the complex: Drive west on SW Jefferson or SW Clay. Either route leads to SW Canyon Road (U.S. 26). Follow Canyon to the Zoo-OMSI-Forestry Center exit. (The floral clock in the formal garden near the entrance is a relic of the Oregon Centennial Exposition of 1959 and really keeps time.) By bus, take #62, the "Discovery" Express, from downtown. The express also serves the Beaverton area.

Oregon Museum of Science and Industry and Harry C. Kendall Planetarium—(248-5900). Hatching

chicks that children can handle, live rabbits (also pettable), a walk-in heart, an authentic ship's bridge, an operating beehive, and reptile exhibits fascinate the youngest members of the family. Others can check out the viewer-operated electricity exhibits, 22 exhibits on fluid mechanics, Oregon fossils, and many other more sophisticated displays. An excellent gift shop sells everything from simulated sea-water crystals to telescopes.

Daily shows are presented in the *Harry C. Kendall Planetarium* and in an auditorium where the "transparent lady" tells the story of the human body. A new planetarium program is produced every three months with dramatic flair. The facility projects approximately 5,000 stars, planets, sun, and moon.

Admission to OMSI: Adults, $1.50; students, 75 cents; senior citizens, 50 cents; members free; group rates on request. Membership in OMSI is $20, $10, and $6, for families, individuals, and students, respectively. Membership privileges include special rates for OMSI's extensive educational programs and classes for adults and children as well as free admission to the exhibits. OMSI also conducts summer science programs at Camp Hancock in Central Oregon.

OMSI is open every day except Christmas.

Summer hours (mid-June through mid-Sept.): Mon.-Thurs. 9 a.m.-6 p.m.; Fri.-Sun. 9 a.m.-9 p.m. Planetarium shows daily at 11 a.m. and 1, 2, 3, and 4 p.m.; additional shows, 7:30 p.m. Fri.-Sun.

Winter hours (mid-Sept. through mid-June): Mon.-Thurs. 9 a.m.-5 p.m.; Fri. 9 a.m.-9 p.m.; Sat.-Sun. 9 a.m.-6 p.m. Planetarium shows, Mon.-Thurs. 1:30, 3:30 p.m.; Fri. 1:30, 3:30, 7:30 p.m.; Sat.-Sun. 11 a.m. and 1, 2, 3, and 4 p.m.

Portland Zoological Gardens—(226-1561) How about testing your reflexes against a mandrill? Or buying a movie ticket for a chimp? These and many other "teaching machines" are in operation at the Portland Zoological Gardens for the pleasure of the animals and the public and, to some degree, for scientific study.

The machines, a unique feature of the Portland zoo, take the routine out of a visit there. But zoo buffs claim the machines prevent boredom among the animals. Teaching machines are in operation at the gibbons, Diana monkey, and mandrill cages. (In addition, visitors can "speak" sign language to some of the chimps.) Other teaching apparatus is operated by the polar bears, seals, and wolves.

Portland's zoo made headlines in 1962 when its Belle became the first elephant in captivity in the Western Hemisphere in 44 years to give birth. The baby, Packy, is still at the zoo, following in the footsteps of his father, the late Thonglaw, who sired 15 elephants there. In summer, you can take a ride on an elephant—with two friends if you wish—for $1 per person.

A free children's zoo, with contact area, and the Zoo Railway, which travels a winding route to a scenic viewpoint in Washington Park, are other features. A children's theater performs on weekends in winter; daily in summer. You can buy food and gifts in the Elephant's Trunk.

The zoo is open every day—even Christmas—from 10 a.m. to dusk.

Two rate structures apply. Residents: adults, 75 cents; children and seniors, 25 cents. Nonresidents: adults, $1.50; children and seniors, 75 cents.

Family and individual memberships in the Portland Zoological Society are available for $15 and $8, respectively. Members receive free zoo admission and a subscription to *Zoo News.*

The Zoo Railway, which travels between the zoo and a quaint canopied station at Washington Park, operates all summer and in winter when weather permits (and at Halloween to give spook rides). Regular ticket prices are adults, $1, children, 50 cents.

Classes are held for adults and children. Call for information.

Western Forestry Center—(228-1367) A 70-foot talking tree and a simulated forest fire dramatize Oregon's No. 1 industry at the Western Forestry Center, a building as architecturally pleasant as it is interesting.

A moving model sawmill, plywood plant, and pulp and paper plant are among the automated exhibits. Outside is a logging locomotive which children can explore inside and out.

The $6 million complex replaced a much-loved giant log cabin museum built for the Lewis and Clark World's Fair held in Northwest Portland in 1905. The old building burned in 1964.

The educational program of the Forestry Center features excellent film showings for groups as small as 10—call the center ahead for arrangements; a landscaping course in the spring and summer; an international forestry lecture series in the spring; and summer tours to tree nurseries, logging operations, and the Redwoods. Woodcarving classes are also offered. For additional information, call the education coordinator. Wooden gift items are available at the Forest Store.

Hours are 10 a.m.-5 p.m. seven days a week. Admission: adults, $1; seniors and students, 50 cents, children under 7, with parent, free. Members are admitted free. Annual memberships are $12.50 for families and $7.50 for individual adults; $5, students, teachers.

North of the Zoo-OMSI-Forestry Center complex on the other side of West Burnside is the *Pittock Mansion* (248-4469). Fate of this French Renaissance mansion, with its fine marbles, cast bronze, hardwoods, and classic plaster work, was uncertain before it and the 46-acre Pittock Acres Park on which it stands were purchased by the City of Portland in 1964. The mansion is now one of Portland's showplace sights because of its fine examples of local craftsmanship.

Rooms are decorated in the style of the period (1909-1914) when the mansion was built by Henry L. Pittock, the founder of *The Oregonian* newspaper. Many fine furnishings have been donated to the mansion by longtime Portland residents and greatly enrich the decor.

Children who visit the Pittock Mansion have to restrain themselves from sliding down the graceful curved bannisters and from turning on Mr. Pittock's private shower, a spectacular example of plumbing "sculpture" which even includes a kidney spray.

Displays of collections and curiosities rotate in the exhibit room. At Christmas time the entire mansion is festively decorated, each year by a different ethnic or social group.

Admission is $1 for adults, 50 cents for students, and 25 cents for children with lower rates on Fridays. Members of the Pittock Mansion Society gain free admission. The grounds are open daily without charge. The mansion is open most days of the week, depending on the season. Phone before you go.

To get there: Follow directions given previously for Pittock park.

Important places to see in the downtown area, moving from south to north are:

Portland Center—a 54-block area south of the Civic Auditorium and SW Market. A city within a city, this glamorous shopping-office-residential complex replaced "Old South Portland," fondly remembered by the city's Jewish and Italian populations as one of their neighborhoods. In the stair-stepped Lovejoy Fountain, you can watch 2-year-olds and a few 20-year-olds splash on hot days. To the north two blocks is **Pettygrove Park**. The fountain and park honor the two Portlanders who named the city.

To get there: Ride free on Tri-Met to edge of Fareless Square at 3rd & Clay (Civic Auditorium and Forecourt Fountain). Walk south through the scenic corridor to SW 2nd and Harrison.

Civic Auditorium and Forecourt Fountain—SW 3rd & Clay, (248-4335, business office, 226-2876, box office).

A delightful contrast: The auditorium, stage for the Portland Opera Association and the Oregon Symphony Orchestra, stands face-to-face with the Forecourt, dubbed "The People's Fountain," a collection of waterfalls cascading over 4,000 tons of concrete. The Forecourt fountain was dedicated in 1970 to complement the newly rebuilt Civic Auditorium.

Because reveling youth spend as much time in the water as out of it in the summer months, the Forecourt is patrolled by lifeguards in the summer.

The Civic Auditorium seats 3,004. Paul Veneklasen, who designed the acoustics for the Seattle Opera House and the Los Angeles Music Center, designed its acoustical shell, the ceiling over the seating area, and the sound system.

Backstage tours of the auditorium can be arranged by calling 248-4335—but are not given during performances or on Sat. and Sun. The tours include a discussion of the auditorium's unusual sound system and visit large and small dressing rooms and other elaborate backstage facilities.

To get there: Follow instructions for Portland Center and Lovejoy Fountain.

Benjamin Franklin Museum—Benjamin Franklin Plaza, SW 1st & Jefferson. This little museum of Franklin artifacts in one of Portland's newest downtown buildings occupies a portion of the Benjamin Franklin Federal Savings and Loan Assn.'s Plaza Branch. Principal piece of art is the porcelain sculpture, "Declaration of Independence," depicting Franklin, Thomas Jefferson, and nine others. Three original signatures of Benjamin Franklin are displayed along with authentic reproductions of several Franklin inventions. Your eyes will blink when you view the custom-made carpeting, featuring a medallion similar to the presidential seal.

The red brick Franklin Plaza building was intended to be the headquarters of a wood products company. The recession hit, the company could not afford its new "house," and thrifty Ben took over.

To get there: Walk from downtown or ride Tri-Met free in Fareless Square.

First National Center—Between SW 3rd & 5th and Jefferson & Columbia (225-2111). For tours (five or more persons), call one day in advance (225-2361). Despite complaints that "it bisected my view of Mt. Hood," First National Center Tower, Portland's tallest building at 40 stories, has become a downtown mainstay. The center, designed by Charles Luckman Associates, who did the new Madison Square Garden in New York, includes two restaurants, a sandwich and coffee shop and take-out food spot (Tower Tote) on the 28th floor, and an elegant dining room, Restaurant 21, on the 21st, both open to the public, but not for late dining. A collection of over 400 paintings, sculptures, and prints is on view throughout the building.

To get there: Walk from downtown locations or travel by bus in Fareless Square.

City Hall—1220 SW 5th (248-3511 or 248-4210 for tours). Portland's unpretentious City Hall, filling the block bounded by 4th and 5th and Madison and Jefferson, squats like a mushroom between the First National Bank Tower to the south and the Georgia-Pacific building to the north.

After adjusting to its scale in relation to its high-rise neighbors you'll admire its Renaissance lines, detailed columns, and marble circular inserts. Much renovation inside and out in recent years has enhanced its clean lines.

City Hall was born in controversy. An onion-domed curiosity was planned for the site, but the city fathers decided it was too costly for the times and abandoned it even though it had been completed to the first floor. The present Whidden and Lewis building was completed in 1894 and has been remodeled several times.

If you tour the building, you will learn that before 1929 its inhabitants included 250 stuffed animals in glass display cases. (What is left of those displays can be viewed at the Children's Museum.)

Tours of City Hall should be scheduled a week in advance and an absolute minimum of two days ahead. Suggested tour days are Wed. and Thurs. when visitors can combine their tour with a visit to a city council meeting. The council of five commissioners meets Wed. at 9:30 a.m. and 2 p.m. and Thurs. at 2 p.m. Visitors are encouraged to attend.

To get there: Ride Tri-Met free in Fareless Square or walk from downtown.

Multnomah County Courthouse—Between SW Salmon & Main and 4th & 5th (248-3511). A full judicial smorgasbord from arraignments to trials and from district court to circuit court is housed in this classic building. The Multnomah County Board of Commissioners and many county services are headquartered here. The building was constructed in 1913 and has been remodeled extensively since—not always for the better.

If you're interested in what trials are "playing," consult a schedule of cases posted in the administrator's office room on the second floor of the courthouse.

The two "showcase" courtrooms in the building are rooms 512 and 544, both good examples of old-fashioned judicial elegance. Notice the portrait of John Marshall above the bench in 512. Wander around the fifth floor and walk in some of the new courtrooms for contrast. Room 526 is a courtroom "in the round."

One floor up, in room 680, the Board of County Commissioners meets Tues. and Thurs. mornings at 9:30 a.m. Citizens are encouraged to attend.

The courthouse is open Mon.-Fri. from 9 a.m.-5 p.m. Visitors are welcome to sit in on most trials and hearings. Special court tours for school children only can be arranged by calling 248-3457.

To get there: Ride Tri-Met free in Fareless Square or walk from downtown.

Georgia-Pacific Historical Museum—900 SW 5th (222-5561-Ext. 7981). Dinner bell is the euphemism for the "gut hammer" you can ring while touring the Georgia-Pacific Corp.'s historical museum depicting old-time logging days and the story of the modern wood products industry. The museum is located in a tunnel under the street between the 29-story G-P building and its parking garage across SW 4th. Exhibits include life-size dioramas of old logging scenes, tools, a logging cart, and other artifacts as well as photographs. A popular feature is an old movie of logging operations in the Oregon woods more than 50 years ago. Another film describes modern reforestation methods. Tours by school or other special interest groups can be arranged by appointment.

Admission is free. Hours: 10 a.m.-3 p.m., Tues.-Fri.

To get there: Ride Tri-Met free in Fareless Square or walk from downtown.

The Old Church—1422 SW 11th (222-2031). An excellent example of "carpenter gothic," the Old Church, built in 1882-83, was a place of worship until the 1960's when its Baptist congregation moved to a new building. The building was saved by a feverish effort of a few dedicated persons. It is now a historic landmark and is supported by the Old Church Society.

Things you can do at the Old Church, besides just look at it, are: Have your wedding there; attend sack-lunch recitals Wednesdays at noon played on the old organ that came around the horn from Boston in 1883; browse in the thrift shop that helps support the church; or attend a political rally or one of the many other public meetings and festivities held there. Phone for special events calendar.

The church is the oldest standing church structure on its original site in Portland. (The oldest surviving protestant church in Oregon, though no longer on its original site, is considered to be St. John's Episcopal Church, now at the foot of SE Spokane St. at the entrance to Oaks Pioneer Park.)

To get there: Ride Tri-Met free in Fareless Square (#60, #21, come closest) or walk from downtown.

Oregon Historical Society—1230 SW Park Ave. (222-1741). Travel back through the long history of the Oregon

Territory and before via the exhibits and research library at the Oregon Historical Center, open free to the public 10 a.m.-4:45 p.m. Mon.-Sat. and some Sundays.

The Indian life exhibit, the society's most elaborate, is among the long-run displays on the second floor. The main floor is reserved for rotating presentations of current interest and an occasional traveling collection.

Life-size dioramas on the second-floor depict the native American way of life on the coast, at the river bank, on the high plateau, and in the desert at the time the first European and American explorers, trappers, and settlers encountered them. A maritime collection features exquisite ship models. A collection of fine wagon miniatures symbolizes the westward movement by land. An original covered wagon, ready to roll, is also part of the long-run exhibits.

The Oregon Historical Society regional research library on the third floor has open stacks for browsing. The society's collection includes rare and general books, manuscripts, maps, microfilm of scores of newspapers, and more than a million photographs. The Society publishes an outstanding illustrated journal of western history, the *Oregon Historical Quarterly*, which is mailed to its 6,000 members.

Almost as interesting as the central museum, is the Bybee-Howell House, a renovated farm home which the society maintains on Sauvie Island, north of Portland.

In addition, the Society sends traveling Oregon history shows into the public schools and, on request, will supply other groups with a free slide program or, for a rental charge, historical films.

The Trappers Rendezvous, for members only, organizes bus trips to interesting destinations around the state.

Memberships in the Society are $10 for individuals and $15 for families. Among the benefits: a subscription to the *Quarterly*, a newsletter, special travel tours, and a discount on publications and items in the gift store. The gift and bookshop offers everything from Portland guidebooks to the Oregon state stone, the thunderegg. Main entrance to the society is on SW Park, just north of Jefferson.

To get there: Ride Tri-Met free in Fareless Square (#60, #21 come closest) or walk from downtown.

Portland Art Museum—SW Park & Madison in South Park Blocks (226-2811). While best known for its outstanding permanent collection of Northwest Coast Indian Art, the Portland Art Museum merits periodic visitations whether to catch the latest exhibit, to rent a painting, buy an unusual gift, attend a class, or view an offering by the Northwest Film Study Center.¶

For the exhibits, guides are available if desired. Other permanent collections include Renaissance, European, African, Oriental, and pre-Columbian art, and the largest single collection of works by C.S. Price. Main floor exhibits change frequently and often include examples of the lively work of the Pacific Northwest's colony of artists. Don't miss the museum's outdoor sculpture mall, a memorable fresh air experience with its waterworks, intended to drown out street noise, and its huge metal "donut." A major work in the mall is "Dual Form" by Barbara Hepworth. Films, programs, and plays rotate in the museum's attractive Caroline Berg Swann auditorium.

Hours—Gallery: daily, noon-5 p.m.; Fridays, noon-10 p.m. Closed Mon. Library: open Tues.-Fri. Rental Sales Gallery: Tues. and Thurs., noon-5 p.m., and Sun., 2-4 p.m. The museum offers a wide selection of gift items, particularly at Christmas time.

Contribution: adults, $1; students, 50 cents. Members, senior citizens, and children, free. Memberships in the Portland Art Association range from $15 and entitle you to discounts in the gift shop and the monthly calendar.

The Museum Art School offers college-level courses as well as a full array of evening and Saturday classes for adults and children.

To get there: Ride Tri-Met free in Fareless Square (#60, #21, come closest) or walk from downtown.

Central Library (Multnomah County)—SW 10th & Taylor (223-7201). The main building of Multnomah County's excellent public library system occupies a full block facing on SW 10th between Yamhill and Taylor. The Georgian-style structure is one of the finest designs of a noted Portland architect, A.E. Doyle. Passersby may test their knowledge of the names of famous authors and other notable persons which are carved on the exterior and on the benches set in a sidewalk balustrade.

Visitors and residents may use the library's large collections of current and old books, magazines, newspapers, art prints, musical records and tapes, and technical reference material.

The lobby always has an exhibit of literary interest and proudly displays one of the rare elephant folios of John James Audubon's paintings of birds. Free film shows and lectures are regularly scheduled in the library's auditorium. The staff maintains a list of current cultural activities in the Portland area.

For visitors to the city, the Central Library can be a place to catch up with hometown papers, to find address directories for Portland and other cities, and to obtain helpful information. Use of the material in the building is free to all. To borrow material for outside use, you need a library card which is issued free at the library to Multnomah County residents. Nonresidents are charged a fee.

The library system also includes bookmobile service and 16 branch libraries. Hours of the Central Library are Mon.-Thurs., 9 a.m.-9 p.m.; Fri. and Sat., 9 a.m. to 5:30 p.m. It is closed on Sundays, but books may be returned to an outside receptacle at the back of the building on SW 11th.

To get there: Ride Tri-Met free in Fareless Square (#21, 36, 37, 34 come closest) or walk from downtown.

Pioneer Courthouse (and post office)—555 SW Yamhill St. (221-3035, post office). Built between 1869 and 1873, the building now known as the Pioneer Courthouse was the first federal office building in the Pacific Northwest and is now the oldest public building in the region. Originally it housed the U.S. district court and assorted federal offices. After the federal courts were moved to the present Portland Federal Courthouse, on SW Broadway between Main and Madison, in the 1930's, the handsome old building continued in use as a postal station and home for various U.S. government agencies under the name of "The Pioneer Post Office."

An extensive restoration program in the 1970s refurbished the exterior. Its interior was extensively remodeled to provide an elegant Victorian Courtroom on the second floor for the 9th Circuit U.S. Court of Appeals, with adjoining offices for judges. Judges of the U.S. Bankruptcy Court occupy chambers and courtrooms on the third floor. The first floor continues to be occupied by a postal station and federal offices.

The structure, built on a slight rise facing east toward the Willamette River was thought by some to be much too far from the business district—then some six blocks to the northeast (now Old Town)—when it was first erected, but the city grew in its direction. Today, the Pioneer Courthouse is Portland's central landmark on its full block bounded by SW 5th and 6th and Morrison and Yamhill.

Rutherford B. Hayes, the first incumbent U.S. president to visit Portland, took in the view from the building's cupola in 1880, and its grounds have been the site of many public gatherings and demonstrations.

To get there: Ride Tri-Met free in Fareless Square or walk from downtown.

Old Town—formerly "downtown," and generally considered to lie between 1st and 5th on either side of Burnside. Many choice buildings have been restored in

this section of Portland which thrives commercially as well as historically. Other choice buildings have not been restored and await an angel.

Throughout the area are specialty craft shops, antique shops, and quaint restaurants, all intended to tempt the strolling sightseer. Anchoring the southwest boundary of Old Town is, ironically, the brand new *U.S. Bank Plaza* on SW Oak between 5th and 6th. In a nice touch of design, its triangular plaza points the way across an urban vista to the bank's revered old main branch, with its ornate Roman Corinthian columns and bronze front doors, which, unfortunately, can only be seen when the bank is closed. Adjoining the temple-like structure to the north is the old Wells Fargo bank, now office space. Look up and notice the "Wells" inscribed at the top in colorful ornamental work just beneath the balustrade. "Fargo" is similarly inscribed on the north face of the building. Inside the old main branch, built in 1917 and added to in 1924, notice the shiny marble columns, each bearing "U.S." eagles in frieze work at the top, and the elegant coffered ceiling. The bank is maintained exactly as it was built.

In contrast, the Plaza building across the street includes a spacious contemporary street-level galleria (inside mall) offering restaurant and retail space while floors above it contain the bank offices and operations.

Still on the south side of Burnside, at SW 1st and Ankeny, is the prim *Skidmore Fountain* set in place of rounded cobblestones said to have come to Portland as ballast on ships. It is considered to be the hub of Old Town. Across Burnside is more Old Town and also *Chinatown,* which extends as far north as the Steel Bridge.

Portland Police Museum—115 NW 1st (223-9353). One of the newest additions to Old Town is the Portland Police Museum, which serves the dual purpose of historical center and working minipolice precinct. Also located there is a crime prevention unit. Hours are 10 a.m.-3 p.m. weekdays; noon-4 p.m. weekends. Groups and individuals may schedule tours by calling ahead.

Fort Vancouver

Fort Vancouver lies across the Columbia River on the Washington State side (use the Interstate Bridge and follow signs). It marks the center of the old Oregon Country.

The replica of the old fort operated by Dr. John McLoughlin for the Hudson Bay Company represents more than 14 years of research by historians, historical architects, and archeologists to determine how and where the original was built. The reconstruction is on the old site and is part of 89 acres administered by the National Park Service.

Diggings have uncovered bits of McLoughlin's china, among other artifacts, all of which are on display at the National Park Service Fort Headquarters. To arrange a tour, call (206) 696-4041, ext. 221 or you can wander the grounds by yourself.

In addition to the restored fort and its buildings, you will pass Officer's Row, a line of two-story houses on Evergreen Blvd. These homes represent an attempt by the Veteran's Administration to keep the street intact, yet allow it to pay its own way. The homes are rented. The row dates from the days of Indian wars in the west, and it is believed to be one of three such rows remaining, although 100 were built at various Army posts in the west before the Civil War.

The oldest house on the row, that of U.S. Grant, was built in 1849, and the newest is a field officers' home built in 1905. Among those who lived to make their mark in history as former residents were George Custer, Phil Sheridan, and the later generals George Marshall and Douglas MacArthur. The U.S. Grant house is open to the public every day but Thursdays from 1-4 p.m. Admission is 50 cents for adults; 25 cents for children.

Sauvie Island

Just north of Portland off U.S. 30, lies Sauvie Island floating serenely on the Columbia River. This pastoral farming area, the largest island in the Columbia, draws up its skirts from the dust of industry and seems to incorporate Mt. Hood into its acreage. A haven for farmers, houseboat owners, and those who just like to do it themselves, Sauvie Island provides a pleasant and secluded day trip for visitors. The dike is a natural for bike trips. Sauvie Island was the headquarters for the now extinct Multnomah Indian tribe.

The island remains ideal for cattle, but it also is a good place for picnicking, fishing, and spending a summer's day. The Department of Fish and Game maintains wild life preserves on the land and several areas are used for dog trails and training.

Commanding a wide view of the river is the *Bybee-Howell House*, administered by the Oregon Historical Society. This restored territorial farmhouse dates back before the Civil War. Open to the public, free of charge from May to the end of September, the restoration proves that all pioneers did not huddle in log cabins.

On the grounds to the rear of the house is a pioneer apple orchard, scions of trees from the Oregon country. Next to the barn is the 100-year-old pear tree—not one of the pears is edible, but each is as large as a quart jar.

Visitors are welcome to see the house at anytime, but the last Saturday of September should be marked on the calendar for the Historical Society's annual "Wintering-In" party. Take a picnic lunch in the morning and spread your cloth on the wide lawns. Local farmers bring in their harvest bounty to be sold, children delight in age-old games and races, and the barn opens its door to sell antiques donated for the occasion.

Cider, made from an old wooden press, proves that the apple trees still fulfill purpose.

Lake Oswego-Oregon City

Macadam Avenue is the easiest route to Lake Oswego and Oregon City, and the old road is shored up by history from start to finish. Passing John's Landing, the newest park on the Willamette Greenway, you will see what merchants have done with an old mattress factory (The Water Tower!) and are doing to return other industrial buildings as well as the river to the people. Condominiums and a boat launch complete the complex at this point with other shopping areas and restaurants to come.

The watery neighborhoods of houseboats along the Willamette at this point represent only one of several such moorings in the Portland area. This particular group celebrates the Christmas season by lighting all the rooftops, chimneys, and porches, giving the Willamette River a special holiday glow.

You will cross *Military Road* along Macadam and the name is justified. Lt. Phil Sheridan and his army used the access from the valley to Fort Vancouver during Indian uprisings.

Lake Oswego is a new community but built upon old foundations. Albert Alonzo Durham named the town in 1861 when he settled there with his sawmill on Sucker Creek (polite society now calls it Oswego Creek). Durham had good reason for his sawmill, for the area was heavily forested and the Portland community was awaiting every board and beam he could cut.

Some 150 Chinese settled where the Bay Roc apartments now rise to dig the many canals necessary to float the lumber to Sucker Lake and to the mill. The canals and the lake, now enlarged, comprise some of the most highly taxed land in the state. Once Sucker Lake was enlarged and its name changed to Oswego Lake, the lavish homes began to rise above the shores.

There is an often-told story, probably true many times over, that an excited Easterner bought a home on the lakefront without consulting his wife. He was so taken with the water view, the waterfowl, and the clean atmosphere that he really didn't pay much attention to the house; he knew that all would be forgiven once she looked out the wide front windows. His wife arrived during the biannual lake drainage, and the front windows stared blatantly upon a wide panorama of mud, old stumps, and last summer's picnic debris. She was able to enjoy this view for six months until the lake was filled again.

Lake Oswego once tried to become "the Pittsburgh of the West" and indeed did cast the first iron stove in Oregon to be used by the Ladd and Tilton Bank. All that remains of that dream is an old stack of basalt rock and the towering chimney on the river bank at the mouth of Oswego Creek (*George Rogers Park*), a spot so returned to nature that the beavers have come back to rebuild their ancestor's homes. If wilderness is appealing, spend a day at *Tryon Creek State Park*, off Terwilliger Blvd., at the entrance to Lake Oswego.

Across Oswego Creek is Portland Blvd. and the route to Oregon City. West of Oregon City, on the opposite bank of the Willamette, is West Linn. The town, a sprawling area of farmland and suburban residences, is marked now by a combination city hall and police station, and the Publishers Paper Co.

West Linn, or Linn City, as it was once called, is remarkable in that it was purchased from the Indians. History does not tell us what Robert Moore paid for the piece of land across the river from Dr. John McLoughlin's sawmill, but it is clear that he paid for it.

Willamette Falls, a natural drop in the river between the two towns, was brought under control by locks in 1868. Visitors to Publisher's Paper Co. are invited to walk through the plant and out under the falls to see the remarkable old locks which control the portage and water flow. For salmon fishermen it is a perfect entrance to the gate of heaven that offers fine Chinook fishing every spring.

Oregon City remains a small town, but its accomplishments will always rank it first in the state. In addition, to becoming one of the first incorporated cities west of the Missouri, the town is the site of the first protestant church, Masonic Lodge, and newspaper west of the Missouri. Oregon City saw the first use of water power in the state, was the first settlement to hear a brass band and had the first mint. It was the second home of Dr. John McLoughlin.

In 1829 he chose a mill site at the falls and started his settlement with the retired trappers and voyageurs of Hudson Bay Company. In 1842 he gave the city its name. He lived there until his death in 1857.

The *McLoughlin House*, restored (it once slipped to shelter the prostitutes of the city), is open to the public Tues.-Sun., 10 a.m.-4 p.m. Admission is $1 for adults, 25 cents for children and students 18 and younger. To make special arrangments for group tours, call 656-5146.

The house is located on the "third" level of Oregon City and can be reached by driving to the top of the hill or by parking on the lower level and riding the city's public elevator (the only one in North America they claim) which connects the downtown business section with the upper streets.

Next door to the McLoughlin house is the home of Dr. Forbes Barclay, Hudson's Bay surgeon at Ft. Vancouver, who resigned and followed McLoughlin to Oregon City.

To reach Lake Oswego and Oregon City by bus, take #36 or #37 from downtown Portland.

Scenic Drives

Portland has three designated "scenic drives"—the west side (15 miles), east side (29 miles), and northwest (25 miles).

Each route is designed to begin at the Chamber of Commerce, SW 5th and Taylor, downtown, where you can pick up a map which describes some of the sights and also lists a number of restaurants found on the routes.

Routes are marked with "Portland Scenic Drive" signs.

Tri-Met buses travel parts of each route, and Tri-Met makes it easy for you to learn how to get the most for your money by providing its "Fun Fare" folder series. To be certain you don't miss anything, pick up these excellent color folders, free, at the Tri-Met Customer Assistance Office, 522 SW Yamhill. Each features a different aspect of Portland sightseeing—water, historical places, gardens, and so on.

Neighborhoods

While taking scenic drives, walks, or bicycle tours, be aware of Portland's many neighborhoods, some of which took root as small river towns or street car line terminals. Landmark buildings are especially noticeable in areas like St. Johns, Albina (now the King, Boise, Eliot neighborhoods), Lents, Sellwood, and Linnton, which once were separate towns. The old city hall in St. Johns is a classic. These signs of the past strengthen neighborhood awareness while the city government encourages neighborhood activism through its Office of Neighborhood Associations. (See phone list under Neighborhood Assns.).

Guided Tours

Port of Portland

The story goes that sea captains sailed to the fresh water Port of Portland to rid their encrusted ships' bottoms of the barnacles that slowed them down.

While barnacles can't survive fresh water, it isn't the reason that today Portland harbor is the third largest on the west coast and first in the Pacific Northwest in the volume of waterborne commerce handled annually.

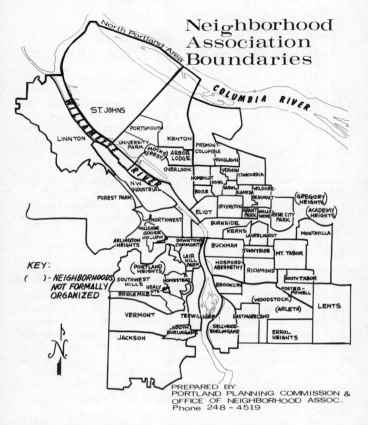

Neighborhood Association Boundaries

PREPARED BY
PORTLAND PLANNING COMMISSION &
OFFICE OF NEIGHBORHOOD ASSOC.
Phone 248 - 4519

The many facilities which the port offers shippers are the magnet, and the casual visitor or the resident can see many of these by courtesy of the port, which offers tours on a regular basis in the summer.

You'll see: The big ships which bring the world to Portland from such far-off places as Japan, Italy, and Germany and which take away Oregon's main agricultural bounty—lumber and wheat—as well as products from other parts of the country; and four marine terminals, two of them near downtown. The port's berths total 29.

While efficiency and containerism have taken some of the romance out of a visit to a large port, you can still see general cargo loaded at the two near-downtown terminals where the sights and sounds of shipping are most accessible to the casual visitor.

The terminals are on SW Front, north of the Fremont Bridge. By Tri-Met, take #55 heading north and get off at SW 18th and Thurman. Walk east to the river.

In the "good weather months," as the port puts it, a free guided tour leaves the Sheraton Motor Inn at 1:30 p.m. and the Hilton Hotel at 2 p.m. every Wednesday and Thursday. Phone 233-8331 for required reservations.

For other months of the year, group tours may be arranged by calling the same number. These tours, which may be scheduled Mon.-Fri., depart from Terminal 1 on NW Front. Groups must provide their own transportation. Mornings (9:45) are reserved for student tours (grade six and above) and afternoons (2 p.m.) for other groups. The tours are all guided by port personnel and are free.

For a do-it-yourself tour, recommended by the port, travel north on I-5 to the Marine Drive West exit. Follow the signs and stop at the check-in gate where you will be directed to the observation tower and administration building of Terminal 6, the port's newest terminal and the most modern container facility on the West Coast. There two 50-ton Hitachi cranes handle large truck size steel containers of goods. In this same area are the *Rivergate Industrial Park*, a former swampland which is being filled by port dredgings, and Kelley Point Park.

Terminal 4 in St. Johns is the most diversified facility, handling autos, lumber and logs, steel, containers, and bulks.

Terminal 5 is home of the fastest grain elevator in the lower Columbia-Willamette region.

Terminal 3? It isn't. A small municipal dock in St. Johns was designated No. 3 when that community was annexed into Portland in 1915. The dock was torn down when the St. Johns Bridge was built.

At Swan Island is the *Swan Island Ship Repair Yard*, located on a 90-acre tract of land at the northern tip of the island in the center of the Willamette River harbor. The yard includes three floating drydocks. The shipyard was acquired by the port following World War II. During the war years, about one ship a week was produced there. Swan Island is reached via the I-5 freeway by taking the Swan Island exit. Take #71 bus right to the drydock. From downtown, catch a #2 and transfer to #71 north of Going at Bess Kaiser Hospital. The #71 stop is across the street.

The bus also stops at **Ports O'Call Village**, a shopping-restaurant complex.

Sometimes at Ports O'Call you can see the sternwheeler Portland, the only steam-powered sternwheel towboat in the world. The 219-foot boat, which is often at work on the river, gives vital leverage when moving ships against the Willamette River current. It is equipped with seven rudders. The port maintains the steamer not only because she is useful but as a tribute to an era when the Willamette and Columbia Rivers were crowded with sternwheelers hauling cargo into the Columbia Basin and carrying passengers to seaside resorts.

Portland International Airport

Daily one-hour tours are conducted at Portland International Airport, also operated by the Port of Portland.

The airport is undergoing a face-lifting, scheduled for completion by early 1977, so if you tour before then, expect some construction sights in addition to the normal aircraft activity. For tour reservations call 233-8331, or if you want to take your chances, inquire at the airport's information booth to learn when the next tour is scheduled. A slide presentation and walking tour are featured; group arrangements can be made—for first graders and up.

To get there: Take I-80N to NE 82nd, travel north on 82nd and follow the signs to the airport. By bus take #14 from downtown to NE Sandy and 82nd. Transfer to a #72 which goes directly to the airport.

The Port of Portland also operates Portland-Hillsboro Airport, Portland-Troutdale Airport, and Swan Island Heliport.

Airplane rides can be arranged by calling Aurora Aviation in Aurora (222-1754); Flightcraft, Inc. at Portland-Hillsboro Airport (648-6631); Western Skyways, Inc. at Troutdale (665-1181). Cost for a half-hour scenic ride varies, but count on spending at least $11 per person.

Gray Line Tours

Tours to Mt. Hood, the Columbia River Gorge, and the Oregon Coast as well as a city tour are offered by the Gray Line (226-6755).

By bus, sightseers may choose a trip to Mt. Hood via the gorge, an overnight visit to Timberline Lodge, an all-day trip to the coast, among others.

Winter and summer schedules differ, so it's important to obtain the latest Gray Line flyer or to phone. Prices vary, but generally, the all-day tours are $15 for adults; half price for children. All tours leave from the Portland Hilton Hotel.

Portland Walking Tours

A group of young Portland women operate this enterprising business. "We believe that a tour without a guide is like a salad without a dressing," says one. "The ingredients may be the same, but something is missing."

You can count on your guide having done her architectural and historical homework whether you take the "City Walk" or the "Old Portland Walk." Each takes two hours and costs $2.50 per person.

"Open tours" during the summer accommodate individuals not associated with groups. For groups of 10 or more, tours may be scheduled throughout the year. A deposit of $25 is required to reserve the time and guides. (If you cancel and don't reschedule, you'll be charged 10%.) Individuals must make reservations as well as groups. Call 223-1017.

The "City Walk" forms on the steps of the Portland Art Museum, moves into the Park Blocks and follows a route which passes the Hilton Hotel to the Pioneer Courthouse. It tours the courthouse. It then heads south past the Georgia-Pacific building, City Hall (to see an Indian rock carving on the site), Standard and Equitable Plazas and concludes at the Forecourt Fountain in front of the Civic Auditorium.

The "Old Portland Walk" begins at the Trader Vic entrance to the Benson Hotel at SW Broadway and Stark, then walks through O'Bryant Square, looks at cast-iron facades on landmark buildings, and discusses the Victorian passion for decoration. The walk continues past boutiques and restaurants and ends near the Skidmore Fountain.

Old Puddletown Tours

This walking tour of 15 blocks into the historic Skidmore Fountain Village/Old Town District considers the history of some of the Old Town buildings, especially the cast iron architecture so prevalent in the area. The tour goes into some shops. Tours between May and December may be arranged by phoning 227-0433. Ticket prices for the summer-fall tours are $1.50, adults; $1, students; 75 cents, children under 12.

Industrial Tours

Oregon business and industry offer tours of their operations, some to groups only and some to groups and individuals.

Most request that persons wishing to tour phone well in advance, although a few—Blitz-Weinhard Brewery, Pendleton Woolen Mills, and Goodwill Industries being notable exceptions—permit drop-in visits at the times listed. Some organizations limit their visitations to educational groups. Individuals can sometimes join already scheduled group tours.

Blitz-Weinhard Co.—1133 W. Burnside (222-4351). The complete brewing process from hops to bottle is covered in this one-hour tour of the oldest brewery west of the Mississippi River. The tour includes a slide show at the beginning and refreshments—beer, if you're over 21, pop if you're not—in the brewery's attractive hospitality room. Tours Mon.-Fri. at 1, 2:30, and 4 p.m. No need to call ahead unless for a group of more than 10. Group tours for adults at night must be arranged for six months in advance.

Crown Zellerbach—(221-7167). The process of turning logs into paper may be viewed at Crown Zellerbach's West Linn and Camas, Wash., paper mills. At West Linn, call 656-2951 to make reservations for tours given Mon., Tues., Thurs., Fri. at 10 a.m. and 2 p.m. Children must be accompanied by parents, and children under 6 are not permitted to tour. School groups must be grade six or older. At Camas, paper is made and then converted into various products such as napkins and facial tissue. Tours are given by reservation Tues., Wed., Thurs. at 1 p.m. No one under 12 is permitted to tour. Tour lasts two hours.

ESCO Corp.—2141 NW 25th (228-2141). Educational tours of the ESCO foundry operation are limited to groups of high school and college students. A slide presentation is also given. Groups must be no larger than 30, and arrangements must be made in advance.

screened, cleaned, and squashed on tour. Visitors receive
a bag of peanuts as a souvenir. Groups are limited in
size to 15 and must start the tour before 2:30 p.m. Call
two weeks ahead for reservation.

Hyster Co.—2902 NE Clackamas (280-7654). The
manufacture of a Hyster lift truck from flat iron to the
finished product is viewed on this tour, limited to educational groups age 16 or older and no larger than 30.
Call two to three weeks in advance for an appointment.

Ice Cream Saloon—3815 SW Murray Rd., Beaverton,
at Tualatin Valley Highway (643-1881). A dish of the ice
cream you've seen in the making is the finishing touch
for this excellent tour of an old-fashioned ice-cream-
making operation. "Our ice creams weighs 40% more than
anyone else's," says the proud proprietor. Tours are
limited to school and youth groups and must be arranged
by phoning ahead. Tour days are Tues., Wed., Thurs. Ice
Cream Saloon is also a restaurant.

First National Bank—1300 SW 5th (225-2202). A
general banking tour is available to groups no smaller
than five or larger than 15. Tour includes a trip to the
observation area on the 30th floor of Portland's tallest
building. In addition, First National offers tours of its
art collection of over 400 pieces. Call at least a week in
advance to arrange for either tour.

Franz Bakery—340 NE 11th (232-2191). Huge amounts
of dough are turned into bread, buns, and rolls at Franz
where groups from age 7 on up can take a 1½-hour tour
Mon., Wed., Thurs., Fri., by reservation. Tours may be
arranged between 9:30 and 3:30 for as many as 28 persons, but allow two to three weeks for an appointment.
The entire baking process, including wrapping, is viewed.

Freightliner—6936 N. Fathom (285-5251). Truck as-
sembly from start to finish—and that means ready to
turn the key in the ignition switch—is viewed here
Wednesdays and Fridays at 1:30 p.m. The tour is open to
groups only no larger than 10 by appointment.

Goodwill Industries—1831 SE 6th (238-6133). This interesting tour visits the facilities where handicapped persons rehabilitate your old castoffs. Tours are given anytime before 2:30 daily and there is no age limitation.
Visitors see shoes being sorted, furniture reconditioning,
the cleaning and laundry operation, the print shop, and
the antique repair shop.

Hoody Corp.—5555 SW 107th, Beaverton (646-0555).

See Hoody peanut butter, jam, mustard, and vinegar in the making on this tour designed for groups of second-grade age and older. You'll also learn that Hoody produces for a number of other familiar labels. Peanuts are

Jantzen Inc.—411 NE 19th (238-5340). Reservations are required for tours of Portland's internationally known sports and swimwear manufacturing company, where visitors see spinning, knitting, fabric processing, cutting, sewing, and finalizing (buttons etc.). Tours are limited to persons 13 or older (no infants). Groups of 6 to 20 are taken through the plant. Walking shoes are suggested for the one-hour visit. Call two to three weeks in advance for reservations.

KATU (Channel 2)—2153 NE Sandy (233-2422). Visit this television studio on a Wednesday morning and you'll watch a live telecast of KATU's "A.M. Northwest" program, featuring Jim Bosley, as well as take a tour of the station. Except in the summer when no tours are given, KATU includes anyone sixth-grade age or older on its tours and accepts groups of 20 or less. Call at least two weeks in advance for a reservation. If you plan to catch the live telecast on a Wednesday, plan to arrive at 8:45 a.m.

KBPS (1450 radio)—546 NE 12th, in the Benson High School auditorium (234-5469). Because of space limitations, the Portland Public Schools station is open only to public school groups for tours.

KGW-King Broadcasting Co. (Channel 8)—1501 SW Jefferson (226-5000). Tours of the facilities for ***KGW-TV*** as well as ***KINK-FM*** (102 radio) and ***KGW-AM*** (620 radio) are given Mon.-Thurs. between 11 a.m. and 2 p.m., by appointment only. The tour is open to seventh graders and older and to groups no larger than 20.

KISN (910 radio)—10 NW 10th (226-7191). Look for your favorite disc jockey while on tour of KISN's radio broadcasting facilities weekdays between 9 a.m. and 5 p.m. Children over 10 only. Groups and individuals should call in advance.

KOIN (Channel 6)—140 SW Columbia (228-3333). KOIN's on-camera newsroom is one of the stops on this tour, limited to fifth graders and older and to groups no larger than 20. The tour also visits the KOIN radio (970) studios. Call two weeks ahead for an appointment.

Lloyd Center—NE 9th & Multnomah (282-2511). Go

behind the scenes of a metropolitan shopping center and see everything from pollution controls in the parking areas to refrigeration equipment for ice skating. Call ahead to make reservations for tours which can be taken Mon.-Fri. betwen 8:30 a.m. and 5 p.m. Lower age limit is first grade. Other features of the popular tour are traveling its network of underground halls and seeing the loading areas in operation. For groups interested in marketing and advertising, a slide presentation is available.

McDonald's Hamburgers—9475 SW Beaverton-Hillsdale Highway, Beaverton (646-1816). This is one of 14 McDonald's restaurants in the Portland area. If another is closer to you, chances are it gives tours, too. One of the most popular youth group tours, this one inspects every square inch of the McDonald's operation. This particular McDonald's uses fresh potatoes for its French fries, so you see potatoes peeled and sliced. At the end, the store supplies each visitor with a hamburger and a shake or soft drink—free. Hats are also provided. The Beaverton McDonald's gives one tour a week, so call at least a month ahead for a reservation.

Memorial Coliseum—1401 N. Wheeler (235-8771). While known best as the home of the Trail Blazers (National Basketball Assn.), the big glass box on the east side near the Broadway Bridge is in almost constant use providing space and seating for everything from ice shows to boat shows. Seating capacity is 13,000 (9,000 permanent seats). Group tours only are given of the behind-the-scenes operation. Call in advance for an appointment.

Nabisco, Inc.—100 NE Columbia Blvd. (285-2571, ext. 66). Nabisco's famous Oreo cookies and Premium crackers are made from the raw ingredients and packaged at this plant, which offers tours by appointment Tues. and Thurs. at 1:15 p.m. Tours are limited to groups (fifth grade and up) of 35 or less. Nabisco asks that you confirm your request to tour by letter.

Oregon Humane Society—1067 NE Columbia Blvd. (285-0643). As popular a part of the tour here as the dogs and cats is a visit to the barnyard to feed the farm animals and poultry which the society has accepted from persons who could no longer keep them. The farm animals are not readopted as are the dogs and cats but are kept in the barnyard to give urban children the experience of seeing and feeding them. Visitors are asked to come with stale bread, but if they don't, the society issues dog biscuits for the barnyard pets. Also on the itinerary is a visit to the pet cemetery, the only one in the Portland area. Flowers and wreaths are regularly delivered to many of the graves which have been purchased for beloved pets. Children get a chance to hold and pet the puppies, dogs, and cats while on tour. The society offers tours for groups only—a minimum of 10 and a maximum of 30—and asks that you call for an appointment two weeks ahead.

Oregon Journal and Oregonian—1320 SW Broadway (221-8336). A press run of the *Oregon Journal* at the Oregonian Publishing Co.'s new offset plant at SW 16th and Taylor is part of this tour for high school and college students above grades eight or nine. After the press run, the group provides it own transportation to the two newspapers' offices on SW Broadway for tours of both newsrooms and display advertising, classified, and other departments. The tour, which starts at 9:15 a.m. and ends at 11:30 a.m., is limited to groups of 15 or less. Call for an appointment at least one month ahead for the Tues. or Thurs. tour.

Pendleton Woolen Mills—(226-4801, ext. 279). See fine woolen sportswear produced from raw wool on tours of these three Portland-area facilities of this famous old Oregon company. No appointments necessary unless for a large group. Children under 12 must be accompanied by parents.

Columbia Wool Scouring Mill, 2030 N. Columbia Blvd. Raw wool right off the sheep is cleaned, washed and dried in this operation. Tours are given from 9 a.m. to 2 p.m. every half hour (except during the lunch hour) Mon.-Fri.

Washougal Weaving Plant, No. 2, 17th St., Washougal, Wash. One-hour tours at 10 a.m. and 2 p.m. Mon.-Fri. view the complete process which the cleaned wool undergoes—dyeing, spinning, carding, and weaving into the finished fabric. When the fabric leaves this plant, it's on bolts, ready for the store or garment factory.

Milwaukie Garment Factory, 801 River Rd., Milwaukie. Complete construction of a man's shirt, from cutting to boxing, is viewed by tours at 10 a.m. and 1 p.m. Tours last 45 minutes.

All of the Pendleton tours are limited to 40, except for the morning Washougal tour, limited to 20. Large groups who wish to make appointments for Pendleton tours should call at least two weeks ahead. The famous Pendleton blankets are made at the company's Pendleton, Ore., facility.

Portland Air Base—5501 NE Cornfoot Rd. (288-5611, ext. 550). Aero-space education tours for high school age youth must be booked far in advance. This excellent tour visits the shops and maintenance area at the base and explores educational opportunities of an air career.

Portland Fire Bureau—55 SW Ash (232-8135). Television's crises are daily routine for the men at the Central Fire Station, and they're happy to tell visitors all about it. An elaborately outfitted emergency vehicle leaves children wide-eyed. Call ahead for a date and time. You can also make arrangements to visit—but not ride on—one of the Fire Bureau's three fire boats—the Spencer, Laudenklaus and Campbell.

Post Office—Main office, 715 NW Hoyt (221-2363). This 1½-hour tour, for fourth-grade age and up, visits workroom floors where mail is sorted both mechanically and by hand as well as other parts of the postal operation. You'll see why it's important to zip-code your mail when you watch the "zip mail translator" in action. Call ahead for a reservation, but avoid the end or beginning of each month, the busiest days at the post office. Tours will take individuals as well as groups. If you're looking for a postal tour for younger children, try calling one of the branches.

Publishers Paper—419 Main St., Oregon City (656-5211). Newsprint for the daily papers is made here as well as paper toweling and fruit wrap. Wood goes in and paper comes out. You see it all on tours Wednesdays at 2 p.m. The tours accept walk-ins but call ahead if you're arranging for a group. Minimum age for the tour is 12.

Reynolds Metals Co.—Sun Dial Rd., Troutdale (665-9171). At Reynolds' Troutdale Reduction Plant you can see aluminum oxide reduced into primary aluminum through an electrolytic process. The molten aluminum is then cast into various ingot sizes. Call ahead to arrange for group tours of the plant during the work week. No one under 12.

Rose's Bake Shop—713 NW 23rd. Tours of this small but very special bakery operation can be arranged for groups by calling Rose's Restaurant (227-5181). The shop is known for its spectacular chocolate cakes, giant-sized cinnamon buns, and braided breads.

Sunshine Dairy—801 NE 21st (234-7526). Milk, cottage cheese, ice cream, yogurt are produced in this complete dairy operation which can be viewed Tues.-Fri. at 10 a.m. Groups only are taken through the dairy by appointment. The tour lasts 45 minutes.

Trojan Nuclear Plant—Rainier, Ore. (556-4741). Trojan Visitors Center at Oregon's first nuclear generating plant features eight exhibits which explain the story of nuclear energy. Visitors may also see the Ecosphere, a multi-dimensional film which places the viewer inside the atom. At conclusion of the tour, test your nuclear knowledge at a bank of computers. Special guided tours for groups may be made by calling ahead. Trojan is or U.S. 30 42 miles north and west of Portland. Landmark is its 499-ft. cooling tower, which tours may now visit. Tours are also now permitted in the main generator building. They are given five days a week, Wed.-Sun., generally mid-morning, early afternoon, late afternoon. Tour is not recommended for children under 12.

U.S. National Bank—Plaza building, SW 6th & Oak, and Main Branch, 321 SW 6th (225-6379 or 225-5750). Learn how computers keep track of your BankAmericard records, see the cash vault, visit the elegant offices on this tour which spans two different buildings, the bank's main branch, a Roman temple-style structure maintained exactly as it was in 1917 when built, and its new Plaza building across the street. Phone ahead for group tours. This is a popular school children's tour.

RESTAURANTS

A Selective Guide to Dining

FEW WILL DISPUTE, in this age of pre-prepared food, that Portland's finest meals are to be found in its homes.

Doug Baker, columnist for the *Oregon Journal*, can cause salivation after a full meal when he discusses a simple supper prepared at his River Place with freshly caught steelhead, a good bottle of wine chilled in the river, and a well-aged piece of cheese.

Amateur chefs know that razor clams must be cooked just until they quiver slightly, strawberries are best eaten warm in the patch, and peas should be picked in the backyard just as the steamer comes to a boil.

Dungeness crab, of course, is best eaten on the beach where it can be mixed with a minute trace of blowing sand for piquancy, and the best lamb and milk-fed pork are found down the country roads from a woman who raises just a few for friends.

Assuming that you know no one in Portland, it is still possible to get a fine meal or plenty of fulfilling servings.

When rumblings begin to drown out your thoughts of other Portland sites, we offer a list of proven restaurants—clean, well-prepared food to fill the family and at least some part of the soul.

This list is by no means complete. Gloria Russakov (*The Oregon Times*) has published a *Guide to Eating Out in Portland*, which grades the last crumb of every stale roll in the city. For those who want to see everything spelled out from antipasto to toothpicks (quality of), pick up her excellent reference. Other penetrating reviews are offered by Mr. Baker, food writers for *The Oregonian*, and Xerpha Borunda of *The Willamette Week*.

Bart's Wharf and Marina—3829 NE Marine Dr. (288-6161). Closed Mon. The rest of the week you can pick out your own fresh Maine lobster from the tank which greets you at the door. Seafood is their specialty and the view (if you can get a table by the window) is of the Columbia River, sailboats, houseboats, and the jets landing at the airport. Complete bar. Reservations suggested. Expensive. Lunch and dinner served. Credit cards accepted.

Benihana of Tokyo—315 SW 4th (226-4754). If you don't want to share your Japanese-modern meal with strangers, take 6 or 8 friends along, although the food is well worth the lack of privacy. An ideal spot for children who can't sit still at a meal. The swinging cleavers will hold them spellbound or terrified, depending upon their temperament. Bar. Reservations required and honored. Lunch and dinner. Moderate. Credit cards.

Bush Garden—121 SW 4th (226-7181). Traditional Japanese food; wear clean socks—you must remove your shoes. Reservations necessary. Cocktails. Credit cards. Moderate.

Canlis—921 SW 6th (228-7475). Closed Sun. On the 23rd floor of the Hilton Hotel. Try Dungeness crab legs with mustard mayonnaise. The sauce is so good you will finish up the shredded lettuce garnish. Good food, good service, and a good view when the smog lifts. Cocktails. Credit cards. Expensive.

Captain Billy Bangs Pub—5331 SW Macadam (227-4663). Sandwiches, pizza, and bar service at John's Landing Water Tower. Good for children, however. Lunch and dinner. Credit cards. Moderate.

Captain's Corner—1201 SW 12th (224-9877). Closed Sun. Owner-host Barney Giansante and head bartender Larry Henderson make this the most popular lunch spot in town. Dinners are also excellent. Don't expect a view; there are no windows. Best for adults because there will be a wait. Reservations. Credit Cards. Moderate.

Carnival—2805 SW Sam Jackson Park Rd. (227-4244). Closed Sun. Hamburgers and hot dogs done on the charcoal broiler. On a hot summer night you can dine by the waterfall outside. Excellent for children with its cafeteria-style do-it-yourself service. And the desserts come last. Lunch and supper. No liquor. No cards. Inexpensive.

Caro-Amico Pizzeria—3606 SW Barbur Blvd. (223-6895). The godfather of all Portland pizzerias. There may be some heated arguments among the staff, but it's all in the family, and you'll still get your pizza. Children welcome. Cocktails. No cards. Moderate.

Casa Molina—107 NW 5th (227-2282). Lunches and dinners with hard-to-find Mexican specialties. Reservations. No liquor. Credit cards. Moderate.

The Castle—18201 SE River Rd., Milwaukie (655-5077). Spin the wheel of fortune and possibly win what will have been a fine meal. Steaks are the specialty. Children welcome. Dinners. Liquor. Credit cards.

Cheerful Tortoise—1939 SW 6th (227-2847). Portland State University area tavern; good sandwiches. Beer. No credit cards. Inexpensive.

Chow's—329 SW 2nd, Lake Oswego (636-0331). Known by some as "the Chinese sandwich shop" because they also serve a decent hamburger. Most regulars order lunch or dinner from the Chinese menu. Food to go. Credit cards. Moderate.

Coco's—11340 NE Halsey (253-7772) and 5457 SW Canyon Ct. (297-2026). Hamburgers plus. Part of the Rueben's group with quality to match. Children will like this one. No credit cards. Inexpensive.

Country Kitchen—10519 SE Stark (252-4171). If you are heading back from a day at Mt. Hood, take on the 72-oz. steak. If you can eat it, it's yours for nothing. Good place for children and family dinners. Credit cards. Liquor. Moderate.

Crab Bowl—7958 SW Barbur Blvd. (246-7797). Lunches and dinners featuring anything that swims. Also take-out service with seafood prepared or raw. No alcohol. Credit cards. Moderate.

Crepe Faire—117 NW 2nd Ave. (227-3365). Offers a variety of filling from main dish to dessert all wrapped in a thin crepe blanket. Lunches and dinners. Beer and wine. No credit cards. Inexpensive.

Dan & Louis Oyster Bar—208 SW Ankeny (227-5906). An institution in Portland. Dine on oyster stew or clam chowder from 11 a.m.-1 a.m. seven days a week. Take the children, they will love the decor. No liquor. Credit cards.

Dandelion Pub—31 NW 23rd Pl. (223-0099). Closed Sun. Hearty sandwiches with beer or wine. No children. No credit cards. Inexpensive.

Dave's Delicatessen—325 SW Morrison (222-5461). A hole-in-the-wall but kosher clean with food to match.

The deli for deli-addicts. Closed Sunday. No credit cards. Inexpensive.

Don Elton—340 N. State St. Alley, Lake Oswego (636-3702). One of a kind. Owner D.E. Foss has decorated freely, and each room is filled with his eclectic tastes as is his menu. What makes this spot remarkable, in addition to good food, suitable also for children, is that everything on the menu will be prepared to go. Walk away with chicken livers wrapped in bacon, salmon steak, or fried chicken. Closed Sun. Wine. Credit cards. Moderate.

Downtown Delicatessen—345 SW Yamhill (227-0202). Offers a 75-cent sandwich which will feed two ladies. Beer, wine, and soda pop to take out along with the sandwich, which can be eaten at the Forecourt Fountain on nice days or in the car during a rushed Christmas shopping session. Closed Sun. No credit cards. Inexpensive.

Elephant and Castle—201 SW Washington (222-5698). Traditional English pub atmosphere complete with fish and chips and dart board. No credit cards.

Farrell's Ice Cream Parlour restaurants serve no alcohol and do not take credit cards, but you will find plenty of entertainment to go along with hamburgers, hot dogs, and ice cream. Great for children. Portland is the home of this fast-growing chain which exploits the all-American American. Visit them for lunch or supper at:
Washington Square, (639-1883)
1600 NE 122nd (255-5776)
4955 SW 76th (292-9103)
1613 NE Weidler (281-1271)

Fish Grotto Seafood Restaurant—1035 SW Stark (226-4171). The least publicized and most consistently good seafood restaurant in Portland for lunch or dinner. Liquor. Credit cards. Moderate.

Foothill Broiler—33 NW 23rd Pl. (223-0287). Hamburgers, hot soup, and homemade pies with orders to go. If you take in your own pie pan, they will bake you a wild blackberry pie for your next dinner. Good for lunch or early supper. Closed Sun. Take the children as they are. No credit cards. Inexpensive.

Genoa—2832 SE Belmont (238-1464). Open Tues.-Sat. for dinners only. They have a recipe for tomato soup beginning, "start with a lot of onions," which should give you an idea of the originality of their Northern Italian menu. Do not take children since this is leisurely dining for a few. Wine. No credit cards. Moderate.

Goody's—10630 SW Canyon Rd., Beaverton (643-4431). Closed Mon. Good spot for breakfast or lunch. Sandwiches feature lox and salami. Small sitting area but large take-out department. No liquor. No credit cards.

Goose Hollow Inn—1927 SW Jefferson (228-7010). No smoking on Mondays, which settles well with the patrons who enjoy the good lunches here.

Grecian Gardens—15 NW 6th (228-7818). Open 7 nights a week with lunches served also. Look for feta cheese in your salad; order shanks and watch the Greek seamen join in the dancing. Liquor. Credit cards. Moderate.

Griffin's Cafeteria—214 SW Broadway (227-0876). For the early riser who doesn't like to eat breakfast at his hotel. Open at 6:30 a.m., closed Sat. and Sun. No alcohol. No credit cards. Inexpensive.

Hillvilla—5700 SW Terwilliger Blvd. (246-3305). Lunch and dinner with possibly the best view of the city. Liquor. Credit cards. Moderate.

Huber's—320 SW Stark St. (228-5686). Closed Sun. If you want to eat in "old" Portland atmosphere, this is the one. For lunch or supper. Their reputation has long been based upon turkey and cole slaw. Liquor. Credit cards. Moderate.

Jade West—122 SW Harrison (226-1128). Across from the Civic Auditorium with complimentary bus service for its pre-performance customers. Cantonese dining 7 days a week for dinner. Liquor. Credit cards. Expensive.

Jake's Famous Crawfish—401 SW 12th (226-1419). In Portland since 1892. Seafood is the specialty, as are the aging waiters and the even older decor. Liquor. Credit cards. Moderate.

John's Meatmarket—115 NW 22nd (223-2119). Good steak and soup with an intimate bar. Prepare to wait there, so do not take children. Open seven days a week for dinner. Liquor. Credit cards.

La Bonne Crepe—5331 SW Macadam (248-9300). Closed Sun. Good French cooking for lunch and supper. Beer and wine. Credit cards. Moderate.

L'Auberge—2180 W. Burnside (223-3302). Open Tues.-Sat. for dinner. French cooking with menu adjusted to fresh market buys of the day. Wine. Credit cards.

L'Omelette—815 SW Alder (248-9661). Closed Sun. Rated by many as one of the best in the city for lunch or dinner. Comfortable atmosphere. Reservations a must, even for lunch. Liquor. Credit cards.

London Grill—309 SW Broadway (228-9611). In the basement of the Benson Hotel. Open 7 days a week, breakfast through dinner. Excellent service and beautiful decor. Moderate to expensive.

Marketplace—4F SW Monroe Parkway, Lake Oswego (635-3456). Lunches and dinners with a wide menu. Elegant, but suitable for children during early hours. Liquor. Credit cards. Expensive.

Monte Carlo—1016 SE Belmont (235-9171). Seven days a week from 11 a.m.-2 a.m. The Italian businessmen still meet for lunch here so it has to maintain its standards. Take the children for pizza. Dancing after 9 p.m. Full Italian menu. Liquor. Credit cards. Moderate.

Nendel's Inn—9900 SW Canyon Rd. (297-2551). Outstanding chicken. Family fare in very nice surroundings. Sun. brunch. Liquor. Credit cards. Moderate.

Old Fashioned Ice Cream Saloon—3815 SW Murray Rd. in the K-Mart Shopping Center (643-1881). Makes its own ice cream on the spot as well as excellent sandwiches. Extra activities for active children. Lunch and dinner. No liquor. No credit cards.

Old Spaghetti Factory—126 SW 2nd (222-5375). Spaghetti for everyone, and no one cares if the children drop some on the floor. Open for lunch and dinner. Liquor. Credit cards. Inexpensive.

Organ Grinder—5015 SE 82nd (771-1178). Seven days a week; open at noon on Sun. Rube Goldberg would be proud of this multi-greeting of pipe organs, drums, and bubble machines which go into action as the pizza cooks. Kids love it, and the noise and commotion drown out the cries and whines. Front row seats in the balcony give the best view if you don't mind eating counter-style with your family. No reservations. Beer and wine. No credit cards. Inexpensive.

Pancake House—8600 SW Barbur Blvd. (246-9007). Check first on this one since the owners often take a month's vacation. For this they are forgiven since they offer the finest pancakes in town. No liquor. No credit cards. Inexpensive.

Pot Sticker and Sizzling Rice—228 NW Davis (248-9231). Closed Sun. Northern Chinese food served at lunch and dinner. No liquor. No credit cards. Inexpensive.

Republic—222 NW 4th (226-4388). Closed Tues. This one is so honorably esteemed that it once bore hatchet marks from a Tong war. Chinese food as Americans like it; reliable and moderately priced. Liquor. Credit cards.

Rheinlander—5035 NE Sandy (288-5503). Just plain hokum and everyone loves it. Steer the children away from the bottle of non-alcoholic wine, it is expensive. Otherwise moderate prices and overwhelming portions in the German tradition. All this is accompanied by an accordionist. Liquor. Credit cards.

John Rian is not a Portland native. But he is such a gentleman, not to mention a conservative, that we are happy to claim him and willing to keep him as one of our own. He has three restaurants and two sandwich stands in the city, all known for being the best of their kind. Any restaurant which bears his name is as good as a guarantee.

Rian's Breadbasket—in the Standard Plaza (223-6111). Open Mon.-Fri. for lunch. Sandwiches, soup, and tamale pie are the favorites. Beer and wine. No credit cards. Inexpensive.

Rian's Eating Establishment—through the wrought-iron gates between Park and Broadway in Morgan's Alley (222-9996). The dark suit member of his group. Closed Sun. Lunches and dinners with a difference are served here. This man has a secret hoard of Dungeness crab and is willing to share it only with his customers. When it comes time to eke out the Dungeness with Snow Crab, he is honest about it. Liquor. Credit cards. No reservations taken. Moderate to expensive.

Rian's Fish and Ale House—6620 SW Beaverton-Hillsdale Hwy. (292-0191). The elder brother in the group featuring an old Rian family recipe for deep fried fish and chips. The menu has been broadened to include sandwiches and other seafood. Wine and ale served. Credit cards. Moderate.

Rian's Sandwich Express—Morgan's Alley and Nordstrom's at Washington Sq. Rian's has a knack for tucking the best into small spaces. Check the Survival Kit for children's and picnic lunches. Unusual sandwiches, plenty of coffee, and blueberry muffins supreme. No liquor. No credit cards. Inexpensive.

Ringside—2165 W. Burnside (223-1513). For steak before the game at the Civic Stadium or any evening of the week. Liquor. Credit cards. Moderate.

Rose's—315 NW 23rd (227-5181). Nonkosher delicatessen with large dining area open 7 days a week, featuring cakes a foot high, lox and cream cheese on rye and blintzes. Good for the entire family. Liquor. No reservations, so you may have a wait during lunch and dinner hours. No credit cards. Inexpensive.

Russian Renaissance—19 NW 5th (228-8215). Closed Sun. Lunch and dinner featuring hearty peasant food. Wine and beer. Credit cards. Moderate.

Skyline—1313 NW Skyline Blvd. (292-6727). Closed Sun. It took him awhile, but James Beard has put his blessing on this renowned hamburger stop. Open Fri. and Sat. until midnight. No liquor. No credit cards. Inexpensive.

Souvlaki Stop—1811 W. Burnside (228-3285). Greek sandwiches 7 days a week in an old gas station. No liquor. No credit cards. Inexpensive.

Steak and Skewer—2913 SE Stark (233-5489). Greek and American food served 7 days a week, along with steak. Liquor. Credit cards. Moderate.

Stock Pot—8200 SW Scholls Ferry Rd. (643-5451). Fine restaurant at golf course. Liquor. Credit cards. Moderate.

Sweet Tibby Dunbar—718 NE 12th (232-1801). Open 7 days a week, Sat. and Sun. for dinner only. Most atmosphere in the city, this restaurant features only fresh fish on its menu, which includes steak and other specialties. The reservation policy saves tables for one third of the house only, so prepare to wait in the English pub bar. It's well worth it for a special night out, but not with the children. Liquor. Credit cards. Expensive.

Taco House No. 1—3255 NE 82nd (252-1695). and *No. 2*—3550 SE Powell Blvd. (234-6401). Mexican food for the Gringo taste. The long waiting lines (no reservations) prove that these restaurants have come up with the right ingredients. Dinners only. Beer. No credit cards. Inexpensive.

Tebo's Famous Hamburgers—19120 SE McLoughlin

Blvd. (655-6333). Long and excellent reputation for charcoal grilled-to-order cafeteria-style food. Pick up your tray and watch the cooks go into action. The hamburger will be done just as you've passed the salad and pie section to stop at the cash register. Lunches and dinners. No liquor. No credit cards. Inexpensive.

Thiele (Henry)—2305 W. Burnside (223-2060). Open 7 days a week from breakfast through 10:30 p.m. dinners. A landmark designating 23rd and Burnside. This white stuccoed building which protrudes on a pie-shaped wedge is all that is left of the "old" business area and is a favorite meeting place for apartment dwellers in the area. Their German pancake has drawn national recognition, and it is a wise place to plan lunch after the Youngland ƒ sales since they have the largest parking lot in the area. Liquor. Credit cards. Moderate to inexpensive.

Thunderbird Downtown—1225 N. Thunderbird Way (just across from the Memorial Coliseum) (235-6611) and *Thunderbird at Jantzen Beach*, 1401 N. Hayden Island Dr. (283-2111). Both are open for dinners 7 days a week, and it depends upon which river you want to see, or where you are, to determine your choice. Both offer dressy dining, the Downtown on the Willamette, the Jantzen Beach overlooking the Columbia River. Both have full bar service. Both accept credit cards. Children do not belong in either, except for lunch. Expensive.

Trader Vic's—309 SW Broadway (228-9611). Closed Sun. In the Benson Hotel. The place to fill up on such tidbits as barbequed spareribs, crab rangoon, and other exotic combinations. At lunch or dinner order the Bongo Bongo soup, an original with this South Sea Island chain. Liquor. Credit cards. Moderate to expensive.

Trees—Hilton Hotel—921 SW 6th (226-1611). The spot to order thin pancakes rolled in lots of melted butter and served with hot maple syrup and crisp bacon or strawberries. Even the friendly waitresses will agree this is the best choice, although the menu is wide. Children eat at half price when accompanied by mother and father. Liquor. Credit cards. Moderate.

Tuck Lung—204 NW 4th (223-1090). Closed Sun. This started out as a Chinese grocery and grew like Topsy Lee. Good lunch spot. No alcohol. No credit cards. Inexpensive to moderate.

Valentino's—555 SW Oak (226-3312). Good Italian food, broad variety with large portions. Cocktail lounge. Slightly noisy. Lunches and dinners. Liquor. Credit cards.

Victoria's Nephew—212 SW Stark (223-7299). Closed Sat. and Sun. Sandwiches and homemade breads and soups. Open 7:30 a.m.-4 p.m. No liquor. No credit cards.

Victoria Station—6500 SW Macadam Blvd. (245-2241). Lunches and dinners featuring a salad bar and prime rib in railroad setting. Plan to wait. Liquor. Credit cards.

West Linn Inn—West Linn (at end of old bridge behind City Hall) (656-2613). Closed Mon. Lunches and dinners. The staff spots children as they enter and immediately serves them a "Shirley Temple." Afterwards the young can visit the salad bar alone. Especially for children is the fried chicken served with ice cream on the same plate. Put them at one end of the table and dine leisurely on scampi, steak, or prime rib, knowing that they will be cared for at their own speed. Liquor. Credit cards. Moderate.

Wilf's in Union Station—800 NW 6th (223-0070). Fine food in historic railway depot. Lunches and dinners. Liquor. Credit cards. Moderate.

Yaw's Top Notch Drive-In—2001 NE 40th (281-1233). The original high school hide-out in the city. Hamburgers are loaded with pickles, relish, and sophomore sensitivity. Good spot to stop for lunch or light supper. No credit cards. Inexpensive.

Ye Old Towne Crier—4515 SE 41st (774-1822). Open 7 days for lunch and dinner served in comfortable "early grandmother" period. Liquor. Credit cards. Moderate.

Yung An—2016 Sandy Blvd. (235-6529). Open 7 days a week. Dinner only on Sun. Northern Chinese food with flair. No liquor. Credit cards. Moderate.

Zapatas—2719 SW Kelly (222-6677). Open 7 days a week, dinner only on weekends, including a Mexican band. Beer and wine. Credit cards. Inexpensive to moderate.

Zen—910 SW Salmon (222-3056). Closed Sun. Open for lunch and dinner otherwise. Japanese full-course dinners in addition to a la carte. Liquor. Credit cards. Moderate.

ENTERTAINMENT

Doing, Seeing, Participating

PORTLAND is alive and well after 5 p.m. From black tie symphony opening nights to a barefoot hassle with an electronic tennis game in the corner tavern, the city provides a wide variety of entertainment for all ages.

Specifics concerning road shows, arias, or drum beats are difficult to generalize, but the following listings contain the most dependable sources to initiate a good evening.

One local publication, *The Performing Arts Index*, available at local book and record stores, will key you in to smaller performing groups. Otherwise, the local newspapers are the best source for up-to-the-minute information.

Theater

In addition to road stars who play the Portland Civic Auditorium, Portland supports several small theater groups that offer a constantly changing script. For information on live theater productions call:

Portland Civic Auditorium—Box Office at 222 SW Clay (226-2876).

Portland Civic Theatre—1844 SW Morrison (226-3048) has a long and excellent reputation for good locally produced shows. Mainstage productions run concurrently with Blue Room theater in the round. Curtain time for each is 8:30 p.m. Children's plays frequently are scheduled for Saturday matinees at this largest of the community theaters.

Present Tense—Dinner theater at the Portland Motor Hotel, SW 5th & Clay. Reservations: 221-1611.

Savoir Fair at the YWCA—1111 SW 10th. Reservations: 223-6281 ext. 36.

Slabtown Theatre Co.—NW 26th & Savier. Always offers an excellent production from the sublime to the ridiculous. Reservations: 228-1969.

Mark Allen Players—Benson Hotel Dinner Theatre. Reservations: 228-9611. Anyone who has ever seen theater in Portland has seen Mark Allen and appreciates his talents.

The New Theatre—0858 SW Palatine Hill Rd. (246-3467). The best in town in intellectual theater.

Oregon Mime Theater—886 SW North Shore Rd., Lake Oswego (636-2068).

Firehouse Theater—Portland Actor's Company, 1436 SW Montgomery (248-4737).

Lake Oswego Community Theatre—156 SW Greenwood Rd., Lake Oswego (635-3901) for reservations.

Paramount Cabaret—1037 SW Broadway (225-0750). Picks up the additional road companies not offered at the auditorium in a dinner show atmosphere.

College Theaters

University of Portland, Lewis and Clark College, and Portland State University have theater schedules during the school year. Portland State now occupies a newly renovated theater in Lincoln Hall and extends its performances to a free lunch box theater of experimental nature during the school year. The lunch box theater plays at noon on Tues., Wed., and Thurs. Call 229-4612 for additional information.

Special Screenings

Several movie houses in the Portland area screen for a selected audience. The Portland Art Museum as well as the main branch of the Multnomah County Library offer out-of-the-ordinary motion pictures from time to time, so check local newspapers for the latest billings.

Especially noteworthy is the *Northwest Film Study Center,* headquartered at the Portland Art Museum (226-2811). The center presents films Thurs., Sat., and Sun.—classics, comedy, retrospective series, and a wide variety of screen drama. Call for the current showings and show times. Prices are reasonable.

These theaters can be counted upon for films with a

difference, whether they be vintage or Renaissance:
Joy, Tigard (639-1482)
Fine Arts, SW Hawthorne Blvd. & 20th (235-5005)
The Movie House, 1220 SW Taylor (222-4595)
5th Avenue Cinema, SW 5th & Hall (224-6038)
Backstage Theatre, 3702 SE Hawthorne Blvd. (236-6116)

Music

Portland is filled with music the year around and the score ranges from Beethoven to Bluegrass, from the preschool set to the Old Time Fiddlers. Four universities and countless auxiliaries see to it that at one time or another every score has its day.

For traveling musical offerings, you can ask to be put on the mailing list of the Portland Civic Auditorium, 222 SW Clay (226-2876) to receive a quarterly calendar of events. For day-to-day listings consult the local newspapers.

Major Groups

Oregon Symphony Orchestra—1119 SW Park (228-1353) was founded in 1896 and presents 11 classical series concerts a year at the Civic Auditorium. The group of 80 permanent members, augmented for special presentations, is heard annually in more than 100 concerts throughout Oregon and Washington. In addition to the classical series (Sun., Mon., and Tues. nights) the orchestra offers a program of pop concerts on alternate Sundays and Mondays. Special youth concerts reach out to more than 40,000 elementary and high school students in the Portland area. Members of the orchestra also perform in a chamber series at Cabell Hall on the Catlin-Gabel campus, 8825 SW Barnes Rd. (297-1894).

Portland Opera Association Inc.—922 SW Main (248-4741) harkens its interest to the first operatic performance given in the Northwest which arrived in Portland in 1867 by a company sailing by steamer from San Francisco. Portland's association with opera is by no means a newly-hatched thought. The Portland Opera Association was incorporated in 1964, the heir of many former interest groups which brought music to the city. Current programs include four productions a year with three performances of each in Sept., Nov., March, and

May. Visiting artists of world stature join an excellent local orchestra and chorus.

Oregon Junior Symphony—922 SW Main (223-5939) was founded in 1924 to provide opportunities for gifted young musicians to study great orchestral compositions. The Junior Symphony, which has had just two conductors in its 52 years, consists of two orchestras: the symphony and the Preparatory Orchestra. Young musicians are heard in four regular concerts at the Portland Civic Auditorium as well as four to five in-school concerts. The orchestras, each with 100 or more players, have no lower age limit. Players are judged solely upon ability and may remain with the group until the age of 21. The organization also offers scholarship opportunities through lessons and summer camps for its members.

New Oregon Singers—Cascade Building (227-5800) is an amazing group of energetic young people who spread the "gospel according to Oregon." This group, which performs contemporary as well as red-white-and-blue tunes, raises its own money through local appearances to tour military installations across the United States and abroad. Their ability to take themselves (not their music) lightly and fill the front row with beautiful faces and figures has made them a part of nearly every hoopla event in the city.

Bureau of Parks and Recreation—1107 SW 4th (248-4287) sponsors more summer music, free of charge, than any other organization. Under their careful planning the public can meet at Washington Park from late July through Aug. for a three-week program of the best in Oregon music. Included on the bill is apt to be a recent musical comedy, the Oregon Symphony, folk dancers, sounds of the big bands, ballet, Old Time Fiddlers, and barbershop quartets. Check the Park Bureau or local newspapers for performance dates and times.

Colleges and Universities

Music is always in the air on college campuses. Following is a list of regular groups, although many offer impromptu groupings. For further information, call the music departments of the college.

Lewis and Clark College—0615 SW Palatine Hill Rd.

(244-6161). Lewis and Clark College Community Symphony, Wind Ensemble, Stage Band. The Lewis and Clark College Choir, Chamber Choir, College Community Chorus and the Collegium Musicum, Renaissance and baroque music for voice and instruments.

Portland State University—724 SW Harrison (229-3011). University Chorus, Chamber Choir, Madrigal Singers. Portland State University Orchestra (combined with the Marylhurst Education Center), Symphonetta, University Wind Ensemble, and the Percussion Ensemble.

Reed College—3203 SE Woodstock Blvd. (771-1112). Collegium Musicum, String Quartet, Reed College Orchestra, and impromptu groups.

University of Portland—5000 N. Willamette Blvd. (283-7319). University of Portland Community Symphony Orchestra, Concert Choir, Chamber Singers, Wind Ensemble, Jazz Ensemble. Solo recitals and mixed groups also are featured. The university will mail out a bi-monthly calendar of activities for those interested.

Other Music Groups

Friends of Chamber Music (229-4081)

Chamber Music Society of Oregon (771-8770)

Portland Chamber Orchestra, P.O. Box 544, Portland, 97207

Chamber Music Northwest, P.O. Box 751, Portland (229-4079)

Civic Choraliers, 7937 N. Hurst St. (284-3294)

Portland Symphonic Choir, P.O. Box 1517, Portland (226-1631)

Portland Chamber Music Northwest (229-4079)

Meister Singers, 125 NW Miller, Gresham (665-3813). Dr. David Quallf

Early Music Calliope, P.O. Box 93, Portland. Timothy Swain

After Dark

Portland offers hot and cool running music all over the town as it continues to prove why musicians are one of the city's major exports.

Now that young men and women are not concerned with preparing for the spring planting, many of them spend the long rainy months experimenting with chords, beats and novel patterns. Unique taverns and lounges display these new talents.

No one knows Portland music like John Wendeborn, critic for *The Oregonian*. A musician himself, this gentle man speaks the language and listens for different beats.

His orchestrations for night life vary from a string quartet through Dixieland, a fast-dying art form in the music field.

Among Wendeborn's choices is one spot for those under 21, **Arbuckle Flat Coffee House**, 1532 SW Morrison (222-5821), where those under age can "go for their kind of music without any hassle."

Musicians often waft away on their own chord process, so the scene in Portland constantly changes. Some of the most dependable include **Riddles**, 1217 SW Stark (224-7650), where Harold Lawrence String Quartet can be heard every Thurs.

Jam sessions are still going Sundays at the **Beachcomber**, 40 N. Lake, Lake Oswego (636-6677) and at **Function Junction**, 426 SE Hawthorne Blvd. (233-0755).

Lounges

Prima Donna, 2015 SW 4th (227-5951). Live music five nights a week.

Bill's Gold Coin, 2050 SW Morrison (228-1189)

Beachcomber, Lake Oswego (see above). Jazz during the week.

Sam's Hideaway, 800 E. Burnside (lower level of the Continental Motel (234-9979). Began as a lounge and restaurant under another "Sam" and continues under Sam-the-second with jazz.

Jazz De Opus, 33 NW 2nd (222-6077). The single listing now offering recorded music. But their quality selections draw approval from the professionals who like the quiet atmosphere and plush decor.

Taverns

Ken's Afterglow, 2229 SW Hawthorne Blvd. (235-7338). The first in the listing to offer what Wendeborn calls pub rock.

Frankenstein's, 737 SW Front (222-5217). Draws a variety of music styles seven nights a week. On Sun. night listen for Dr. Corn's Bluegrass Remedy.

Old Town Strutter's Hall, 120 NW 3rd (224-3285). Dixieland.

Belmont's Inn, 3357 SE Belmont (232-1998). Jazz.

Buffalo Head Tavern, east side of the I-5 freeway at
Tualatin (638-8232). Rock.

PC and S Tavern, corner SW 11th & Morrison (no
telephone). Folk music.

Claudia's Tavern, 3006 SE Hawthorne (232-1744). Folk
and folk rock.

Earth Tavern, 632 NW 21st (227-4573). Multi-media
tavern with plays, music, and films. Once a month they
shut down the bar, serve cider, and ask children to
enter through the Irving Street door.

Euphoria Inc., 315 SE 3rd (236-0883). Multi-media including traveling names, touring bands; some jazz,
mostly rock and roll.

The Faucet, 6821 SW Beaverton-Hillsdale Hwy. (297-
2702). One of the biggest taverns in the state, featuring
dancing with rock and a game room.

Darcel XV, 208 NW 3rd (222-5338). A gay tavern which
caters to straights during a female impersonator show
once a week.

Flight 181, 1116 SW Washington (248-0398), folk and rock.

Gazebo Gallery, 11 SW Mt. Jefferson Terr., Lake Oswego
(635-2506). Open seven days a week with a particularly
soft atmosphere on Fri. nights—wine and music in a
gallery situation.

The Sanctuary, NE 181st & Glisan. Large with rock
music.

Reuben's 5 Tavern, 1235 SW Jefferson (227-2283). Folk
singer and guitars.

Questing Beast Palace, 2845 SE Stark (233-8197). Multi-
media two-story tavern; no live music upstairs but the
coffee shop does stay open until 5 a.m.

Old Irish Inn, 7850 SW Barbur Blvd. (245-2711). Receives
the Wendeborn 4-star rating for its Irish food and Irish
music six nights a week; rock and roll on Sunday.

Silver Moon Tavern, 432 NW 21st (227-9012). Combination of rock on some nights, jazz on other.

Sopwith Camel Tavern, 1128 SW Jefferson (223-4807).
Singles and duos with folk rock.

Local Gentry, 4108 NE Sandy Blvd. (288-0920). Live
music on weekends.

Louis XIV, 2140 NE Sandy Blvd. (234-5629). Bluegrass
  every Saturday night.

Discotheque
Peter's Habit, 7 NW 3rd (228-3906)
Slabtown, corner of NW 16th & Lovejoy

Electronics

Television Stations
KATU-TV Channel 2, the ABC affiliate
KGW-TV Channel 8, the NBC affiliate
KOIN-TV Channel 6, the CBS affiliate
KPTV Channel 12, independent station
KOAP-TV, Channel 10, the educational station

Radio Stations

Easy Listening
KXL—95.5 FM 750 AM
KUPL—98.5 FM
KQFM—100.3 (Muzak)
Listener Supported
KBOO—90.7 FM
Middle of the road
KEX-1190
KJIB—99.5 FM
KOIN—970 AM 101.1 FM
KUIK—1360
Country & Western
KWJJ—1080
KRDR—1230
KPOK—1330
Educational
KOAC/KOAP—550 AM,
  91.5 FM
KBPS—1450

Talk
KKEY—1150
KYXI—1520 (all news)
Rock
KGON—92.3 FM
KGW—620
KPAM—97.1 FM
KINK—102 FM
KISN—910
KVAN—1480
Religious
KPDQ—800
Jazz
KLIQ—1290

SHOPPING

A Guide to Buying

SHOPPING is a fine art, honed to the last checkbook decimal and shaved to the tune of an exhausted partner's final plea. Portland is rich in shopping experiences and environments.

Its residents maintain the shrewd New England attitude of their forbears. They look for the best buy, regardless of where a store is located. Generally, one good store will draw others into its area, however, some remain smugly isolated, alone in their exceptional quality.

In this section you'll find individual services, regardless of location, a listing of shopping centers or areas, and finally thrift-minded stores, out-back ventures.

Stores sometimes resemble the circuit rider; just as they begin to spread a particular gospel, they move on. So check, by telephoning, before you head into the hinterlands.

Antiques

Is it an antique, is it junque, or is it just second hand? Only the dealer knows for sure, so be sure of your dealer. Some reliable sources include:

Baker's Bridge Farm Antiques, Carver (658-3563). Take 82nd Ave. south to Estacada and turn on 224th. Call first on this one, or you will find yourself out in the cold with your nose pressed to a tempting window of furniture.

Cast Iron and Cast-offs, 14941 S. Henrici Rd., Oregon City (656-0193). Warm yourself by one of the great variety of woodburning stoves for sale. During sunnier days you will see the best collection of carousel horses anywhere. Even their oddments are endearing.

Cathy's Antiques, 2425 NW Lovejoy St. (223-1767). Excellent collection of fine glassware and china.

China Gate Antiques, 1024 SW Alder St. (222-2541). Some excellent jade pieces and some old furniture.

Arthur W. Erickson, 630 SW 12th Ave. (227-4710). Has the best collection of Indian baskets in the city.

Evilo Eaton Antiques, 7825 SE 13th Ave. (235-6414). Respected name in the business. English pieces and good jewelry as well as doll house memorabilia are included in her specialties.

Greenville Station, 2440 SW Vista Ave. (227-2721). Interesting assortment.

Joneses Antiques, 9661 SW Canyon Rd. (292-1797). Primitives, postcards and excellent selection of old hardware.

Marneff Antiques, 6515 N. Interstate Ave. (289-2645). Museum quality for some things; leave your children elsewhere.

McDuffee-Mongeon Galleries, 115 SW Ash St. (223-9093). Estate appraisers bring in many fine pieces including silver, glass, and furniture.

Oak Tree Antiques, 7783 SW Capitol Hwy. (244-4536). Furniture and stained glass.

George Root Jr., 2381 NW Flanders St. (223-7834). Call before on this one also. Fine collection of brass and furniture.

Second Hand Rose, 2168 W. Burnside St. (227-5282). Begins to lead us into the funquey junque, but there are some definite buys scattered about. For others of varying ilk, try the yellow pages in the telephone directory.

Books

Abigail Brown Books, 1975 SW 1st. (222-3942). At Portland Center which includes other specialty shops.

B. Dalton Bookseller, 530 SW 5th Ave. (222-3851), Lloyd Center (288-6343), and Washington Square in Tigard. (620-3007). A chain, but it distinguishes itself by knowing what books are in the store.

Brian Thomas Books, Galleria, 921 SW Morrison (222-2934).

Children's Book Store, 148½ SW B St., Lake Oswego (636-5438). Some books autographed by the authors.

J.K. Gill Co., 408 SW 5th Ave. (224-2800). Branches at Eastport Plaza, Jantzen Beach Center, Lloyd Center and Washington Square. This store, one of the "pioneer" firms in Portland, now has included office furniture, games, stationery, and art supplies in its inventory.

Graham's Books, 460 SW 2nd St., Lake Oswego (636-5676).

Green Dolphin Bookshop, 215 SW Ankeny St. (224-3060). Marvelous assortment of old and rare books.

House of Titles, Water Tower, 5331 SW Macadam (228-0290).

Katharine McCanna Book Counselor, P.O. Box 13534 (234-7664). The lady to call when you know what you want but can't find it. She and Edith Bristol, both retired from local bookstores, represent nearly a century of involvement in literature.

Midway Bookstore, 2532 SE 122nd (761-4155).

Old Oregon Book Store, 610 SW 12th Ave. (227-2742). Rare books, especially dealing with the Oregon country.

Portland State University Book Store, SW 6th & Hall St. (226-2631). Not just for the intelligentsia.

Skidmore Village Children's Books, 50 SW 3rd Ave. (222-5076). Probably the largest inventory of children's books in the state.

The Book Cellar, 267 SW A St., Lake Oswego (636-7403).

The Book Vault, 3125 SW Cedar Hills Blvd., Beaverton (646-0396).

Volume I, Mall 205, 10018 SE Washington (252-7122).

Walden Books, Jantzen Beach Mall (289-3319).

A Woman's Place Bookstore, 1300 SW Washington (226-0848).

Nor'wester Book Shop, 222 NW Davis (228-2747).

Bakeries

Bohemian Pastry Shops (see Yellow Pages for locations of 11 shops) Each offers its own specials plus chocolate whipped cream and banana cream cakes.

Helen Bernhard Bakery, 1717 NE Broadway (287-1251). An institution in Portland.

Jenkinson-Ikeda Pastry Shop, 6330 SW Capitol Hwy. (244-7473). Customers argue over whether the cake donut or the raised donut is better. Everyone agrees on the black bread and the pink champagne cake.

Middle East Bakeries, Inc., 8005 SE Stark St. (252-3006). Makes the unleavened Middle and Far East breads which have become so popular. It's a special treat to get it right out of the oven.

Rose's, 715 NW 23rd Ave. (227-4875). Home of the giant cinnamon roll and twelve million calories, every one of them worth it.

Children's Clothing

Without doubt, the finest and most extensive shop for children is:

Youngland, 30 NW 23 Pl. (227-1414) which outfits children from the bib stage to the junior prom. This store has gained a west coast reputation for its boys' sport coats, beautifully tailored and proportioned. Everything, including these famous coats goes on sale twice a year. Anyone not afraid of a determined horde of mothers should make the sale a must.

Cooking Supplies

Cook Shack, 515 SW Broadway in Morgan's Alley (224-1360). French cookware.

The Kobos Co., The Water Tower, 1553 SW Macadam (222-5226). Freshly ground coffees and many teas, spices and herbs plus a multitude of cooking aids from small accessories to large wrought iron pot hangers.

Kitchen Kaboodle, 8788 SW Hall Blvd. (643-5491). Newcomer on the kitchen scene, but what it lacks in seniority, it makes up for in availability.

Kitchen Kupboard, 5027 NE 42nd Ave. (284-7023). Specializes in hard to find kitchen tools.

Lakeside Drugs, 464 SW 1st, Lake Oswego (636-4593). Almost half of this large pharmacy is given to baskets, French cookware and unusual oddments to perk up your interest in cooking.

Copies

J.Y. Hollingsworth, 104 SW 2nd Ave. (223-8181). Instant copying service and the home of Portland calligraphers at Christmas time. These gentlemen are most helpful when it comes time to reproduce a homemade card.

Crafts

J.K. Gill Co., 408 SW 5th Ave. (224-2800). Entire basement level has art materials, including engineering supplies at one end and handmade paper at the other with craft items in between.

J. Thayer Stationer, 12220 SW 1st, Beaverton (646-9191). Usually has an "artist in residence" in addition to two floors of supplies.

Reed College Book Store, 3203 SW Woodstock Blvd. (774-2826). Treasure trove for serious calligraphers. The college is the home ground of now retired Lloyd Reynolds, "the father of 20th century calligraphy." It rises to the occasion.

Macramé

You can pick up macramé supplies nearly everywhere, but two shops deal in nothing else.

Let's Knot, 702 5th, Oregon City (655-2385). Has a very unobtrusive sign since it is in an old residential area of Oregon City and is the home of Connie Nicoud. Her main floor rooms are filled with baskets of tempting beads of all types and string of every possible color.

Two Ladies—218 NW Couch (223-9155). Natural wood beads, imported beads, silver, turquoise, coral, special orders.

Spinning and Weaving

Arachne Webworks, 2930 NW Thurman St. (227-0134). Indigo as well as other hard to find dyes and wool.

Wildflower Fibres, 211 NW Davis St. (222-4044). Looms, wool, and specialty yarns as well as many wood and china bits for macramé or weaving.

Robin and Russ, McMinnville (472-5760). Draws the serious spinners just south of Portland for a wide assortment of wheels, looms, wool carders, and other weaving accessories.

If all you lack is the inspiration, drive to the Pioneer Craft School at the Damascus barn (658-2704), Damascus, about 15 minutes from 82nd Ave., to see classes in progress. Two dozen different spinning wheels are chattering in a great circle while the looms, both traditional and Navajo, clack away in another room. The barn also offers classes in quilting and is an inspiration in itself should you be tempted to tear down an old building of your own. The shop sells swifts and other spinning and weaving accessories as well as some fine handmade items. Open weekdays until 4 p.m.

Fabrics

Calico Corners, 8526 SW Terwilliger Blvd. (244-6700). See "Thrifty Places to Shop."

Daisy Kingdom Wholesale Fabrics and Trims Inc., 217 NW Davis St. (222-9033). The unusual, the usual, and everything in between.

June's Fabric Shop, 429 SW 1st, Lake Oswego (636-5505). Probably the widest selection in the greater Portland area.

Fish and Seafood

To live less than two hours from the ocean and not know where to find fresh fish is ridiculous. But if you have no time to cross the mountains, several stores will do it for you on a daily basis. Incidentally, never look for sole two days after a storm at sea. The sole is a shy fish and will not rise in rolling waters.

Plancich Fish Co., 300 NW 13th Ave. (227-6416). The last of the colorful fish markets; located in the warehouse district. Just pull over the train tracks and park between the box cars.

Tony's Fish Market, 14th & Washington Sts., Oregon City (656-7512). This market is so particular that owners have their own crab pots. Like Frank Buck, they "bring them back alive."

Florists

We're not called the City of Roses for nothing. Some specialty shops go a scent further.

Burkhardt Florist Inc., 2405 W Burnside St. (223-6151). Has been in Portland since 1882. The shop includes an incredible array of pots, planters, and china elephants to carry them.

Flowers by Dorcas, 617 SW Washington St. (227-6454). Complete turnover of merchandise with every season. Specialties include imported silk flowers, imaginative

dried arrangements year around, and special gift items
for children. At Christmas look for decorated Yule logs
to be delivered as hostess gifts.

Tommy Luke Downtown Shop, 625 SW Morrison St. (228-
3131). Owner Charles Koefler has made the pages of
House Beautiful with his Victorian floral arrangements
for old Portland homes.

Wildwood Weeds, 2036 W. Burnside (228-0325). Great
varieties of indoor plants. Proprietor is happy to advise
you on your sick ones at home as well as to sell you
new ones.

Gift Shops

Anyone, and usually his mother, can operate a gift
shop. But some do it with flair, such as the woman who
had just finished decorating a birthday cake for her
grandson. A customer dropped by as she added the last
slap of icing, and it was love at first sight when he saw
the cake. Of course she sold it to him and then rushed out
to a nearby supermarket to buy another for her grandson.
That's what gives a gift shop owner elan.

Others, who might do the same, include:

And Things Inc., 3125 SW Cedar Hills Blvd. (646-7613).
Baskets, jewelry, pottery, toys, and lots of imports from
European gift markets.

The Calendar, John's Landing (227-5855). Christmas year
around.

Carl Starker Shop, 5220 SE Hall, Milwaukie (654-6361).
A literal pioneer in the area with an eye and a shelf for
anything interesting.

Carriage House Boutique, 629 SW Washington St. (227-
3077). Hand-blown eggs with a porcelain quality. They
will mount your child's picture on an egg of heirloom
quality; handmade patchwork skirts, and other extra-
ordinaire.

Raleigh Hills Rexall Drugs, 7306 SW Beaverton-Hillsdale
Hwy. (292-3539). You could go Christmas shopping for
a family of 12 on December 24 and make it seem that
you had been hand picking all over the city for a year.

Red Wagon Store, 19730 NE Sandy Blvd. (666-4561).
Freshly ground coffees, rare teas, and the pots and
cups to serve them both in.

Kathleen Rockwell, 734 SW Morrison St. (223-6235).
Exquisite dolls and porcelain eggs.

Elsie Ames Gifts, 12300 SW Bull Mountain Rd., Tigard
(639-1802). Open just before Easter and Christmas with
appropriate and special trimmings and gifts.

Gourmet Shops

An over-used word if ever there was one, but the en-
ticing odors wafting from these doorways would probably
draw you to them if we did not:

Anderson's Delicatessen, 9575 SW Beaverton Hwy.,
Beaverton (643-5415). Owner Verne Anderson has built
a following with his wines and cheeses. He assembles
both for entertaining, or you can browse his shop and
gain 25 pounds just by looking. (Lox lovers, stop here.)

Anzen Oriental Foods and Imports, 736 NE Union Ave.
(233-5111). Everything, including fresh vegetables, for
the wok.

Harris Wine Cellars Ltd., 210 NW 21st Ave. (223-2222).
The late Bert Harris taught many Portland businessmen the right way to smell a cork. Now the shop has expanded to cheese and wine and sandwiches.

Pieri's Delicacies Inc., 3824 SE Powell Blvd. (232-7003).
Memorize this telephone number, and call ahead for the
finest pizza ever assembled to be taken home and baked
in your own oven. While you wait for the final touches,
browse through marzipan and dried mushrooms, wine
and cheese.

Strohecker's Inc., 2855 SW Patton Rd. (223-7391). Far
more than a delicatessen. It is the last of the neighborhood grocery stores—but what a neighborhood. Here
you can find strawberries, out of season, and many
other foods to tickle a tired palate. Liquor store on
premises.

Tuck Lung Co., 205 NW 4th Ave. (223-1090). The next time
you return from the grocery store and your husband
says, brightly, "did you have a nice time, dear?" make
sure that you have been to Tuck Lung and for once you
can say "yes." Sit down for a cup of tea and an
excellent Chinese lunch before or after you shop in this
unique combination restaurant-grocery.

Imports

Import items are available all over the state. Several stores such as Import Plaza (1 NW Couch St., Lloyd Center, and Washington Square), H-K Limited (1002 SW 6th Ave., Jantzen Beach Center, Washington Square, and Eastport Plaza), and Pier One Imports (14410 SE Stark St., 9307 SW Beaverton-Hillsdale Hwy. and 5331 SW Macadam at John's Landing) contain everything that can be crammed on a ship.

Individual foreign specialty shops are best. Among them:

China Gate Antiques, 1024 SW Alder St. (222-2541)

Designs of Scandinavia, 2173 NE Broadway (288-3045)

Eye of Ra (native Greek imports), John's Landing (224-4292).

Kathleen Connolly Irish Shop, 725 SW 10th Ave. (228-4482)

Quintana's Indian Arts and Crafts, 139 NW 2nd Ave. (223-1729)

Kennels

Since some accommodations do not welcome Fido, this seems like a promising spot to include kennel boarding services. Two of the best:

The Charlton Kennels, Sauvie Island (621-3675) also trains gun dogs and those for field trails. In addition the Charltons will give boarders extra love and attention as well as a good run in the open fields. Dogs once boarded there will return to jump from the car and run in eagerly. Call ahead several weeks for reservation, if possible.

GG's Dog Inn, Rt. 1, Box 276, West Linn (638-4101) boards dogs and cats and offers heated and air conditioned runs with piped-in music to sooth the nervous beasties. Grooming pickup and delivery available on request.

Jewelers

Jerome Margulis, 701 SW Broadway St. (227-1153). Has some estate jewelry.

Zell Bros. Jewelers, 800 SW Morrison St. (227-8471) and
Washington Square in Tigard (620-3610). Both stores do
custom work and repair in addition to carrying a fine
selection of jewelry.

Men's Specialty Shops

All but one of the following men's stores originated
in Portland.

Estes, 2364 W. Burnside St. (227-0275). Is not complete
without a word with owner Este Morrison. An avid
golfer, he has designed his own "wet suit" and can run
through the hazards and handicaps of any west coast
golf course. Custom tailoring.

John Helmer, 969 SW Broadway (223-4976). Wears all the
hats in town. If you want one, go see him.

Norm Thompson, 1805 NW Thurman St. (221-0380). Low
on decor, high on the unusual. Look for shearling
jackets and Irish tweeds.

Rosenblatts, corner SW 6th Ave. & Alder St. (226-4701).
Very complete men's haberdashery.

M and HH Sichel, 519 SW 6th Ave. (223-1800). Solid con-
servatism in the best English tradition.

Albert Ltd., 900 SW 5th Ave. (224-2020). Began in Seattle,
but we will forgive them since they stock such smash-
ing tartan trousers.

Miniatures

Miniatures (don't call them doll house furniture) have
become the third largest hobby in the United States.

Card and Candle Miniatures, 521 SW 10th (227-4997).
Largest assortment in the city.

Enchanted Doll House, 625 SW Washington St. (224-
3322). It is.

Nurseries

Gerber Gardens, 15780 SW Boones Ferry Rd., Lake
Oswego (636-5565). This garden center plants hanging
herb baskets which flower into beautiful meals. Come
summer, when the fields are yielding the best produce,
Gerber's cannily gathers just the best and displays
freshly washed carrots in a granite bowl, just-picked

blackberries, and pickling cucumbers wood-crated by size.

Kasch's Garden Center and Nursery, 8135 SE McLoughlin Blvd. (235-5424); 3250 SW Cedar Hills Blvd., Beaverton (644-1640). More than 200 varieties of rhododendrons, large supply of young trees. If you can't find what you want, they will get it for you if it's still growing anywhere.

George L. Routledge Co., 1852 SE Hawthorne Blvd. (232-7111). The place to go with garden questions. Mr. R. has all the answers.

West Linn Garden Center, 5605 W. Portland Ave., West Linn (655-4577). Don't bother to call here, just drop in seven days a week to see what the owners have found. One year it was patio climbing tomato plants, already deep red for picking; another time it was hanging strawberry gardens, a third year brought 7 yr. old blueberry bushes.

Wishing Well Farm and Garden Center, 599 SW A, Lake Oswego (636-7744). Home gardeners count on them for good seed potatoes, Oregon Giant green bean seeds, and other hard-to-find garden starts—all hidden behind a commerical atmosphere of bird baths and geraniums.

Pharmacies

Irving Street Pharmacy, 638 NW 23rd Ave. (223-6297). Keeps its prices down by doing a high volume business. And it isn't hard to find out why once you've met owner Milt Olshen, a Portland landmark in himself. He opens his store every day but Sunday to dispense drugs and philosophy.

Medic Pharmacy Inc., 1016 SW Clay St. (222-9611). Open Monday through Friday, offers economy in prescriptions also.

Sporting Goods

Caplan Sport Shop, 521 SW 4th Ave. (226-6467). Larger than two basketball courts and has everything at every price.

Larry's Sport Center, Oregon City Shopping Center, Oregon City (656-0321). Hunter's and fisherman's paradise (fishing licenses available here).

Stationers with Style

Helen M. Clark Co., 811 SW Broadway St. (222-5666).
Small but select and very friendly.

Zell Bros. Jewelers, 800 SW Morrison St. (227-8471). A
most traditional stationery department on the 2nd floor,
including engraved monogrammed notepaper, and hard-
to-find heavyweight blank place cards.

Tailors

Bee Tailors and Cleaners, 1222 SW Salmon St. (227-
1144). Eventually gets most of the alterations in town
anyway so you might as well meet Heinz, the magician,
who can make a pair of pants fit right just by looking
at them.

Toys

King Norman's Kingdom of Toys, Washington Square,
(620-3700). A child's paradise. King Norman offers
weekly specials which are way below discount house
everyday prices.

Mrs. Tiggy-Winkles, Water Tower Building, John's Landing (227-7084). Some say, the best teddy bears in town,
toys, children's clothing, hand-crafted items.

Thinker Toys, advertised as Oregon's own educational
toy store, 10655 SW Greenburg Rd., Tigard, (639-2511).
Custom products for those who think learning can be
fun.

Toyland, 1305 Lloyd Center (284-6414). Still ranks high in
its assortment of toys. Model train buffs will like the
display.

Callin's Novelties, the House of Magic, 412 SW 4th Ave.
(223-4821). Where you take a bored boy on a rainy day.
In addition to the Atlantic City poo-poo cushions and
the joy buzzers, look for magic tricks (which employees
will demonstrate) and small party favors. Tell them the
theme and they will dig in the deepest boxes, cheer-
fully. The help will steer children from the center aisle,
which contains some off-color items for the boys who
never grew up.

Women's Apparel

Fifth Avenue Shop, 711 SW 10th Ave. (223-8127). Very old Portland.

I. Magnin, 930 SW 6th Ave. (226-7811) is I. Magnin is I. Magnin with possibly the prettiest women's restroom in town.

Nordstrom's, 655 SW Broadway (224-6666), Lloyd Center, and Washington Square, carries the usual throughout the store and the unusual in the Collector's Corner. Clerks are very helpful in telephoning to other branches to find the correct size.

Norm Thompson, 1805 NW Thurman St. (221-0380) has built its reputation on English shearling coats, Irish woolens, and safari pants.

Simi's, Washington Square (620-0282). When this shop says "designer," you had better believe it. The word is out, among the women, that this is the spot to check, but take a good look at your checkbook balance first. Many one-of-a-kind fashions and an unusual sales force. After fitting you, they will be the first to tell you "that is not for you."

Traveler's Choice, 459 SW 2nd, Lake Oswego (636-3310). Specializes in packables, including several well-known imported knit and woolen labels.

Shopping Centers and Special Spots

Rumor raced the streets of Portland in 1893 that this small port town would soon face what the rest of the nation felt—the closure of banks and a collapse of the economy. A young merchant, Aaron Meier, who had come to Portland from Germany the year before, paid a late evening call upon his friend, Henry Corbett.

"I have gold and it is at your disposal," Meier offered.

The next morning Henry Corbett, clad in frock coat and starched shirt front, stood amid bags of gold in the lobby of his bank. Those who had come to take their money out stayed to invest more.

You may draw whatever parable you wish from this story, which happens to be true, but it is a dandy lead-in to major stores and shopping centers in the Portland area.

Counting downtown Portland as a shopping center, which it has become since so many merchants allow free parking with a stamp of a sales slip, the Portland area claims 19 centralized areas for shopping. Some seem to be stretching the word a bit, by including a strip of stores strung along a parking lot.

Downtown

This is where you will find main branches of the largest department stores in the city. Saturday is the best day to visit this area since suburbanites flock to the outlying areas on the weekend swelling the parking to mile wide perimeters.

Lipman's, 521 SW 5th Ave. (228-8111). Offers nine floors of general merchandise including its own tea room, chocolate lounge, and Perkin's Pub in the basement, a spot for hearty sandwiches and home-style soups.

Meier and Frank, 621 SW 5th Ave. (227-4400). Ten floors (not counting the basement and sub-basement levels) of general merchandise. Famous for its Friday Surprise sales. Look in its bargain basement for seconds. Waitresses at the tea room (10th floor) have been serving luncheons on white linen cloths with silver settings since the store's beginning.

Nordstrom, 625 SW Broadway (224-6666). The new newcomer but holds its own in the women's fine apparel line. It also has the largest shoe department in town. Plans are under way for an even more extensive store in the downtown area, much to the relief of other merchants in the area who work 24 hours a day to promote the inner city concept.

J.C. Penney Inc., 638 SW 5th Ave. (221-6520).

Quick Turns Down Narrow Streets

Morgan's Alley—Enter at the Pot Shop, 515 SW Broadway or turn down the brick steps to Rian's Eating Establishment off Alder St. Either way you will run into a subterranean honeycomb of fine specialty shops and restaurants. Spend a rainy day as well as money here.

Old Town—Reaching from SW Ankeny to NW Everett Sts. along 2nd Ave. Old Town is a monumental effort to restore Portland's old iron front buildings and other early structures. (See Old Town walking tour).

Uptown Shopping Center—One of those "strips along a parking lot," but has spread well. This area, located at W. Burnside & 23rd Ave. includes three specialty women's wear shops, a good men's store, children's wear, The Coffee Bean Coffee Co., Uptown Hardware, which is more than tacks and nails, and on and on. This one grew like Topsy, park your car and walk it. Several restaurants will sustain your tour.

Outlying Shopping Centers

The Lloyd Center—NE 10th Ave. & Weidler St. At last count this center contained more than 140 stores and a covered ice arena. Free parking for 8,000 cars. Shoppers will find enclosed pedestrian malls, landscaped with trees, flowers and fountains. The largest store in the development is Meier and Frank, followed by Penney's and J.J. Newberry Co. Other large stores include F.W. Woolworth, Nordstrom, Lipman's, Rosenblatt's, and Roos/Atkins.

Jantzen Beach Center—Just south of the Interstate Bridge. Small but fun for children, since developers have retained the original amusement park features. Carousel rides are a quarter, and the old automatic fortune teller still plies her cards for a dime. Liberty House is the largest store in the center, which includes many small specialty shops.

Ports O'Call—4555 N. Channel St. Seems to be doing a brisk turnover in leases, but the brick structure with breathtaking glimpses of the river make it a pleasant place to stroll on a warm day. Scattered among the import shops are several restaurants.

Washington Square—9585 SW Washington Square Rd., off Hwy. 219. Newest of the centers. Completely enclosed and built around California-style concourses planted with trees and flowers, the multitude of department stores and small shops have no doors but open onto temperature-controlled walkways.

The Water Tower—5331 SW Macadam Ave. First in a series of Willamette riverside enterprises which abut the newest greenway on the water's edge. The building itself was once a mattress factory, and architects left the old hardwood floors and other structural devices when they added more than 40 specialty shops at interesting angles. The Water Tower also houses six restaurants.

Thrifty Places to Shop

Once-a-Year Sales

Ascension Attic Treasure Sale, 1823 SW Spring St. (227-7806). Held every May. The ladies of the chapel do a fine job of assembling antiques and lesser objects from Portland's older homes.

Bybee-Howell House Wintering-Inn, Sauvie Island. Sale held by the Oregon Historical Society the last Saturday in September.

Catlin-Gabel Rummage Sale is such a Portland institution that the date is set a year in advance. The sale runs three days at the Memorial Coliseum. One year the offerings included an entire room of used bicycles. Call the school (297-1894) or watch the newspapers for the dates.

Oregon Episcopal Schools' Country Fair. Last Saturday in April on the school grounds at 6300 SW Nichol Rd. Children can ride the carnival midway attractions while you shop the rummage and antique sale. Book buyers bring their own empty cartons to carry away the vast selection of used books and records.

Also noteworthy are the sales held by Temple Beth Israel (222-1069) and Trinity Episcopal Church (222-9811). Call for the dates or watch the newspapers for announcements.

Thrift Shops

Assistance League Thrift Shop, 735 NW 23rd Ave. (227-7093).

Bargain Tree (Junior League), 912 SW 3rd Ave. (227-7413)

Bluejay Wear Haus, 5335 NE 42nd Ave. (282-2126)

Canterbury House, 1604 SW Boones Ferry Rd., Lake Oswego (635-5023)

Christie's Attic Thrift Shop, 7907 SE 13th Ave. (236-0222)

Council Thrift Shop, 300 SW Stark St. (227-2877)

Goodwill Industries of Oregon, 1831 SE 6th Ave. (238-6165; Lents Store, 9130 SE Woodstock Blvd. (774-7503); St. Johns Store, 8641 N. Lombard St. (286-5646); Walnut Park Store, 5270 NE Union Ave. (281-7323)

J and O's Thrift Store, 6712 NE Sandy Blvd. (287-1583)

Nearly New Shop (Portland Chapter of Hadassah) 3415 SE Hawthorne Blvd. (235-8053)

Old Church, The Church Mouse Thrift Shop, 1422 SW
11th Ave. (222-2031)
Parry Center Thrift Shop, 709 NW 23rd Ave. (227-6201)
Red White and Blue Thrift Store, 19239 McLoughlin
Blvd., Gladstone (655-3444)
The Resale Shop, 12505 SW Broadway, Beaverton (644-
6364)
St. Vincent dePaul, 2740 SE Powell Blvd. (234-0594)
Union Gospel Mission, 140 SW Yamhill (228-4529); SE
store, 5615 SE 82nd Ave. (771-3510); NE store, 5620 NE
Union Ave. (287-0910)
Value Village Thrift Store, 5050 SE 82nd Ave. (777-4736)
Veterans Rehabilitation and Thrift Centers, 12415 SW
Powell Blvd. (760-1676); 7720 SE 82nd Ave. (775-4343)
Young Women's Christian Assn., Y's Buys Shop, 1127 SW
Morrison (222-2669)

Reduced and Resale Clothing, Women

As one husband was heard to roar, "women's clothing is the biggest racket in the world." Which is not to
say that these shops do not have a finger in the pot, but
at least they only dip into the second knuckle.
Act II, 1139 SW Morrison St. (227-7969). Designer clothing often.
Cinderella Samples, 8101 SE Stark St. (252-0408). Brand
names, not all sizes.
Clothes Closet, 425 2nd St., Lake Oswego (636-5932). Resale, often current styles.
The Clothes Out, 9525 SW Beaverton-Hillsdale Hwy. (646-
0400). Separates of brand name sportswear. Save 75%
during sales.
Julie's Resale Shop, 6920 NE Sandy Blvd. (284-1336).
Select stock.
A.G. Sacks, 8855 SW Beaverton-Hillsdale Hwy. (292-
2119). New styles, some labels cut out. Well-known
brands.
Sally's Sample Shop, 7776 SW Capitol Hwy. (244-6403).
Overstock, sizes 6-24.
Sample Nook, 6307 SW Capitol Hwy. (246-9363). Sales-
men's samples, sizes 7-12.
Sample Shack, 1804 NE 40th Ave. (284-3330) and 430 SW
2nd, Lake Oswego (636-3922). Wide range of sizes
jammed into these stores. Sports to dress styles.

Mens, Children's Clothing

If you are going to come home from a shopping spree laden with bundles for yourself, it's a good idea to tuck in a few things for the rest of the family. To give you that "selfless" appearance, try these stores.

Clothes Line, 16585 SE Milwaukie Blvd., Milwaukie (654-2722). Whistling clean new shop with name brand children's clothing. New shipments made weekly, so keep in touch.

C/Y's House of Samples, 6800 NE Killingsworth St. (287-5770). Largest sample store in Northwest, includes women and men's clothing, children and infants, and ski wear.

Dehen Knitting Co., 404 NW 10th Ave. (222-3871). This local firm specializes in school sweaters and athletic jackets. The outlet store carries mostly adult sizes.

The Fabric, 8624 SW Hall Blvd. (Progress Plaza) (644-3410). Women's wear, junior sizes, coats and ski wear.

House of Uniforms, 811 SW Morrison St. (223-9993). Budget store for the other branches, including discontinued styles for men and women.

Jayvee R.N. Inc., 113 SW Foothills Rd., Lake Oswego (636-9691). Infant clothing at 50 percent reduction.

Pendleton Mills, Washougal, Wash. (take I-5 north to Camas exit on Washington State side. At Washougal you can see the name on the watertower.) All seconds and irregulars made by Pendleton are sold here. Woolen yardage available also.

The Sales Room, 11875 SW Pacific Hwy., Tigard (620-5456). Casual wear for the family; irregulars marked.

The Tailor's Touch, 3849 SE Powell Blvd. (233-5365). Obviously not the hub of the fashion world, but low overhead in this shop means men's suits, slacks, and sport coats at considerable savings. Also custom work.

Shoes

Al's Shoe Store, 5811 SE 82nd Ave. (771-2130). Men's and boy's shoes.

B and R Family Shoe Store, 2940 NE Alberta St. (281-5819). Includes famous names in tennis and athletic shoes at 50 percent off.

Discount Shoe Center, 13815 SE McLoughlin Blvd. (654-0729). Family shoes at a saving. Discontinued women's shoes at one price.

Doane's Shoe Box, 7116 NE Sandy Blvd. (282-6845). Keep
checking in; this is a sample shop with sizes 4-12.

Hank's Family Shoe Store, 8878 Sandy Blvd. (253-7098).
Biggest selection in men's shoes, but good range of
sizes from infants on up.

Books

Armchair "Family" Bookstore, 3205 SE Milwaukie (236-
0270). Comic books and paper backs. Especially nice to
children.

Cameron's Books and Magazines, 336 SW 3rd Ave. (228-
2391). Takes a lot of browsing.

Old Weird Herald's, 6804 NE Broadway (254-4942). Even
conducts a mail order business which includes children's books, comics and paper backs.

Powell Books, 1207 W. Burnside St. (228-4651). More than
100,000 books.

General Merchandise

This covers everything you want and some things you
haven't thought about. Most are at a better price than
you will find elsewhere.

A-Boy Electric and Plumbing Supply, 1701 SW Jefferson
(222-1914). Electric fixtures for less.

A-1 Electric and Plumbing Supply, 3910 SE 82nd Ave.
(775-3616). Even the electricians use this one for low
cost standard fixtures.

Andy and Bax, 324 SE Grand Ave. (234-7538). Army and
Navy surplus and then some. Everything from clothing
(fatigues and wool caps) to odd lots of plexi-glass which
makes great palettes for Sunday painters.

Bargains Galore, 1425 NW Glisan St. (222-2185). Clothing, sporting goods, hardware, etc.

Bee Company, 800 N. Killingsworth St. (283-3171). The
grandaddy of the railroad salvage business. Includes
freight-damaged groceries, furniture, clothing, and
more.

Captain Whiz Eagles, 535 SE Grand Ave. (233-0079).
Creative Playtings at a lower price.

Discount Wallpaper, 10510 NE Halsey St. (256-3400). Discontinued patterns at 50 percent reduction.

Golden's Inc., 825 SE Madison St. (233-6593). Cheaper
by the dozen or the case—glasses, mixes and bar
supplies.

Jafco, 619 SW Alder St. (221-0844) and 10500 SW Beaverton Hwy., Beaverton (643-6771). Brisk catalog business, particularly during the holiday season. Visit their showrooms for everyone in the family.

Kida Company, 127 NW 23rd Ave. (227-2544). Small appliances, housewares, luggage, and cameras at discount catalog prices.

Meier and Frank Co., 621 SW 5th Ave. (227-4411). Bargain basement for many irregulars and discontinued items, especially linens.

Montgomery Ward and Co. Bargain Annex, 2301 NW 26th Ave. (227-7631). Catalog returns, discontinued items, and who knows what else.

Mountain Shop, 628 NE Broadway St. (288-6768). Ski equipment resales, every October through the Schnee Voegli Ski Club.

Oregon Retired Persons Pharmacy, 1501 SW Taylor St. Worth special mention since it caters exclusively to retired persons passing on savings in prescriptions, over the counter drugs, and other geriatric supplies.

Sealco, 209 SW 1st Ave. (222-9293). Roll up your sleeves and have at this show room, which includes diamonds behind the counter and seconds in luggage. There is no charge for the dust on some items.

Sears Roebuck and Co. Outlet Store, 5230 N. Basin St. (Swan Island). Carries the store's furniture and large appliance rejects.

Sears Roebuck and Co. Surplus Store, 718 NE Irving St. (238-2080). Catalog returns, discontinued stock, etc.

Standard Brands Paint Co., 20 NE Hancock St. (287-8098). Arts and craft items, floor coverings, paint, and wallpaper.

United Glass and Bottle Co., 335½ SE Morrison St. (235-4214). Canning jars, wine bottles, and lids for both.

Village Store, 6108 NE Glisan St. (236-5071). Everything from jam and jelly to nuts and bolts.

Wholesale Fountain Supply, 936 SE Clay St. (233-6411). What would you expect? Glasses, napkins, straws, all by the case lot of 500.

Zidell Explorations Inc., corner SW Gibbs & Moody (228-8691). Largest salvage yard in the city. Mostly marine goods—take your choice of hatch covers, lockers, shipboard safes, and mess kits. Leave little boys at home or take them as a birthday treat—it can be expensive.

Fabrics

American Fabrics, 308 NW 11th Ave. (222-3665). Drapery and upholstery goods.

Barton Fabric Shop, just across from the general store, Barton, may prove worth the drive along the Clackamas River to find doubleknits at very low prices. Check each piece carefully.

Calico Corner, 8526 SW Terwilliger Blvd. (244-6700) Drapery and upholstery fabric. Smart hostesses look for the extra wide chintz to make tablecloths.

Discount Fabrics—all these shops have somewhat lower prices: Gateway Shopping Center, 1408 NE 100th Ave. (253-5710) Main Store, 900 SE Sandy Blvd. (234-7433) Raleigh Hills Shopping Center, 4790 SW 76th Ave. (292-4887) Rockwood Plaza Shopping Center, 2240 SE 182nd Ave. (665-5070) Southgate Shopping Center, 10405 SE 82nd Ave. (774-3388)

Jantzen Fabric Outlet, 2012 NE Hoyt St. (238-5396). Not all fabrics are from Jantzen but everything is of good quality.

John Gilbert Manufacturing Co., 9009 SE 82nd Ave. (774-0630). Everything for upholstery.

Oregon Leather Co., 110 NW 2nd Ave. (228-4105). Whether you plan to bind a book or patch a jacket, you will find assorted bits of beautiful leathers in the barrels at this old Portland firm.

Records

CrystalShip, located in the old Rhodes building, SW 10th & Morrison St. (222-4935). Pioneer tenant in what promises to be an interesting shopping arcade.

Everybody's Record Co., 8660 SW Canyon Rd. (297-4141) or 7901 SE Stark St. (255-4141)

Long Hair Music, 915 SW 9th Ave. (224-8542)

Food

The price of eating is becoming a little hard to swallow. If you keep your appetite down and your ears open you may hear of several other spots to cut grocery bills.

Bakery Thrift Stores—With the exception of a new car, nothing depreciates so quickly as bakery goods. Your freezer will rejuvenate breads and pastries.

American Bakeries (Langendorf Divison), 14510 SE Stark St. (254-5476) 1711 SE 10th Ave. (234-6421) 16585 SE McLoughlin Blvd. (659-5722)

Oroweat Bakeries, also carry whole wheat and other whole grain flours: 17450 SW Boones Ferry Rd., Lake Oswego (635-3796) 10750 SW 5th, Beaverton (643-5541) 1100 SE 199th, Gresham (643-5541 ext. 37) 8308 SE Woodstock Blvd. (643-5541 ext. 51)

Franz, 300 NE 11th Ave. (232-2191)

Pfaff's (broken cookie shop), 2132 SE Division St. (232-4292)

Sweetheart Bakeries, 1403 SE Stark St. (235-4145)

Wonderbread and Hostess, N. Cook and Vancouver Ave. (no telephone)

Canned Goods—You can buy canned goods at special caseload savings once a year at several grocery chains. At least three businesses deal in case lots the year around.

Cannery Outlet, 4010 SE 114th, Beaverton (646-3288)

Harold Bettis Canned Goods, 135 SE 135th Ave. (760-1991)

Northwest Canners Outlet, 8600 SE 82nd Ave. (775-1750)

Soda pop—Cases are available at The Pop Shoppe. After the initial deposit, you can save on their own brand at 1313 SE 82nd Ave. (252-7063) or 118 E. Oak St., Hillsboro (648-8155).

Produce—Less expensive produce and bulk items are a definite savings at Corno and Son, 711 SE Union Ave. (232-3157). Southern cooks find items not ordinarily available elsewhere at this large store.

Back Road Bargains

The family who picks together, stays together—at least for another winter. For who can say which box of strawberries was his and which jar of grape juice was hers, when everyone works the row? And somehow the squabbles in the pumpkin patch are remembered fondly by the time the east winter wind whistles down the Gorge.

Preserving the produce you find can be very simple with the use of a freezer, canning kettle, jars, and Zip-Lok bags.

Green peppers go slightly lower than 10 cents each in the supermarkets during the summer. You can find them in some U-pick fields for less. With half an hour out of a summer's day you can snub the produce section when the price soars to 89 cents a pound the following winter.

Peppers lend themselves beautifully to freezing. Rinse off the outsides, top them, and pull out the seeds. Stack the peppers, just like cups, in Zip-Lok bags, zip up and toss in the freezer. To stuff them later, fill while still frozen. They will maintain their shape. Take a few more minutes and dice up the tops, sans stems, for seasoning and color in other dishes. If you find a good buy on *red peppers*, you can confuse the crowds by freezing these to use as pimento.

Raspberries, the envy of Southern California residents, can be frozen in Zip-Lok bags. Just rinse and drop them in gently; sprinkle a little sugar over the top (or not) and freeze. Serve them while still touched by frost, and they will maintain their firmness.

Blueberries will freeze in a large Zip-Lok bag. Fill the bag to the top, then as you need the berries, give the bag a slight tap on the drainboard and the berries will come loose just as they did from the bush. Drop them into muffin or pancake batter in their frozen state—it makes no difference.

Corn is so simple to freeze you will be sorry if you don't do it. Drop the ears into boiling water for a minute (the corn will turn a brighter yellow). Remove to cold water. Get out your angel food cake pan and a sharp knife. Poke the stem of the corn cob into the funnel part of the pan and scrape away. The corn will fall all around you, hopefully into the pan. This is a good project to do before you mop the floor, however. Empty the cut corn into a large Zip-Lok bag and freeze it en masse. To prepare, just smash the bag against the drainboard and drop what you need into a little boiling water.

Mushrooms will freeze well if you sauté them a minute in butter. The oil seems to keep them from going "leathery." However, one thrifty housewife says she freezes hers dirt and all and then cleans them up as she needs them. She has her own theory about dirt as a preservative. Do bag them up, though, regardless of your method.

Blackberry juice is time consuming, but delicious when mixed half and half with frozen lemonade. Since blackberries are free for the picking in many parts of the state, it all depends upon what you think your time is worth. (Do not pick close to a busy highway. Studies show that lead content may be dangerous.)

After you have put up your share of jelly, bring the rest of the washed berries up to a simmer in a little water (very little). Drop them into a heavy sieve and grind away. There is a special conical sieve sold with its own wooden pestle and stand which is perfect for drawing out juices and very few seeds. It also works well for fast jelly, although purists will say that the jelly will not be "clear." But who can taste "clear" anyway? Fill fruit jars with heated juice and drop into a boiling water bath in the canning kettle for 10 minutes to seal.

Squash, potatoes, and *dry onions* need little care. Find a cool place and store them in baskets which let them breathe.

Eggs, naturally, cannot be "preserved" unless you are doing the Ukrainian variety. But those purchased directly from under the chicken are good for three weeks or better under refrigeration. Only the grocer knows for sure how long he has had his in his dairy case.

Apples can be canned as sauce or in pieces for pies, but one of the quickest methods for pies is to freeze them up in the Zip-Lok bags. They will turn a bit brown as you slice them but after you have baked them in a pie, with cinnamon and sugar, no one will know. Toss them into the pie pan in their frozen state and reserve what won't fit for another batch of pastry.

Come June, keep a couple of flat boxes and brown paper bags in your car. Otherwise you may find yourself looking wistfully over a fence as someone else gathers the fruits of the field.

Oregon strawberries begin in June with the Marshalls, known throughout the state for their ability to produce the best jam. They have a short but sweet season. The Portland area growing season runs through October when you will find squash, pumpkins, potatoes, and nuts. Naturally, the more labor you provide, the more you will save.

On the road to Carver is a sign for filberts: 59 cents picked, 49 cents you pick. If nothing else, one U-pick season will help you to appreciate the high price of labor.

One word of caution: some transitory vegetable stands, including those by the "truckload" can be factory seconds for the vegetable market. A dead give-away is a large sign reading "oranges." Science has yet to introduce the orange tree to Oregon orchards. With this sort of operation, you pay your money and hope.

You will find oranges, early on in the season, at the *Canby Fruit Stand*, between Oregon City and Canby on 99E. The honest ladies who run this fresh air market will tell you flatly that it is too early for Oregon produce, and they open as soon as the Sunday drivers begin. This stand sells some of the plumpest blueberries in the state, as well as cantaloupes with great taste. As the summer progresses, all the out-of-state produce is replaced by local produce of the finest quality. It pays to make this a regular stop.

Drive on south, after filling your trunk at this stand, and turn right at the sign for the Canby Ferry. Along the road, a couple of small farm stands offer corn, potatoes, and onions at varying times. *Country Produce* comes just before the long descent to the ferry. The barn is filled with freshly-picked vegetables from surrounding fields. Late in the season the owner allows U-pickers to glean his fields at a lower price.

Cross the ferry—it's free—to find *Weber's* corn patch. It must be the river silt, but the corn grows as high as a dinosaur's eye, and it is easy to become lost in the stalks. One veteran picker noted that it is easier to walk in with the basket and pick your way out. Corn should be processed immediately for the best results, so this should be a pick-and-prepare day.

The *Stafford area*, south of Lake Oswego, is abundant with U-Pick fields. One of the largest belongs to the *Wilhelm* family and includes raspberries and strawberries. If you time it just right and have the stamina, you can pick both in one day.

Fiala's on Johnson Road, just off Stafford Road, does a brisk business in broccoli and beans. Incidentally, you can get there from here. Stafford will connect with the Canby Ferry and is signed.

If you must go through doors to purchase fruits and vegetables, a rural atmosphere continues at the *Big E Market* in Gladstone, where strawberries can be as big

as half dollars and the prices are a little less. They
also have the best geraniums in town.

Frankie's Market, 2717 NE Columbia Blvd., is a good
starting place on the eastside. They carry a wide variety
of fruits and vegetables. Afterward, take Marine Drive
east, heading toward the Gresham-Sandy area and keep
your eyes open for U-pick signs. *The Barn* at 1511 SE
122nd Ave. (771-1552) sits in the middle of its own fields
and offers fresh produce through the summer months.

Rather out of the way, but worth knowing about, is
McCormack's in Woodburn (981-1863). Fussy house-
wives telephone orders for broccoli, among other
vegetables, and McCormack's picks to order by the hour
to insure freshness. Take the Woodburn exit on the I-5
freeway heading south. McCormack's is at the exit going
south just at the curve of the road.

As long as you've driven to Woodburn, you might take
another quarter tank of gasoline and push on to Salem
to visit the *West Mushroom Farm*, 255 50th NE (581-
2471). The plant's salesroom is open Monday through
Friday, and you can buy five pound crates of freshly
picked mushrooms for less than supermarket specials.

Check valley fruit stands for peaches, an item rarely
found "up north" out of the orchard basin. Brooks prunes
are a treat worth taking home and can be found fresh
off Salem trees late in the summer.

There is no easy way to get to Logan, but the trip is
worth it if you map the course and run off copies for three
or more drivers. *Logan Egg Farms,* which sells fresh
eggs to a large dairy, also sells at a considerable reduction to customers willing to drive to their door. The outlet
store is open Monday through Friday and has no telephone. Eggs are sold by the 2½ dozen flat; small ones can
go for 25 cents a flat, the large and jumbos are always at
least 30 cents below supermarket price.

The way to make a Logan trip pay is to vary the trip
with other drivers. Each adult is allowed 30 dozen eggs,
which sounds like a great number, but 5 dozen will hold a
family of 4 nicely for about 3 weeks and the eggs which
are laid the day you purchase them will remain fresh for
that amount of time in the refrigerator.

To reach Logan, take 82nd Avenue to Clackamas River
Drive, follow the drive to the combination service station-

grocery which is the settlement of Logan. Go past the "city limits," taking the road to the right and turn left at the Community Church which is about one mile up the road. The gravel road in front of the church will lead you directly to the egg farms. An alternate approach to Logan is through Redland and Fischer's Mill.

Out beyond the St. John's Bridge lies Sauvie Island,¶ and in late October it means just one thing: the *Pumpkin Patch*. Everyone becomes a child again when he sees acres of roly-poly pumpkins lying in the muddy reaches. Wear your boots and take the children. At these prices everyone can have a jack-o'-lantern. After the pumpkins have been gathered in, check out the barn for every sort of squash imaginable, including some crosses unheard of, and potatoes by the 50-pound bag. Potatoes come in gunny sacks, which later become fine far-West costumes, and carrots come by the 25-pound bag. If that amount tends to over-kill your creative ability, take a friend along. Old timers say that carrots, as well as other root vegetables, will keep well if buried in a foot of straw. At these prices it's worth being a pioneer again.

Which leaves nothing more for the table but the center-piece. Mrs. John Anicker, 13856 SW Beef Bend Rd., Tigard, grows a garden which is a garden. She won't charge you to look at it (stay out of her husband's dahlias), and she will sell dried flowers for a most reasonable price. If you're taken with iris or chrysanthemums, ask her to call you when hers are in bloom. She will mark varieties to be transferred to your garden at the right time.

TRANSPORTATION

Getting Around Is Half the Fun

EVER SINCE the covered wagons rolled across the Oregon Trail from Missouri, Portland has been luring travelers over the mountains. Successor to the Old Oregon Trail is I-80N, which, interestingly enough, carries transcontinental motor and bus traffic along an approximate version of the covered wagon route.

Remnants of the Oregon Trail and the Barlow Road, which provided wagon passage over Mt. Hood to Portland, are marked for motorists as they whisk in or out of Portland via I-80N or U.S. 26.

More recently Portland has become a major west coast terminal for air travel to and from the Orient and other parts of the world.

A railroad center, Portland is not. Those once-glamorous east-west trains, the City of Portland and the Portland Rose, have disappeared like the covered wagons before them. AMTRAK completely eliminated transcontinental passenger travel to and from Portland, except via Seattle, and now only provides service north to Seattle and south to San Francisco.

Airlines

Portland International Airport is emerging from a major terminal expansion with minor headaches—and a sense of humor.

Airport expansion is always disruptive so the Port of Portland, which runs the airport, capitalized on the inconvenience and invited its patrons, the customers of eight major and three commuter airlines using the facility, to have their say in poetry.

Poetic barbs were inscribed in large print on the temporary construction tunnels leading to the terminals. Though now gone, the light verse expressed travelers' universal irritation with airport remodeling, so we quote one here by Portlander Elaine Cogan:

"She came here to meet her beau, but never found the plane. The signs just led her round and round and straight back home again."

The new terminal, to open in the spring of 1977, will feature underground escalator service to and from the parking areas and a children's area with semiprivate facilities for parents with infants, including child-size furniture. Decor is distinctly Northwest in mood—red cedar paneling, warm red and blue carpeting, suspended fabric panels illustrating Oregon wild flowers, and natural plantings typical of Oregon.

Major airlines serving Portland are: Braniff (224-5030), Continental (224-4560), Eastern (224-7550), Hughes Air West (224-5252), Northwest Orient (226-3211, domestic; 226-6091, international and Hawaii), Pan American (227-6671), United (226-7211) and Western (225-0830).

Commuter airlines flying out of Portland International are: Columbia Airlines (249-4750), to towns in eastern Oregon; Execuair (281-0340), to Seattle and other points; and Cascade (249-4920), to central and eastern Washington.

Airport Transportation

DART (Downtown Airport Rapid Transportation) offers the most convenient way to get to the airport, short of a free ride with spouse or friend. DART sends 16-passenger Mercedes-Benz buses back and forth frequently for $2.50 a passenger ($1.25 for children 6-12; free under 6). Office is at 617 SW 17th (223-2139).

If you're staying near the airport, the new Sheraton Inn and most other hotels and motels provide transportation to and from the terminal.

If you choose to drive yourself to the airport and "board" your car there while you're away, you can park for a reasonable price in the long-term parking facility operated by the airport. A free shuttle bus will take you to the terminal. Plenty of short-term parking is also available. None of the airport parking is under cover. Private shuttle parking is offered near the airport.

AMTRAK

Portland's revered red brick Union Station, 800 NW 6th (248-1146) is more interesting as a landmark than as AMTRAK's passenger station. Built in 1890, the station has a 150-foot clock tower and a red tile roof visible from many downtown sites. AMTRAK sends three trains daily to Seattle from the station; the Coast Starlight leaves daily for San Francisco. And that's it. Call this toll-free number for AMTRAK Intercity Rail Passenger Service Information and Reservations (1-800-421-8320). Baggage room number is 223-2663.

Busses

Tri-Met

Tri-Met, the Portland metropolitan area's excellent tri-county public bus system, is trying harder and harder to lure commuters out of their automobiles—and seems to be succeeding.

Of the many new services and features Tri-Met has initiated, the Portland Mall, to be completed by late 1977 or early 1978, is making the greatest impact on the downtown scene.

Wide brick sidewalks, planters, park benches, information plazas, flower stalls, kiosks for public notices, and passenger shelters are intended to make the mall a place where people want to gather, shop, work—and board the bus.

When the mall is complete, Tri-Met's orange and silver busses will travel exclusively on two of the three lanes on 5th and 6th from Burnside to Madison, whisking passengers through downtown more quickly. Streets crossing the mall will continue to carry cars and other vehicles.

While construction continues, downtown bus patterns keep changing, so call Tri-Met's 24-hour information service (233-3511) if you have questions about where your bus stops.

Fareless Square—Complementing the mall scheme is Tri-Met's already established, popular Fareless Square policy. Fareless Square is a 288-block area downtown where you can ride free (see map.) It extends from the river west to the Stadium Freeway (SW 13th or 14th) and from Market north to Hoyt.

Let's suppose you're staying at the Congress Hotel on 6th and want to have lunch in the Old Town area. Just hop any bus in front of your hotel (when the mall is completed) and travel north to Oak. Walk through the U.S. Bank Plaza east toward the river and you're in the heart of Old Town—free.

Generally, all southbound busses travel through downtown on 5th and all northbound busses on 6th; generally all go the entire length of the mall.

Get a Fareless Square map for details on free travel outside the mall.

Two things are important to remember about Fareless Square, especially if you learned as a child to exit from the rear of a bus:

This is Fareless Square

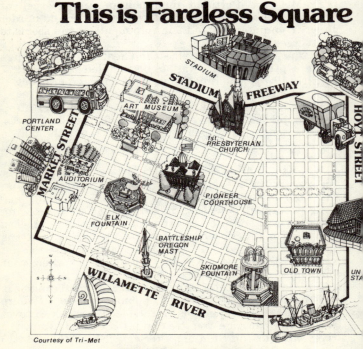

Courtesy of Tri-Met

Ride for Free.

1. If you board the bus free in Fareless Square and are leaving it outside the square, break that old habit and exit from the front because you must drop your money in the fare box as you leave.

2. If you board a bus outside Fareless Square that is traveling downtown, pay when you board and exit conventionally, from the rear.

Customer Assistance Office—Located in the center of downtown at 522 SW Yamhill, this handy drop-in center is staffed with clerks who sell tickets, monthly passes, and are generally helpful. The center is stocked as full as a magazine stand with all of Tri-Met's schedules and other information. There is a free direct telephone line for route and schedule information.

Fares—Except for Fareless Square, which is free, you pay 40¢ to ride Tri-Met. Exact change must be dropped in the fare box. Students and senior citizens (Tri-Met calls them Honored Citizens) ride for less.

The rate for high school students with ID cards is 30¢. The rate for younger students is 20¢. Children in grades one through six need not carry ID cards, but seventh and eighth graders must. ID cards are available at schools. Children under six riding with an adult ride free.

Honored citizens may use an Honored Citizen card or Medicare card to qualify for 10¢ fares during weekday nonrush hours (9 a.m.-3 p.m.) and free rides on weekends and evenings after 7 p.m. The rest of the time they pay the regular fare. Honored Citizen cards, which are issued to disabled or legally blind persons, as well as to persons over 65, are available at the Customer Assistance Office.

Books of tickets may be purchased at the Tri-Met Customer Assistance Office or at any of more than 90 ticket outlets around town. BankAmericard is accepted at the Tri-Met office but not, generally, at other outlets. Nor can you charge you Tri-Met ticket book on a downtown store account.

Monthly passes, costing $14, are also available at the Customer Assistance Office. They are transferable so anyone in the family can use them.

Transfers are issued to passengers who must take more than one bus to reach their destination. All transfers are good for as long as two hours to provide for shopping time in between busses.

Pets—No animals are allowed on Tri-Met busses unless they are in a container or cage.

Tri-Met Routes—Covering three counties, Tri-Met obviously operates plenty of routes. You can ride the air-conditioned busses as far as Canby, Molalla, and Estacada to the south, Hillsboro and Forest Grove to the west, Sauvie Island to the north, and Boring and Troutdale to the east. Get one of the system's excellent route maps for more details. A smaller version is in the Portland phone book. In addition, there are 130 places around the city which stock all Tri-Met schedules. By perusing them, you'll be amazed at all the places Tri-Met goes and the schedules it keeps at odd hours (i.e.) Early Bird Expresses and Owl Service.

Park-and-Ride Stations—Many areas are designated around the metropolitan area. You may park your car free all day and ride Tri-Met wherever you want to go. For the Park-and-Ride nearest you, call 233-3511.

Freeway Travel—Whether you're bussing or driving, if you've been on I-80N, locally known as the "Banfield," you've noticed the signs that say "Busses and 3-Person Carpools Only." These signs designate a special lane which Tri-Met uses for express "flyers" weekdays on the busy Banfield. The special lanes run from NE 39th to 82nd eastbound and from NE 82nd to Holladay westbound. Restrictions are imposed only during rush hours.

Tri-Met Publications—Tri-Met printing presses must run over-time getting out materials to help make bus travel fun and easy, so take advantage of it. Worth noting, in addition to the route map previously mentioned, is *The Bus Rider's Guide*, a revision of an outstanding manual written for Tri-Met in 1974 by a 14-year-old travel buff, David Bragdon, who entertained himself by riding busses. (Now he's into trains.) The guide has a light touch, is easy to understand, and is written for the person who has never stepped on a Tri-Met bus before.

Tri-Met also publishes an attractive series of color "Fun Fare" pamphlets that suggest various sightseeing excursions—industrial tours, historical places, gardens, fountains, night sights, and walks.

Sports and Special Events Shuttles—Tri-Met operates shuttle busses for sports and special events. Call before the event for details.

Handy Phone Numbers—Route Information (233-3511); Lost and Found (238-4855), Charters (238-4853), Senior Citizen Escort Service (238-4914), Complaints and Suggestions (238-4909).

Inter-City Busses

Two transcontinental bus lines serve Portland: Greyhound Bus Lines, 509 SW Taylor (228-5171, for nationwide information; 228-9481, Seattle only) and Trailways Bus System, 1010 SW 6th (228-8571).

Important to Portland-Vancouver commuters is the Vancouver-Portland Bus Co., 807 Jefferson, Vancouver, WA (Portland phone: 285-8210).

Taxis, Limousines

Biggest cab companies in town are Broadway Cab (227-1234) and Radio Cab (227-1212). Don't try to hail a cab in Portland; phone ahead. Special phones are provided in many busy locations for ordering cabs.

Coach Limousine Service (235-2173) provides 24-hour service with a 3-hour minimum charge.

PLACES TO STAY

"Room service, please..." to "Tenting Tonight"

PORTLAND HOTELS and motels are located for convenience. With the exception of the Benson, built by retired logger Simon Benson following the opening of the Lewis and Clark Centennial exposition in 1913, those standing are there just because they are there.

When President Gerald Ford first visited Portland he greeted locals at the Benson; being a good politician, he crossed the river the following year to shake hands at the Lloyd Center Sheraton. The National Trust for Historic Preservation ironically chose the contemporary Hilton Hotel for its meeting a few years ago. Zsa Zsa Gabor called for hairdressing services to her suite at the Benson, while George Hamilton held court at the Jantzen Beach Thunderbird not long ago. George Washington did not sleep in any one of them, but for the most part local facilities are clean, well-managed, and the hallways are safe at night.

Following is a selection of tested, expensive to inexpensive accommodations, all of which are friendly and comfortable. Rates are subject to constant change along with the U.S. dollar but quality is not. For your convenience we have arranged them by area.

Hotels and Motels

West Side (downtown)

The Benson on Broadway—309 SW Broadway (228-9611). 342 rooms. Ask for the new section, with apologies to Simon. A Western International Hotel, home of Trader

Vic's, and the Holiday-award London Grill. Pay garage. Expensive. All credit cards, including United Air Lines.

Congress Hotel—1020 SW 6th (228-0181). 150 rooms, some air conditioned. Dining room and cocktail lounge. Pay garage. Moderate. Credit cards.

Hilton Hotel—SW 6th & Salmon (226-1611). 500 rooms. Canlis restaurant on the 23rd floor, not open Sundays. Outdoor swimming pool on the terrace also caters to guests and to the delight of the employees of the Public Service Building across the street. On the main floor find The Trees (see Restaurants). Although this hotel is part of an international chain, the waitresses have learned to "speak Portland." Waitress Kay Scroggins crocheted all the bright potholders for the individual coffee pots. Pay garage. Credit cards. Moderate to expensive.

Imperial Hotel—400 SW Broadway (228-7221). 170 rooms which still serve as a stopping place for eastern Oregon cattlemen. Comfortable with room enough to swing your lariat. Restaurant and bar. Credit cards. Moderate.

Mallory Motor Hotel—729 SW 15th (223-6311). 144 rooms. Quiet, out-of-the-way home-away-from-home (NYC) for gourmet James Beard; also where Medford, Oregonians stay when they visit the Portland Clinic. Credit cards. Moderate.

Portland Motor Hotel—1414 SW 6th (221-1611). 180 rooms near downtown area; restaurant, bar, and coffee shop. Credit cards. Moderate.

Ramada Inn—Portland Center, 310 SW Lincoln (221-0450). 245 rooms in this fine motor inn located in the heart of the urban renewal area. Within a short hike (downhill) to middle of shopping area. Three restaurants, live entertainment. Credit cards. Moderate to expensive.

Riverside West Motor Hotel—50 SW Morrison (221-0711). 137 rooms, some overlooking the Willamette River. Close to shopping areas. Dining room and lounge. Credit cards. Moderate.

East Side (Coliseum-Lloyd Center)

Cosmopolitan Motor Hotel—1030 NE Union (235-8433). 175 rooms. Rooftop pool and dining. Best Western Motel. Credit cards. Moderate to expensive.

Hyatt Lodge—431 NE Multnomah (233-5121). 80 rooms. Close to Memorial Coliseum and Lloyd Center. Credit cards. Moderate.

Royal Inn of Portland—420 NE Holladay (233-6331). 97 rooms in the tradition of all Royal Inns, moderate prices for the whole family. Credit cards.

Sheraton Inn—Lloyd Center (288-6111). 280 rooms. Outstanding east side hotel with two restaurants, live entertainment. Features cabana rooms around swimming pool. Convention facilities just across the street from the Northwest's largest shopping center.∫ Credit cards. Moderate to expensive.

Thunderbird Motor Inn Downtown—1225 N. Thunderbird Way (235-8311). 220 rooms opposite the Memorial Coliseum. Dining room and cocktail lounge overlooking the Willamette river. Meeting facilities and banquet halls. Credit cards. Moderate.

Travelodge at the Coliseum—1441 NE 2nd (233-2401). 243 rooms. Unlike the average Travelodge, this is a fine motel. Restaurant and lounge with live entertainment; within walking distance of the Coliseum and the Lloyd Center. Credit cards. Moderate.

Airport

Cosmopolitan Airtel—6221 NE 82nd (255-6511). 100 rooms, three minutes from the airport. Indoor-outdoor pool and tennis courts. Credit cards. Expensive.

The Fortniter—4911 NE 82nd (255-9771). 52 suites with kitchenettes. New; close to airport. Credit cards including Exxon. Moderate.

Rodeway Inn—7101 NE 82nd (255-6722). 140 rooms adjacent to airport. Restaurant and lounge with live entertainment. Credit cards. Moderate.

Sheraton Inn Airport—8235 NE Airport Way (288-7171). 152 rooms built in 1975. Although this is located at the end of the runway, the rooms are sound-proofed and beautiful. Lobby, cocktail lounge, and restaurant feature all Oregon woods. Meeting facilities. Credit cards. Moderate to expensive.

Outlying Innkeepers

Greenwood Inn—10700 SW Allen Blvd., Beaverton (643-7444). 200 rooms located well out of the downtown area but close to Washington Square.¶ Live entertainment with "name" celebrities. Convention facilities 15 minutes from city center. Credit cards. Moderate to expensive.

Nendel's Inn—9900 SW Canyon Rd. (297-2551). 108 rooms, outstanding restaurant. Heated pool and convention facilities 10 minutes from downtown. Credit cards. Moderate to expensive.

Motel 6—3104 SE Powell Blvd. (233-8811).

Motel 6—17950 SW Lower Boones Ferry Rd. (639-0631). Both are inexpensive, comfortable motels located out of the downtown traffic pattern. Good lodging for family on a budget. No restaurants. No credit cards.

Ramada Inn—7125 SW Nyberg Rd., Tualatin (638-4141). 104 units in sylvan setting just south of Portland on I-5. Coffee shop, restaurant, live entertainment, pool. Credit cards. Moderate.

Thunderbird Motor Inn at Jantzen Beach—1401 N. Hayden Island Dr. (283-2111). 347 rooms in this new motor inn built on the banks of the Columbia River. Luxurious accomodations, fine restaurant, and cocktail lounge. Large convention center. Located on I-5 just 10 minutes from the airport. Credit cards. Expensive.

Mobile Homes and Trailer Parks

All State Overnighter Park, 6645 SW Nyberg Rd., Tualatin (638-7304). RV's and tents along the Tualatin River.

Cedar Shade Trailer Park, 2130 NE Killingsworth (254-1692). RV's.

Fir Grove Trailer Park, 5541 NE 72nd (252-9993). RV's on city bus line.

Fir Haven Trailer Court, 17007 SE Stark (253-4770).

Lawn Acres Mobil Home Park, 11421 SE 82nd (654-5739). Adult permanent living on bus line; overnighters welcome with children.

LeRose Mobil Court, 18040 SW Boones Ferry Rd., Tigard (639-1501).

Rolling Hills Mobil Terrace, 20145 NE Sandy Blvd., Troutdale (666-7282). Summer and winter rates.

Town and Country Mobile Estates, 9911 SE 82nd (771-1040).

Oxbow County Park (Multnomah) (663-4708 or 248-4308) about 20 miles s.e. of Portland. Take SE Division east through Gresham to Section Line Rd.; turn right and travel several miles to Hosner Rd.; turn left to Oxbow. 42 tent campsites and 44 trailer sites. No hookups. No reservations. Pets and alcohol not allowed. Park is locked each night. Open year round. $2 per night. Maximum stay is five nights. Good fishing.

State Parks

Lewis and Clark State Park, off I-80N, 16 miles east of Portland; tents.

Champoeg State Park, off US 99W, 7 miles east of Newberg. Tents and trailers; trailer dumping station but no hookups.

Fort Stevens State Park, off U.S. 101, 10 miles west of Astoria, tents and trailer sites with hookups. Trailer dumping station. Reservations: 861-1671. Open year around.

Beverly Beach State Park, U.S. 101, seven miles north of Newport. Tents, trailer sites with hookups. Reservations: 265-7655. Open year around.

Listed immediately above are two of the largest state camping facilities on the Oregon Coast. There are many others and not all require reservations.

Fees at state parks range from $1 per night for primitive tent campsites to $4 for a trailer campsite with hookups and sewage disposal.

A State Park Campsite Information Center operates weekdays from 8 a.m. to 5 p.m. from mid-May through August to provide current information on the availability of campsites. You may cancel reservations through the center but must make them directly at the parks. The number, toll-free from anywhere in Oregon, is 1-800-452-0294.

Destination Resorts

Coast

Inn at Otter Crest offers 300 rooms and suites. Park your car at the office and be shuttled down wooded paths to the rooms which climb the cliffs. Facilities include year around swimming, tennis, saunas, a putting green, and trails. Restaurant and cocktail lounge. Reservations: Otter Rock, 765-2111.

Salishan Lodge rooms are on the 18-hole golf course*f* and tucked up in the kinnikinnick. Restaurant, coffee shop, lounge, year around covered swimming pool, sauna and hydro-therapy pool, men's and ladies gym, playground, and covered tennis courts. (764-2371).

Mountains

Kah-Nee-Ta Vacation Resort affords an opportunity to spend some time with the Indians. Stay in a tepee (complete with firepit and cement floor) or take one of the 90 rooms with air conditioning. Heated pools, hot mineral baths, golf, and a restaurant with Indian and "international" cuisine. For reservations, call: 553-1112.

Sunriver Development, 15 miles south of Bend. 211 guest rooms and suites. Swimming, golf, tennis, fishing, horseback riding, boating, nature tours, skiing (at Mt. Bachelor just 20 minutes away), bicycling (they rent them), restaurant, coffee shop, and cocktail lounge. Private landing strip for small aircraft. (593-1221).

Timberline Lodge,f offers overnight accommodations on the slopes of Mt. Hood. Activities include heated pool, day and night skiing all week, a ski shop with ski rental and school, a restaurant, and convention and banquet facilities. For reservations, 226-7979.

Valley

The Village Green blossomed into a multimillion dollar resort simply because Oregonians were intrigued with luxurious accommodations in the middle of nowhere. Located just off I-5 (south of Eugene), this development includes 96 luxurious rooms and suites, swimming pool, a 9 hole pitch-and-putt golf course, tennis, bowling, and a visit to Railroad Town, USA. (942-2491).

WALKING TOURS

Seeing Things & Places In-Depth

IF YOU REALLY want to learn something about your city at close range, a guided walking tour, such as those given by Portland Walking Tours, is the best way. Short of that, we recommend four do-it-yourself tours.

Park Blocks-PSU-Portland Center

Two tours are suggested if you start from the vicinity of SW Clay and Park.

Tour #1

Head south through the South Park Blocks into the Portland State University campus. As you enter, notice old Lincoln High School, now a PSU hall, on your left. As you pass Smith Memorial Center, consider a look at the latest art exhibit inside, at the White Gallery. Continuing south on the campus mall and still favoring the east (left) side, pause at Neuberger Hall to see one of the campus show pieces—the sculptured bronze panels by Tom Hardy depicting flora and fauna of Oregon. Continue your walk past Shattuck Hall, another old Portland school building, the Park Theater, and through a playground where you will find it hard to resist a climb up the "Lincoln Log" structure leading to the top of a slide. At SW Jackson turn left (east) and proceed east across Park and Broadway. As you walk, look to the southwest at Piggott's Castle on the hillside. The residence was built in 1892 by an eccentric. At SW 6th turn left (north) and walk two blocks. Turn right (east) at SW Hall, but as you do, look north to locate the *Portland State Bookstore* and *Sam's Hofbrau*, a good sandwich

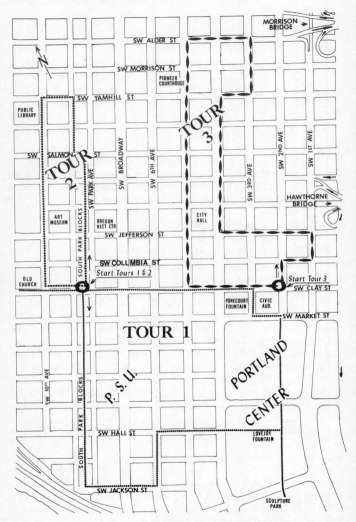

spot. On SW Hall, you'll pass the 5th Avenue Cinema on the south side of the street. Cross SW 5th and SW 4th and enter a brick plaza leading into Portland Center ◀ Walk straight ahead past an orange tile "smokestack," clever camouflage for a Pacific Northwest Bell air intake shaft, until you reach the top of the Lovejoy Fountain.◢ From the base of the Lovejoy, you can walk the mall to the south to see the Lee Kelly Sculpture Park,◢ which lies between the American Plaza apartments and the Ramada Inn, and then return to tour the attractive avenue of shops and services east of the Lovejoy. Follow the mall north all the way to Market where you will see the rear of the Civic Auditorium at Market and 2nd. Turn left (west) and pass between the auditorium and the Forecourt Fountain◢ on 3rd. At Clay, turn left (west) and walk to SW 11th where you'll find the Old Church.◢ Take Clay east to your starting point at Park Avenue.

Tour #2

Head north through the South Park Blocks past the equestrian statue of Theodore Roosevelt, the Oregon Historical Center◢ at SW Jefferson (on your right), and the Portland Art Museum and Sculpture Mall on your left. Be sure to enter the Sculpture Mall,◢ which is between the museum and the Masonic Temple to the north. In the Park in front of the Masonic Temple is a bronze statue of Abraham Lincoln. Tulips, roses, and joggers bloom in the Park Blocks in spring and summer.

Continue to the next Park Block to view the delicate bronze maiden in the Shemanski Fountain, named for a grateful immigrant who donated it.

At Salmon Street (you'll find the *Zen Restaurant* to the west), take a jog to the left to SW 9th and continue north past the red brick Arlington Club (last stand for the male establishment in Portland). Across from the Arlington Club on SW 9th are *Longhair Records* and *Art Craft Silversmiths*. Cross SW Taylor and continue north to SW Yamhill. Turn left (west) and walk to SW 10th. Facing 10th between Yamhill and Taylor is the Multnomah County Library, main branch.◢ To vary your route back, go south on the east side of 10th past a variety of small shops and businesses. On the west side between Taylor and Salmon you'll find the *Rice Bowl.* You'll pass the YWCA before reaching Clay. Turn left (east) and walk to SW Park.

Downtown

Tour #3

Buildings and sights north of the Civic Auditorium may be taken in either on an extension of the Park Blocks-PSU-Portland Center tour or on a tour beginning at SW 2nd and Clay. Walk north on 2nd one block and turn right (east) on Columbia. Walk to the Benjamin Franklin Plaza and Museum. Museum entrance is at 1330 SW 1st. Turn left (west) on SW Jefferson. Head west past the offices of Pendleton Woolen Mills and continue to SW 4th where you'll see Portland's tallest building, the First National Bank Tower. Turn right (north) and stop at Federal Park to see a replica of the Liberty Bell (3rd Avenue side) or to rest in the miniamphitheater. Federal Park provides a vista for the graceful rear entrance to City Hall. Cross Madison into Chapman Square, where the benches are marked "women and children only" and there is a well-maintained women's restroom. Continue north across Main, past the Elk Fountain into Lownsdale Square, paired with Chapman as the men's park. Here is the Spanish-American War Memorial defended by "Howitzers used in defense of Fort Sumter 1861." You might see men playing chess in the park, and, appropriately, the men's restroom is here.

As you continue north on 4th, you'll see the Multnomah County Courthouse between Main and Salmon and next, the Georgia-Pacific Building with its redwood and bronze sculpture "Perpetuity". At Yamhill take a detour, if you wish, to the right (east) and go to the Mohawk Gallery building between Yamhill and Morrison on 3rd. Wander through the main level to enjoy the sculpture and fountains. Stay on 3rd for one more block, then turn left (west) on SW Alder. Walk west to 5th and turn left (south). You are in the heart of downtown Portland, within view of *Meier and Frank* and *Lipman's*, two large department stores. Continuing south on 5th, you'll pass the Pioneer Courthouse at Yamhill, on the west side of the street, and the outdoor market, the Chamber of Commerce Visitors' Information Center and the front of the Georgia-Pacific Building with its marble fountain, all on the east side of the street. At Salmon you may detour one block west to *I. Magnin* on the northeast corner of 6th and Salmon. Continue south on 5th past the County

Courthouse and the main entrance of City Hall. Across from City Hall on the diagonal to the northwest is the Standard Plaza building and *Rian's Breadbasket.* Continue your march south until you reach Clay. Walk east to your starting point. (Remember, you are in Tri-Met's Fareless Square so if you want to skip some of the suggested sights, board a bus headed in the right direction and ride free.)

At 5th and Clay consider walking two blocks further to Mill to see the charming early-Italian style Church of St. Michael and the Archangel at 424 SW Mill.

Old Town

Tour #4

The remains of early Portland lie in the area along the west bank of the Willamette River now known as Old Town. Although the metropolis of the small port town once lay along the harbor and on First Avenue, that enemy called progress has removed most of the original city.

Several preservation-minded groups are working to upgrade what remains from SW 2nd and Oak and north to Everett.

Three major parking lots will accept your cars on Saturdays and Sundays with no charge—also assuming no liabilities. All make excellent starting points.

For the longest walk start from the parking lot on SW 2nd and Oak (across from the Police Station), and while you are there, step around the corner to 3rd to search out the *Portland Outdoor Store*, a one-of-a-kind enterprise which stocks western and eastern riding clothing, gear, hunting and fishing equipment, and even some Indian jewelry.

Just south from the parking lot is *Victoria's Nephew,* an excellent stop for lunch or high tea, either at the end or the beginning of your trip.

As you walk along 2nd, you will pass the Hazeltine Building, where local historians have recorded high-water marks from flooding during the 1800s. Flood control is one of the kinder changes brought to this original city of iron fronts, Victorian lace, and Gothic arches.

The brightest star in the area is the Skidmore Fountain,⸸ located just at the end of Ankeny. This narrow lane transports you back to the days of horse and buggy or the earliest Model As.

The fountain splashes next to the newer fire station on 1st and is well worth a stop, but first duck down the alley toward *Dan and Louis' Oyster Bar.* The oyster shells tucked neatly around the bases of young trees as well as the scent of salty seafood will lead you there.

Just across 2nd, on the river side, is the New Market Theatre, now a parking lot. The lot outside to the north, as well as the one directly across the street, will accommodate your car if you would like to make the walk a shorter one.

Heading west on Ankeny (Dan and Louis' is a good lunch stop), just across the street is the *Green Dolphin Book Store* as well as *The Source,* a mixture of new and old oddities. This cluster provides an especially good side trip for a rainy day since many of the doorways are canopied, and the narrow street will cut the cold wind.

Don't think that all has ended with these three stops. Turn the corner of Ankeny on to 3rd to the left and discover the *Tucker Toy Co.* and *Skidmore Village Books.* This is easily the best short walk of the area and will provide an afternoon of browsing if you like to search out every shelf of a shop.

With energy to spare, however, retrace your steps back down Ankeny, put your fingers to the wind to find the river, and head east toward 1st. This is a walk to the main shopping area of Old Town which avoids crossing Burnside, the main intersection of the city which flows heavily with traffic during all waking hours.

At the Skidmore Fountain if you look up and to the right, you will see the top of the mast of the Battleship *Oregon* and next to it the American flag, giving you a good idea of the strength of the wind as well as the patriotism of city fathers.

Turn left, walk under the bridge, and be sure to stop for a tour of the Saturday Market (providing that it is Saturday), Old Town's newest addition and a mecca for young artists. If you covet a piece of pottery, a bit of wood carving, or anything else for sale, give in to your whim and buy it. Many of these artists travel considerable distances for the market and do not return every

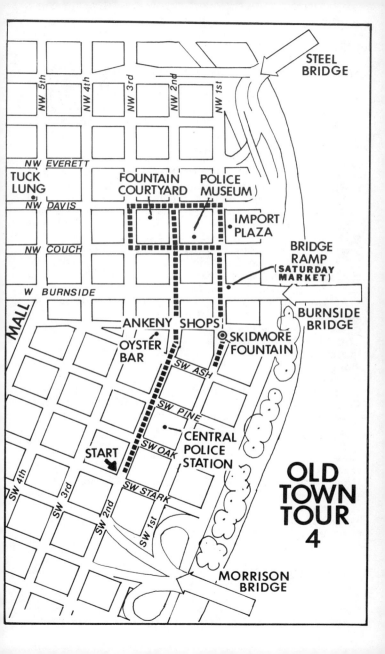

STEEL
BRIDGE

NW 5th
NW 4th
NW 3rd
NW 2nd
NW 1st

NW EVERETT

TUCK
LUNG

FOUNTAIN
COURTYARD

POLICE
MUSEUM

NW DAVIS

IMPORT
PLAZA

NW COUCH

BRIDGE
RAMP
(SATURDAY
MARKET)

W BURNSIDE

BURNSIDE
BRIDGE

ANKENY SHOPS

OYSTER
BAR

SKIDMORE
FOUNTAIN

SW ASH

SW PINE

CENTRAL
POLICE
STATION

START

SW OAK

OLD
TOWN
TOUR
4

SW 4th
SW 3rd
SW 2nd
SW 1st

SW STARK

MALL

MORRISON
BRIDGE

week. Certainly their wares vary with their moods, which makes the market a new experience every week. The market is open Saturdays 10 a.m.-5 p.m. May to mid-Dec.

Coming up under the bridge, you will face the bright light and Couch Street. Just beyond the traffic light on the right is *Import Plaza,* the largest of the direct shipment stores in the city. Import Plaza has a large and free parking lot to the north of the building as well as one across the street. These will be the first to fill up, so if you start your tour at this end and cannot find a parking spot here, drive on south to Oak Street.

But before you load yourself down with baskets, pinatas, and other bulky items which may make you a sidewalk hazard, take a quick left across Couch and head toward the tiny alley marked by pseudo-gaslights. This brick alley leads to the Police Museum,¶ and the renovation looks as though the Keystone Kops will be tumbling out the door any minute.

At the end of the newly-made alley stand the two smokestacks from the Battleship *Oregon*, the "Bull Dog of the Navy" whose 14,000-mile dash from San Francisco around South America to join the fleet off Cuba was a celebrated event of the Spanish-American War. Decommissioned, the *Oregon* was a floating museum in Portland from 1925 until it was cut up for scrap in World War II.

Just across the parking lot with the stacks, to the west, lies the heart of the shopping center known as Old Town. It says so in bright red letters, so don't worry, you can't miss it.

What you may miss, however, are some of the shops you found the last time you visited. Like the breeze from the river, some of these owners drift back and forth and sometimes away all together, so it is pointless to locate many specific shops.

Do cross the street at NW 2nd and Davis. On 4th near Davis lie most of the Chinese restaurants of the downtown area. Squint a little and you will see the green and white sign marking the *Tuck Lung Grocery* on the right.

The Fountain Courtyard proves that many beautiful moments lie behind the old brick facades in the area. Enter this center of calm which is the core area for four buildings, either on Davis between 2nd and 3rd or on 2nd between Davis and Couch. Either way you will pass a variety of stores on the way to the fountain. It still seems that there should be some laundry flapping in the breeze about four stories up, but the courtyard has become park-like.

Another innovation around the corner to the south is *Couch Street Galleries,* a combination of you-name-it decor with a nonsexist restroom labeled "Ye Old Outhouse," which might come in handy. Like most of the old buildings, the restroom has a skylight, keeping it bright, and is reasonably clean.

There are two ways to return to your car, if you left it across Burnside. You can make this same trip in reverse, reworking the many shops and picking up those items you admired the first time around. Or you can head directly south on 2nd, crossing Burnside. There is a safety island in the center of Burnside, and if you are counting on crossing with young children, you will need it. The route along 2nd will take you past a couple of "antique shops."

Walking Tour Postscript

Portlanders are encouraged to cross the Columbia to Vancouver, Wash., to take a five-mile historical walking tour of that city. A map and brochure are available from the Parks Department, Box 1995, Vancouver, WA 98663.

SPORTS AND RECREATION

Fun and Games for Every Season

SNOW IN THE MOUNTAINS, fat salmon and trout in the clear rivers, lots of water for boating, and thousands of miles of scenic hiking trails are persuasive reasons to choose Portland as a place to live.

Many do and then want to seal the state off from more newcomers. You won't hear them boasting that in Oregon you can golf year-round and ski in June—on real snow. But, you can.

With all of this plus a fair-sized shopping list of spectator sports, Portland is the kind of place where even the nonathlete has to read the sports pages to survive in social conversations.

Spectator Sports

Professional Franchises

Portland supports two major league professional sports franchises, the Portland *Trail Blazers* of the National Basketball Assn., with home games played in the Memorial Coliseum, and the Portland *Timbers* of the North American Soccer League, home games played in Portland Civic Stadium. Portland is also the home of the Class A baseball *Mavericks*, who have been the subject of two Joe Garagiola national television programs.

The Portland *Buckaroos,* formerly champions of the Western Hockey League, are now, because of the influx of the NHL in Vancouver, B.C., a semipro team playing at the Jantzen Beach Ice Arena.

Portland *Trail Blazers*—Season runs October through March; tickets at the Memorial Coliseum, 1401 N. Wheeler (235-8771) or at the Trail Blazer Ticket Office, 700 NE Multnomah (234-9291).

Portland *Timbers*—Season runs May-Sept., games played at Portland Civic Stadium, 1844 SW Morrison (248-4345). Tickets are sold at the stadium and Timbers ticket office, 806 SW Broadway (245-6464).

Portland *Mavericks*—Season runs June-Aug., games played at Portland Civic Stadium, 1844 SW Morrison (228-7234). Tickets are sold at the stadium.

Parimutuel Betting

Portland Meadows Horse Race Track, 1001 N. Schmeer Rd. (285-9144). Season runs Jan.-May.

Multnomah Kennel Club Dog Race Track, 223rd Ave., Fairview, about 15 miles from the city (665-2191). Season runs May-Sept.

Other Athletic Events

Basketball—The Memorial Coliseum reverberates each Christmas season with the Far West Classic, recognized nation-wide as the finest college basketball tournament going. Pacific-8 Conference University of Oregon and Oregon State University host the annual affair. During the regular college season, the many fine smaller schools in the area play regularly. The best of these are Portland State University, University of Portland, and Lewis and Clark College.

Track and Field—During the second or third week of January each year, the Memorial Coliseum hosts the Portland Invitational Indoor Track and Field Meet, which normally plays to a packed house. The best athletes from all over the world compete in one of the slickest track meets in the nation.

Auto Racing—Portland Speedway, 9727 N. Union (289-2322). Begins its super stock, jalopy, and speed-stock racing the last of March and programs, sometimes including dragsters and formula road racing (particularly through the summer months), continues into late fall. The facilities are good and the track is easily accessible.

Wrestling—This sport can be seen weekly at the Portland Sports Arena, 8725 N. Chautauqua (289-4222). If you like to spend an entertaining two hours watching Tough Tony Bourne, Lonnie Mayne, Wild Bill Savage, and other wrestlers with colorful names, this is the place.

Participant Sports

Archery

Public archery ranges are available at Washington Park in Southwest Portland and Delta East Park in North Portland. Bring your own targets. Visitors or new residents from the more populous eastern parts of the country might be interested in knowing that archery is more than just a fun and games sport in Oregon. Our hunting season includes a special month-long period for bowhunting. Call or write the Oregon Fish and Wildlife Department, 1634 SW Alder, P.O. Box 3503, Portland 97208, for details.

Baseball, Softball

Portland Park Bureau offers a full range of fastpitch and slowpitch softball programs for adults and children throughout the city.

In addition, Portland has one of the bigger and better Little League Baseball programs in the country. As well as pee wee, minor, and major league teams, the Portland Little League sponsors a Little League softball program for girls. (Girls also play on regular Little League teams.) Other baseball programs include Babe Ruth, Pony League, and American Legion, for youth, and Casey Stengel League for adults.

Additional information about Little League and other baseball programs is available from the Park Bureau sports office (248-4325).

Basketball

In 1975-76, a total of 160 Portland Basketball Assn. teams competed in the commercial, industrial, church, major, 6-foot and under, and 35 and older divisions at Portland high schools. Sponsored by the Park Bureau, this city league was described in a local newspaper, *Willamette Week*, as "the Park Bureau's answer for frustrated, aging athletes with a lust for competition." In addition, the Park Bureau offers competition in Golden-ball Basketball for grade and high school teams. For information about basketball for grade school girls and adult women, call the Park Bureau (248-4325).

The YBA (Youth Basketball Assn.), sponsored by the YMCA, the National Basketball Players' Assn., and Equitable Savings and Loan, offers an after-school program of instruction and play at various public school buildings for boys and girls in the third through sixth grades. Call 636-1212 for more information.

Bird Watching

Wintering area for ducks and geese and stopover for migrant birds, including sandhill cranes, is the Sauvie Island Wildlife Management Area, operated by the Oregon Fish and Wildlife Dept. A recreational officer conducts group tours. Call 621-3173 to make arrangements. Best time to bird watch at the area is in late winter and spring.

Other close-in watching areas are:

The Crystal Springs area surrounding the lake at the Rhododendron Test Gardens¶ (Feb.-April).

Pittock Wildlife Sanctuary, ¶ a good place to see the pileated woodpecker.

An area known as the Oaks Bottom, which is still being developed in Southeast Portland as a wetland bird sanctuary. Call the Audubon Society (292-6855) for more information.

Bicycling

Bicycle touring in the Portland area has become more popular and enjoyable since state funding became available to construct bicycle paths. Bike routes are well marked throughout the city, but you need not confine your riding to these. Many roadways without bike paths are perfect for cycling if you follow the safety rules for cyclists.

One tip from the Portland Traffic Safety Commission is worth quoting here: "Bridges are something special in Portland. Burnside Bridge is the safe one—on the sidewalk. Morrison and Steel Bridges, because of on-ramps, cloverleafs, and lane mergers, are pretty much nightmares. Broadway Bridge is passable, depending on the direction of travel and the time of day. Hawthorne, Sellwood, and St. Johns Bridges are safe if you use the sidewalk and can pick your way through the approaches."

For persons unfamiliar with cycling routes in Portland, an excellent map is available for the asking at the Portland City Planning Commission, 424 SW Main (248-4517). It is published by the Citizens' Bicycle Advisory Committee.

Bicycle Trips

Some popular bicycle trips and bicycle areas are listed here—a compilation of the favorites of a number of cycling friends. If you're serious about touring, buy *55 Oregon Bicycle Trips*, by Nick and Elske Jankowski (Touchstone). It is full of pictures, maps, and helpful suggestions.

Blue Lake Ride—Views of cathedral-like St. Johns Bridge, river traffic, air traffic, and Mt. Hood are all rolled into one bike trip on this scenic ride for the experienced cyclist. For west-siders, a crossing over the St. Johns Bridge to Ivanhoe is suggested. Head east on Ivanhoe,

with a jog to Jersey, to Buchanan. Turn left (north) on Buchanan and ride to Columbia Boulevard. Get on Columbia. Ride to N. Macrum and turn right (south) until you come to Columbia Way. Travel east on Columbia Way until you hit N. Portland Road. (These directions are important because the route to N. Portland Rd. is not clear on the bike map.) Follow Portland to Marine Dr. Turn east and follow the Columbia River past Portland International Airport to Blue Lake Park for picnicking and swimming. Marine Drive is considered by some to be one of the most beautiful and interesting rides in Portland. It has a good shoulder. Traffic can be heavy. This is about a 40-mile tour round-trip. You can shorten it by starting from any of a number of city parks in the north or northeast areas.

SW Fairmount Boulevard—Fairmount Blvd. in southwest Portland is a winding road which draws a 4-mile circle around Portland Heights and borders the base of Council Crest Park. You can start at any point on the circle. Fairmount is a lovely, wooded road edged with hillside residences. It's narrow, and though not too heavily traveled by automobiles, stay alert on the curves. The grades are gentle.

Scenic Figure-8 Trip—Travel the Fairmount circle and then take SW Talbot Rd. to SW Patton where Patton joins Humphrey Blvd. at St. Thomas More Church. Travel Humphrey northwest to Hewett Blvd. Follow Hewett back to Patton.

Multnomah Falls Ride—For the rider who is in good condition, a beautiful ride is to Multnomah Falls, 35 miles east of Portland in the Columbia Gorge. Cyclists recommend going to the Columbia River Scenic Highway via SE Stark and returning to Portland via NE Halsey.

Terwilliger Boulevard—You can park near the Carnival Restaurant, 2805 SW Sam Jackson Park Rd., where Terwilliger begins its incline toward the University of Oregon Health Sciences Center, to begin this lovely park-lined ride of about 3 miles (one-way). This is an established bike route and is well signed. To avoid the rather steep incline at the beginning, you can leave your car at a scenic parking area about 1½ miles up the road from the Carnival. Travel through Terwilliger Blvd. Park and past the Health Sciences complex. Notice the Totem Pole at the Hillvilla Restaurant on your left. Your path will pass under busy SW Capitol Hwy. and put you on the boundary of peaceful George H. Himes Park, a good picnic spot. You'll find tables at Terwilliger and SW Nebraska. The bicycle path ends at Barbur Blvd.

Terwilliger-Tryon Creek State Park—An extension to the Terwilliger ride takes you on to Tryon Creek State Park ƒ to the south. To achieve this, cross a major intersection at Barbur (where the Terwilliger bike path ends) and continue south across a bridge over I-5. You're still on Terwilliger. Continue on it through the Burlingame shopping area, past Collins View School to a fork at Boones Ferry Rd. At this point, a bike route (well marked) begins which takes you into Tryon Creek State Park. The distance from the end of the Terwilliger bike path to the beginning of the Tryon path is about 1½ miles.

Sauvie Island—Country roads and pleasant beaches are your reward for pedaling on Sauvie Island, ƒ a rural agricultural retreat formed by the confluence of the Willamette and Columbia Rivers. To get there, take U.S. 30 (one of the roads to Astoria) going northwest to the Sauvie Island Bridge about 10 miles from Portland. Immediately after crossing the bridge, you'll see a park, where you can leave your car if you're not cycling all the way. Follow Reeder Rd. to the beaches on the northeast side of the island. One of these is dubbed "Social Security Beach" because it is a pensioners' favorite fishing ground and the "headquarters" for "plunking," a peculiar technique of angling using a rod, rod holder, and cow bell, which is rigged to ring when a fish strikes the line. Unfortunately, salmon fishing has been curtailed on the Sauvie Island beaches and plunking may become a lost art.

Mary Young State Park—Three miles south of Lake Oswego between State Hwy. 43 and the Willamette River is Mary S. Young State Park, which contains a designated bike path.

Bike Postscripts

• For bicycle spectators, the Portland Rose Festival offers an exciting event: the Bicycle Road Races at Mt. Tabor Park. Also scheduled during the Rose Festival, held each June, is the Bicycle Track Race at Alpenrose Dairy. Rose Festival events are widely publicized in the metropolitan press.

• Portland Wheelmen Touring Club is the major bike organization in town. To join, you must be at least 16, but younger persons may ride with their parents or guardians. The club is associated with the League of American Wheelmen. If you're interested in membership, write to club at 7850 SE Stark, Portland 97215 and enclose your phone number.

• For information about bicycle racing clubs, check with Northwest Bicycles, 2108 NW Glisan (248-9142). Northwest's repair service, by the way, is fast and, happily, does not favor racing machines. The proprietors are just as nice to you when you bring in a child's broken one-speed. Other recommended bicycle shops are:

Cycle Craft, SW 12th & Morrison (222-3821) and SW Capitol at Sunset (246-8419). Cycle Craft rents bikes.

The Bike Gallery, 5211 NE Sandy (281-9800), open Sun.

Hook's Cyclery, 7850 SE Stark (253-1191), and in Gresham, 1045 E. Powell (665-5408).

Action Sports Inc., 12467 SW Broadway, Beaverton (644-3636).

• Classes in bicycle maintenance are frequently sponsored by the Park Bureau at various community centers.

Boating

Portland's riverways are wide enough and deep enough that small recreational craft, from sleek rowing shells to power speedboats, can "live" compatibly with the barges and ships that comprise the every-day river traffic.

Many of the big yacht clubs and moorages are located on the Columbia River along NE Marine Drive between NE Union and points east of the Portland International Airport. Other moorages are located on Sauvie Island, Hayden Island, and on the Willamette south of downtown Portland.

For general information about boating in the Portland area, read the boating column each Wednesday in *The Oregon Journal*.

"Boating is a way of life for those who take it seriously," says the columnist, Ed Goetzl, who has observed that Portland is one of the few places where you can catch a 30-pound salmon during your lunch hour—if you have a boat. (*The Portland GuideBook* makes no guarantees.)

In a motorboat, sailboat, or canoe, you can explore 200 miles of shoreline in the metropolitan area alone. Favorite haunts of boaters include Ross and Hard Tack Islands between the Ross Island and Sellwood Bridges, south of the downtown area; Coon Island and Collins Memorial Marine Park (Columbia County) in the Multnomah Channel opposite Scappoose, north of Portland; Sturgeon Lake on Sauvie Island, also north of Portland; and Government Island and Lady Island on the Columbia. The locks at Willamette Falls at Oregon City and at Bonneville Dam east of Portland on the Columbia are free and easily negotiated.

Boaters who know the river shoreline say a good place to moor your boat temporarily for downtown access is at the old harbor patrol dock on the west side of the river at the foot of Clay. There is no boat-launching ramp there.

Houseboat communities in the Portland area are not unusual and are often regarded as closeknit and chic. The houseboat colony that calls itself the Portland Rowing Club (it still owns some shells) is moored on the east side of the river above the Sellwood Bridge. Others moor at Oaks Park and at Hayden Island in the Columbia.

Courses in basic safe boating, varying from one to 13 weeks in length, are conducted by U.S. Power Squadron Units of the area and by the various flotillas of the Coast Guard Auxiliary. In addition, the Coast Guard Auxiliary offers a sailing course. The classes, usually taught in public school buildings, are conducted in spring and winter. Beginning courses are free and open to the public. Watch the newspapers for announcements. Learn-to-sail courses are also offered by Portland Community College (244-6111). PCC also offers canoeing instruction at Tillicum Lake.

Every motorboat and every sailboat 12-feet long or longer—and any sailboat with auxiliary power—must be registered with the State of Oregon Marine Board. After receiving your title and registration number, you must renew your registration yearly. How much you pay depends on the size of your boat.

Every powerboat must carry at least one fire extinguisher and one Coast Guard-approved personal flotation device for each passenger. It's hard to believe 40,035 registered boats call Portland home.

An *Oregon Boaters Handbook* is issued by the Oregon

State Marine Board, 3000 Market, NE, No. 505, Salem 97310.

For water skiing, the Willamette, south of Sellwood Bridge, and the Columbia are popular as are the lakes and reservoirs of the Portland area. Central Oregon and the Coast have many lakes where powerboat owners in the Portland area go for skiing and pleasure boating.

Sailing

"The Willamette River is a good place to learn to sail because you have to be alert every minute," counsels one sailor. Most sailing in the metropolitan area is confined to the Willamette and Columbia Rivers, and most boaters agree that river sailing is tricky. On the Columbia, when the northeast breezes combine with the current to take you downstream in a hurry, it's a hard tack back.

Nonetheless, sails dot the river in summer, many of them flying from small boats. Favorite small boat classes are *Thistle, Lightning, 470, 505, Coronado, C-Lark, Karalle, Laser,* and *Sunfish.* A popular small craft sailing club is the Willamette Sailing Club at 6336 SW Beaver, north of Willamette Park on the Willamette River's west side. Take time on warm, breezy summer evenings to watch a race there.

One of the most popular sailing reservoirs for small sailboats near Portland is Yale Lake, Wash., which can be reached via I-5 north of Portland 22 miles to Washington 503. The lake is about 30 miles east.

While sailing and powerboating seem to dominate the local water scene, the Willamette, Sandy, and Clackamas Rivers and nearby lakes and reservoirs provide good water for canoeing and rowing.

Canoeing

If you're planning to canoe on the Willamette, write for the *Willamette River Recreation Guide,* published by the Oregon State Highway Division, State Parks and Recreation Section, Salem 97310, or pick up a copy at the Portland Chamber of Commerce Visitors Information Service, 824 SW 5th. The *Guide* is an excellent annotated chart of the river from Cottage Grove, south of Eugene, to a point north of Sauvie Island. Boat-launching sites, marinas, camping facilities, fishing "holes," trails, and picnic areas are marked. Launch your canoe upstream and paddle downstream to any of a number of destinations.

If urban sightseeing by river is your desire, try putting in at Mary S. Young State Park near West Linn and paddling downstream under bridges, past river-bank homesites to the highrises of downtown Portland. The working cranes at Zidell Explorations Inc. (a sophisticated junk yard) are an interesting sideshow. You'll get a different perspective of the Portland skyline than you do by car. The St. Johns Bridge Ramp is probably the best spot to take out. Watch for debris in the river there. The whole trip will take a full day. For a shorter trip, take out at one of the many boat ramps south of the city.

For a rural Willamette River drift, try a trip from the Newberg boat ramp at Newberg (near the Herbert Hoover house) downstream to Willamette Park in West Linn, at the mouth of the Tualatin River. Bass fishing is good here. River enthusiasts warn: watch out for poison ivy on the tempting islands that dot the river course.

A good drift on the Sandy River is from Oxbow County Park⌂ to Dabney State Park.⌂ Both parks provide good facilities for putting in and taking out. The drift is about six miles.

In the Sauvie Island area, a pleasant one-day outing is from the Gilbert River Landing at the end of Reeder Rd. up the Gilbert River to Sturgeon Lake. The Oregon Fish and Wildlife Dept. maintains a two-lane paved ramp and a parking area at the landing.

Ramps, Rentals, Charters

Following is a list of boat ramps in the Portland stretch of the Willamette:

St. Johns Bridge Ramp (east side)
Willamette Park (west side, south of downtown)
Staff Jennings Ramp (west end of Sellwood Bridge)
Sellwood Bridge Ramp, (end of Spokane under east end of the Sellwood)

Many more ramps are available in the Milwaukie, Oswego, and Oregon City areas to the south and in the Sauvie Island area to the north.

Canoe rentals are common in the Portland area. For the Sauvie Island area, try Brown's Landing (1-543-6526) and for the Oregon City area, Sportcraft Landing (656-6484). For canoe drift parties, Sportcraft will truck canoes up the Willamette. In addition, you can let Yachts-O-Fun do all the work for you and charter the Cruis-Ader Princess (285-6665).

Oregon River Tours, by John Garren (Touchstone), $4.95 provides detailed information about river running.

Rowing

A rowing renaissance is under way in Portland. An enthusiastic group of adults and students have organized the Station L Rowing Club, which takes its name from a steam plant at its moorage beneath the east end of the Marquam Bridge. The club was formed to promote the return of intercollegiate rowing to the Willamette. Reed and Lewis and Clark College students pay $25 a year as student members; adults, who make up the "Cardiac Crew" of recreational rowers, pay $50. The club's membership is open. For further information call Andy Rocchia (228-6994).

Bowling

More than 25 bowling alleys are operated in the Portland area, many of them offering food service and child care. Billiard facilities are available at some bowling alleys. For more information about bowling, call: Portland Bowling Assn. (288-6597) or Greater Portland Women's Bowling Assn. (288-5089).

Boxing and Wrestling

Boxing and wrestling programs are offered through the Park Bureau at a number of community centers and high schools. Call the Park Bureau (248-4325) for more information. A Wrestling Fitness and Development Program for grade school youth is sponsored by the Park Bureau in cooperation with the Portland high school wrestling coaches.

Bridge

In addition to Park Bureau bridge programs at some community centers, there are at least three bridge clubs in Portland: Cavendish Bridge Club, 624 SW 13th

(228-7942); Gateway Bridge, 10751 NE Fargo (252-5630); and Portland Bridge Club, Inc., (287-4445).

Chess

Portland Chess Club, 420 SW Washington (228-1785). Each spring some 5,000 high school students compete for a chance to play in *The Oregonian*-OMSI annual chess tournament, a big event in the northwest. OMSI also offers chess instruction.

Curling

Portland Curling Club, 1210 NE 102nd (255-4644)

Fishing

Salmon, steelhead, and rainbow and cutthroat trout are the glamour fish from the lakes and streams.

Willamette River—Famed for its run of spring chinook salmon in March, April, and early May and for sturgeon from Feb.-May. The fishery is the length of the lower river and Willamette Slough.

Clackamas River—Steelhead in the lower river, from River Mill Dam to Clackamas, in Nov.-March, and for rainbow trout in the upper river, May-Sept.

Eagle Creek—This Clackamas tributary near Estacada is good for winter steelhead Dec.-Feb., and for jack salmon and coho, late Oct.-Dec.

Sandy River—Fish the lower river from Marmot Dam to Troutdale for steelhead, Dec.-March, and for coho and fall chinook, Oct.-Nov.

Molalla River—Above Wagon Wheel County Park, steelhead, March-Apr., and rainbow trout, May-Aug.

Salmon River—This tributary of the Sandy is good for rainbow trout from June-Sept.

Sauvie Island Wildlife Management Area Lakes and Sloughs—Panfish, bass, catfish, March-Sept.

Sauvie Island Beaches (Columbia River side)—Steelhead, salmon, jack salmon, and searun cutthroat (harvest trout). Seasons have recently been curtailed on spring and summer runs of salmon.

Licensed fishing guides in the area include:

Ray Dunigan (292-5531)
Dud Nelson (654-5311)
Dennis Mobley (761-1310)

For more information about guides, write for the *Oregon Guides and Packers Directory*, P.O. Box 722, Lake Oswego, Or. 97034.

Charters

The cost of salmon at your neighborhood market is out of sight, you say? You can't get it at all in the inland states. So you decide you want to charter a boat to hook fresh fish and have some fun at the same time.

Nearly every town on the coast berths charter boats, but there are charters and then there are charters. Charters by the hour are a poor investment, for the captains rush to return to shore and pick up the next load whether or not you've limited out. We offer you the very best in two areas. If they're full, they'll recommend someone else. Wise fishermen who take the recommendations usually take home a limit of chinook or silvers.

Prices for salmon excursions run out of the economy class, but you'll get your money's worth with the better skippers. Small boats, four to six passengers, usually cost about $33 per person, larger boats, eight to 12 passengers, about $30 each. Pick up one- or three-day licenses and salmon tags at a modest fee from sport shops and most charter-boat operators on the coast. The season usually runs from May 1 to Oct. 15, give or take a couple weeks.

Boats usually leave dockside between 5-6 a.m., so a word of warning: easy on the drinks the night before. Get as least six hours of solid sleep. If you've never been on the ocean, take a motion sickness pill (*Dramamine* or *Marazine*) at least an hour before leaving the dock as insurance. Your stomach will thank you for it.

Bring your own lunch and beverages, other than coffee, aboard. Most cafes open at 4 a.m. on the coast and will prepare a lunch for you while you eat breakfast.

Astoria-Warrenton-Hammond—The top independent small charter boat in this area is "The Fancy," skippered by Maury Weis. A former Portland grade school principal, Maury will hunt fish until you're exhausted or limited out, whichever comes first. He hops around better on his one leg than you can on two and his beautiful 36-foot Chris-Craft is outfitted to the gunwales with safety equipment. Berthed at Warrenton, Maury can be reached in Portland off-season for scheduling (235-8118) and in the evenings. He provides the tackle and the bait; you bring your lunch and beverages. Pay attention to his advice and you'll not only catch fish, you'll have the outing of a lifetime. Boat capacity is six fishermen. Reserve well ahead for this popular boat.

For larger groups who want to be together in one boat and don't want steerage treatment, Bud Charlton's "Warrenton Deep Sea Charters" is the answer. Capt. Charlton operates three boats for 12 passengers and a couple with smaller capacities. Like Weis, Charlton is in the business for your enjoyment, not his profit and loss statement. He is a pro's pro and will get you fish if there are any in the ocean. He furnishes tackle and bait. Again, reserve well ahead (861-1233).

Depoe Bay—This is a unique area for deep sea fishing. From Depoe Bay the fishing waters are only a 10-minute boat ride, compared to approximately one hour from the Astoria area. For this reason, Depoe Bay charter-boat skippers offer four-hour trips, and these can be worthwhile. Charter costs are somewhat less expensive here and most boats get in two trips a day.

Stan Allyn's Depoe Bay Charters (765-2345) is one of the best known among the large operators in the area, although there are many other worthwhile skippers. Allyn is usually booked well ahead of time, so call in advance to be sure of your trip time.

Bud Romans is a former power company engineer who flicked the corporate rat race to captain his own charter boat. The fishermen are better off for it. He can be reached in Portland throughout the year at 252-1398 or (765-2713). When he's on the ocean, his wife does the booking for him.

Fly Fishing

When the Cascade rivers have expended their rush of cold, spring snowmelt, fly fishing picks up and is best during summer evenings. Closest to Portland for the fly angler in July and August is the Clackamas above North Fork Reservoir along with its tributaries, Oak Grove Fork and Collowash Rivers. A run of summer steelhead is now being established in the Clackamas. Summer steelhead are available in the Big Nestucca and Wilson Rivers on the Northern Oregon Coast.

There is also nearby fly fishing for these wild warrior steelhead in southwest Washington on the Toutle, Kalama, Washougal, and Wind Rivers during spring and summer months.

East Fork Hood River, Badger Creek, and White River on the east side of Mt. Hood National Forest are pleasant streams, but the most noted is the lower Deschutes River which has a special fly-only area.

After a brief sojourn in the saltchuck the searun cutthroat return to the coastal rivers. Fly fishing with bright attractor patterns is pursued in the lower reaches, near tidewater, for cutthroat starting in August and continuing into September. Nearest Portland or west of the Coast Range are the Kilchis, Big Nestucca, Little Nestucca, Trask, Wilson, and Necanicum Rivers for these searun trout.

The *Oregon Journal* and *Oregonian* both carry weekly fishing reports. Detailed information can be obtained from the Oregon Fish and Wildlife Dept., 1634 SW Alder, Portland, 97201 (229-5403).

A large casting pool in Westmoreland Park is available for bait, spin, or fly casting practice.

Shellfish

Going after Pacific shellfish is something to tell the folks back east about. Try digging for razor clams on a minus tide along the Pacific surfline, or venture onto the bay flats in search of cockle, butter, littleneck, softshell, or gaper clams. Some are best steamed or eaten on the halfshell, others are great for chowder, and the razor clam is the prize when quick-fried in butter and a fresh bread crumb jacket.

Dungeness crab is considered superior to all others by epicures, and moorages on Nehalem, Tillamook, Netarts, Siletz, Yaquina, and Alsea bays offer crab rings and bait plus friendly advice on how to use them.

Or, consider a "crabbing package" such as that offered by the Embarcadero Resort Hotel in Newport. The package includes complete crabbing gear and an excursion on Yaquina Bay.

Football

Pop Warner football (tackle) for 6th, 7th, and 8th grade boys is conducted through the Park Bureau program. Sponsors pay team fees of $250. The Park Bureau also coordinates seven-man touch football competition for adults and sponsors nine-man flag football programs for grade school boys. Call 248-4325 for more information.

Golf

The Portland metropolitan area supports more fine golf courses per capita than nearly any other city in the United States. Many public courses are available for play, and a number of the fine private clubs are accessible if you're a member of a club in your home town or know a member of one of the local clubs.

Nearly every course is playable year-round. A broad spectrum of challenges faces the hacker or the scratch player. Greens fees are generally quite reasonable at the public courses and only slightly more expensive at the private clubs.

Listed below are public courses in order of toughness:

Meriwether Country Club, Hillsboro (648-4143)— About 15 minutes from downtown. 18 holes, 7042 yards, par 72. Long, lots of water, bunkers, limited clubhouse facilities; plan to shower at your motel.

Forest Hills Country Club, Cornelius (648-8559)—20 minutes from downtown; 18/6244/72; best manicured of all public courses with rolling hills, many bunkers, and quite a bit of water and tall fir trees. Local favorite. If you have time, it's worth the drive. Good clubhouse facilities. Call ahead for tee time.

Eastmoreland Municipal Golf Course, 2425 SE Bybee Blvd. (775-2900)—18/6522/72. A contrast in nines; one fairly mundane, the other beautiful with water on every hole. Gets heavy play, so call ahead. Modest clubhouse facilities. Plan to shower at motel.

West Delta Municipal Golf Course, 3500 N. Victory Blvd. (289-1818)—18/6397/72. Robert Trent Jones designed course; many bunkers, not too long or too many trees or water; lots of doglegs. Needs to mature and get more attention from city fathers. Modest clubhouse.

Gresham Golf Club, 2155 NE Division, Gresham (665-3352)—18/6500/72. About 18 miles from downtown. Challenging course with a little bit of everything for the golfer. Fun to play, and at times can be an ego builder. Good clubhouse facilities.

Rose City Municipal Golf Course, 2200 NE 71st (253-4744)—18/6493/72. Rather pedestrian layout with about five interesting holes. Lots of trees, little sand or water. Gets heavy play. Modest clubhouse facilities. Shower at motel. Close to town.

Colwood National Golf Club, 7313 NE Columbia Blvd. (254-5515)—18/6432/72. Fun course for average golfer; a little sand, a little water, a lot of trees. Jets at nearby Portland Airport sometimes make the hearing difficult. Very friendly people; shower facilities adequate.

Broadmoor Golf Club, 3509 NE Columbia Blvd. (281-1337)—18/6155/72. Sporty, tight course with a little sand and quite a few trees; slick greens. Close to town; also close to airport. Shower facilities adequate.

Mt. View Golf Club, 27195 SE Kelso Rd., Boring (663-4869)—18/6214/72. Tight course with some beautiful holes. About 22 miles from town. Some sand, some water.

Progress Downs Golf Course, 8200 SW Scholls Ferry Rd. (646-5166)—18/6496/72. No sand, no water, little trouble except for a few small trees. Does have one of the city's finest restaurants, The Stock Pot. If you like to golf, then eat, with the emphasis on the latter, this is your course.

Glendoveer Golf Club, 14015 NE Glisan St. (253-7507)—Only 36-hole course in Oregon. 6368/74; 6066/72. Gets heavy play and little maintenance from county. Beautiful fir trees and narrow fairways provide most of challenge. Not very long and has very little sand; lots of rough, some intended, some unintended. Shower in your room.

Top O'Scott Golf Club, 1200 SE Stevens Rd. (654-5050)—18/5544/70. If you like to see a view of the city along with a pleasant outing while swinging a golf club, this is the place. Not a great challenge, but a fun course— good for the ego.

Executive Courses

Charbonneau Golf Club, Wilsonville (638-7606)—

18/4260/64. New, beautiful executive course running through a fine housing development. Lots of sand; good challenge despite short length. Off I-5 about 15 minutes south of downtown. The course will fool the good golfer and bedevil the average one.

Portland Meadows Golf Course, 901 N. Schmeer Rd. (289-3405)—9/2180. Nine holes inside a horse race track. If you have some time before the races, during the season, this is where the action is.

King City Golf Course, Tigard (639-7986)9/2442/32. Tough, tight, and tempting.

Par-three Courses

Hoyt Park Pitch and Putt, near the zoo at 4001 SW Canyon Rd. (222-5144)—18/1322/54. The place to take the children; club rental. Interesting but very short course, although hilly. Portland Zoo, OMSI, and Forestry Building all within a block. Great for a family afternoon.

Rivergreens Golf Course, 480 River Rd., Gladstone (656-1033)—18/2380/54. Along the Willamette River about 12 miles SE of town. Easy to reach and fun to play.

Lake Oswego Municipal Golf Course, 17525 Stafford Rd. (636-8228)—18/2725/54. Very similar to Rivergreens except it is on a hill, overlooking Portland.

Private Golf Clubs

Portland has some of the finest private clubs in the Northwest and all are accessible to the traveler, providing he belongs to a reciprocal private club in his home town or knows a member in Portland. Listed, in order of toughness, are:

Portland Golf Club, 5900 SW Scholls Ferry Rd. (292-2778)—18/6714/72. Robert Trent Jones re-designed course; lots of trees, water, and sand. Location of several PGA tournaments; beautifully manicured, torturous greens; superb facilities; some caddies; electric carts. Call ahead for starting time.

Oswego Lake Country Club, 20 SW Iron Mountain Blvd., Lake Oswego (636-5933)—18/6584/71. Beautiful, exquisitely manicured hillside course with very tight fairways, abundant sand, water, and small, slick greens. Outstanding facilities, some caddies; gasoline carts.

Willamette Valley Country Club, 2396 Country

Club Dr., Canby (655-4013)—About 25 miles from downtown Portland. 18/7200/72. Long and treacherous with lots of sand and water. Fairly new course; when it matures it could be best in area. Adequate clubhouse; electric carts.

Waverley Country Club, 1100 SE Waverly Dr. (654-6521)—18/6324/72. Oldest course in Oregon (1913). Site of National Amateur in 1972. Comparatively short; very tough with lots of bunkers and trees. No water, but vicious greens. Magnificent colonial clubhouse with all other facilities to match. Caddies, carts.

Riverside Country Club, 8105 NE 33rd Dr. (282-7265)—18/6467/72. Long, narrow, well trapped and watered. Gets heavy ladies' play. Excellent pro shop. Electric carts, some caddies. Fine facilities.

Columbia-Edgewater Country Club, 2138 NE Marine Dr. (285-8354)—18/6598/72. A fine all-around challenging golf course with abundant sand and water as well as trees. Site of many PGA tournaments. Very friendly membership. Carts, some caddies. Fine facilities.

Rock Creek Country Club (645-1101)—12 minutes from downtown on Sunset Highway 26; 18/6916/72; long, narrow, not heavily bunkered, large greens. Good clubhouse facilities. Generally tough course.

Tualatin Country Club, Tualatin (638-5432)—About 15 minutes from downtown. 18/6324/72. Demanding tight course, well bunkered. Well manicured. Nice clubhouse. Carts, some caddies.

Pleasant Valley Country Club, 12300 SE 162nd, Clackamas (658-3101)—About 15 minutes from downtown. 18/6530/72. Fairly new club, moderately trapped, some water, fairly tight. Clubhouse facilities adequate. Course sporty, challenging. Electric carts.

Coastal Golf (Astoria to Newport)

Astoria Golf and Country Club (private), Warrenton—18/6486/72. Outstanding course laid out on rolling sand dunes with water, sand, and sometimes wind that provides the ultimate challenge to all golfers. Well manicured in a beautiful setting. Probably the best coastal golf north of the Pebble Beach area. Fine, new clubhouse with excellent facilities. Electric carts. Call ahead.

Gearhart Golf Club (public), Gearhart—18/6147/72. Challenging, windswept seaside links. Not much sand or water, very dry fairways. Nice greens. Gets heavy play during the summer months. Carts available, showers not. Pleasant cocktail lounge and coffee shop.

Seaside Golf Course (public), Seaside—9/2610/36. Pleasant, fairly easy family-style golf course. Some challenging holes to help while away a pleasant afternoon. Good restaurant, no showers.

Neah-kah-nie Golf Club (public)—Along the Coast Highway at Manzanita. 9/1804/29. Sidehill course best suited for family play. Good view of the ocean. Can be an interesting challenge for medium to long iron players.

Alderbrook Country Club (public), Tillamook—18/5810/72. A truly fun golf course. Don't let the shortness of the course fool you. There are some holes that can bite you. This course requires good, strong legs or an electric cart. Good clubhouse facilities.

Neskowin Golf Course (9/3021/34) and *Hawk Creek Hills Golf Club* (9/2910/34) (public), Neskowin. Both in a small, isolated resort area. Both courses are sporty with no overwhelming challenges. Shower in your motel.

Salishan Golf Club (public), Gleneden Beach—18/6437/72. Bring lots of golf balls. If you hit into the rough, you probably won't find your ball. Long, well-trapped course with a little water. Beautiful view of ocean. Some holes on course, particularly the 7th, border on the unfair. Course is absolutely unforgiving. Fine pro shop and coffee shop. Electric carts are available and almost a necessity, considering the steepness of the front nine.

Agate Beach Golf Club (public), Agate Beach—9/3002/36. Pleasant course to play. Host pro and owner, Bill Martin, is very accommodating with well-stocked pro shop and pleasant coffee shop. Last four holes quite sporty. Ideal for the golfing family. On a windy day, it's a tiger. Change and shower in your room.

Salem Golf

Illahe Hills Country Club (private)—18/6716/72. Truly a beautiful golf course. Exceptionally well manicured; heavily trapped, fair amount of water. Mostly open except for a few fairways framed in filbert trees.

Large, slick, tricky greens. Fine dining, cocktail, and locker room facilities. Phone ahead.

Salem Golf Club (public)—18/6302/72. A finely crafted and manicured old public course that's home to 1975 L.A. Open champ Pat Fitzsimons. He holds the course record at 58. Nicely bunkered, with a little water and lots of trees. You'll use every club in your bag; some to play with, some to throw in frustration. Adequate pro shop and shower facilities.

McNary Golf Club (public)—18/6718/72. Young course with few bunkers but quite a bit of water. All greens are elevated and undulating. Several long holes with 600-yard-plus 18th, which is a monster. Fine clubhouse, restaurant, and pro shop facilities.

Gymnastics

As demanding as it is, gymnastics is a surprisingly popular athletic activity among young people in Portland. Most Park Bureau programs offer classes as do the YMCA (223-6161) and YWCA (223-6281).

Handball, Squash, Racquetball

Nerve center of squash in Portland is the private Multnomah Athletic Club, or if you're not a member, the YMCA, which is opening a new building at Duniway Park, with excellent squash and handball facilities. Neighborhood House, a community center, has handball courts which are leased to the Neighborhood Athletic Assn. Call Neighborhood House (226-3251) for more information. The Jewish Community Center, 6651 SW Capitol Hwy. (244-0111) has handball and racquetball facilities which are restricted to members. Call the membership secretary for further information.

Hiking

Oregon hiking trails are so popular in summer that many appear to be pedestrian freeways. The true wilderness seeker soon learns to hike midweek or in places that have not been publicized in books like this. The crowd thins in proportion to the number of miles you're willing to hike, but not necessarily when you're mountain climbing. Even though proportionately fewer persons bag peaks, climbing routes become congested, as there are only so many ways to the top. Literally hundreds of people will reach the summit of Mt. Hood on any number of good climbing days during May and June.

Because there is so much to learn about hiking, backpacking, and climbing, we recommend good books, maps and equipment, and membership in one of the climbing and hiking clubs in the Portland area. Hikes are sponsored by various Park Bureau community centers. Hiking information and guidance are also available from the YMCA and YWCA.

August is the most popular hiking month in the mountains because by then, in a typical year, the snow has melted from the trails and the mosquito hatch has passed. September is an ideal month to hike—no mosquitoes and fewer people. Trails in the Columbia Gorge and at the coast can usually be used year-round.

Clubs

Most widely known mountaineering club in the area is the 2600-member *Mazama Club*, 909 NW 19th (227-2345). To become a member, you must climb a peak with a living glacier. This sounds rather restrictive but Mazama programs are geared to helping potential members reach the top and return. When you see a new crop of Mazamas headed for the top of Mt. Hood in late spring or early summer, it's "like the Himalayan Army," someone once said.

Also worth noting are the *Trails Club* of Oregon, P.O. Box 1243, Portland, 97207, and the *Sierra Club*, which has an Oregon office at 2637 SW Water (222-1963). Both the Mazama and Trails Clubs have lodges on Mt. Hood.

Gear, Guides, Books

Where to go for climbing and hiking gear? Mountain shops offer equipment to buy or rent and fancy freeze-dry food at fancy prices. Worth special mention are:
Alpine Hut, 1250 Lloyd Center (284-1164)
Howell's Uptown Sport Centre, 21 NW 23rd Pl. (227-7910)
Mountain Shop at three locations: Cloud Cap Chalet, 625 SW 12th (227-0579); Mountain Shop West, 3225 SW Cedar Hills Blvd., Beaverton (643-5693); Mountain Shop, 628 NE Broadway (288-6768)

Oregon Mountain Community, 222 SW Main (227-1038)
    If you need a professional leader call:
Johann Mountain Guides, 7808 SW 40th, Portland, 97219
    (244-7672)
    Many beautiful guidebooks are available to Oregon
hikers. Among them:
    100 Oregon Hiking Trails, by Don and Roberta Lowe
(Touchstone), an excellent all-round hiking guide; *70
Hiking Trails, Northern Oregon Cascades*, also by the
Lowes (Touchstone); *Hiking the Oregon Skyline,* by
Charles M. Feris (Touchstone); *Short Trips and Trails,
The Columbia Gorge*, by Oral Bullard and Don Lowe
(Touchstone).
    For mountain climbers, *Freedom of the Hills*, published
by the Mountaineers in Seattle, is considered the classic
hiking-climbing text for the area.
    Some of the best hikes in Oregon are in national forests
in the Cascade range. To acquaint visitors and residents
with the features of these areas, the U.S. Forest Service
(USFS) and the National Parks Service (NPS) jointly
maintain an information office on the ground floor of the
Multnomah Building, 319 SW Pine (221-2877). Many
maps of wilderness areas are available there, some free,
some for 50¢. (Especially good is *Forest Trails of the
Columbia Gorge*, free.) Maps that provide the most detailed hiking information are U.S. Geological Survey
topographic maps. Some are available from the USFS-
NPS information office. They are also sold at J.K. Gill
Co., 408 SW 5th, and Captain's Nautical Supply, 832
SW 4th.

Short Hikes

    The Portland-area is blessed with a seemingly endless
list of day hike destinations, most of them suitable for
spring, summer, and fall months. Here are a few day
hikes, suitable for family outings. In the Forest Park area:
    Wildwood Trail—Within the city limits, huge Forest
and Macleay Parks offer 30 miles of hiking trails, including the 14½-mile wooded Wildwood Trail, which
begins at the Western Forestry Center and winds through
the Arboretum and Pittock Acres¶ and ends deep in
Forest Park on Saltzman Road. The Wildwood Trail has
been designated a scenic trail by the National Trail Act.

Upper Macleay-Wildwood Loop—A lovely wooded loop hike, particularly in spring when the trillium and elderberry are in bloom, is on the Upper Macleay Trail to a junction with the Wildwood Trail which brings you into the Macleay Trail and back to your starting point. To reach the start, take Burnside west. Turn right on Macleay Blvd. (about half a mile west of 23rd) and wind uphill past Warrenton to a cul de sac where Macleay terminates. Find good parking and trail markers. Follow the Upper Macleay Trail about ¼ mile to a three-pronged junction. Take the center trail winding downhill and looping back to a junction with Wildwood and Macleay (not to be confused with Upper Macleay) Trails. Follow Macleay back to your car. Allow one hour at the most for this 1½-mile hike.

Arboretum Trails—Start at the Western Forestry Center(on the Wildwood Trail, which parallels the pitch-and-putt golf course and leads you to various trails that lace the Hoyt Arboretum.

Group tours on the Forest Park trails and arboretum trails can be arranged by calling 228-1223.

Some short hikes in the spectacular Columbia Gorge area are:

Wahkeena-Perdition Loop—For this 3-mile hike which takes in views of Wahkeena and Multnomah Falls, park your car at the Wahkeena Picnic Ground on the Columbia River Gorge Scenic Highway. Follow Trail #420 for nearly half a mile to a junction with Perdition Trail #421. Take Perdition for nearly a mile to a view of Multnomah Falls. Continue on to the junction with Larch Mountain Trail #441, 1.1 miles from Multnomah Falls Lodge. Follow #441 north to the lodge. Follow trail #442, which parallels the highway, west to Wahkeena Picnic ground.

Horsetail Falls-Oneonta Gorge Loop—Your departure point for this spectacular 2.5-mile waterfall hike can be reached only via the Columbia Gorge Scenic Route. Park at Horsetail Falls, two miles east of Multnomah Falls. Trail #438 climbs via switchbacks for about ½ mile to a passage behind Upper Horsetail Falls. Children love this. After passing "through" the falls, proceed less than ½ mile to a viewpoint overlooking deep, dark Oneonta Gorge, a narrow cleft in a basalt bluff, and

Eagle Creek Trail in the Columbia Gorge leads to Punch Bowl Falls—a 2-mile easy hike.

the Columbia Gorge. Continue another ½ mile to Oneonta Trail, #424, which descends in an easterly direction to the Columbia River Scenic Highway, ½ mile west of the Horsetail Falls parking area. A very abbreviated version of this is to Upper Horsetail and back.

Eagle Creek and Punch Bowl Falls—Eagle Creek Trail in the Columbia Gorge (not to be confused with Eagle Creek, a tributary of the Clackamas River) will take the serious hiker as far as Wahtum Lake, 13 miles away. For the family day hike, however, we recommend a 2-mile trip up the Eagle Creek Trail to Punch Bowl Falls, a wonderful geological "waterworks." To get to your departure point, travel east on I-80N to the Eagle Creek Fish Hatchery, a mile east of Bonneville Dam. Travel south to the end of the dirt road and park. Trail #440 rises through forest and past mossy rock walls. After 1½ miles, you'll reach a short side trail to Metlako Falls. A half mile further you'll see the side trail to Punch Bowl Falls. This trail descends to the river for a close look at the punch bowl as it receives a massive spill of water from a spout in the basalt. At this point, you can either return or proceed 1.7 miles further to Tenas Campsite.

Watch small children on all hikes in the Columbia Gorge. Trails often wind up and down steep canyons, and the very features that provide interesting and spectacular viewpoints can make the terrain dangerous for unpredictable youngsters.

In the Mt. Hood National Forest, we recommend these easy day hikes:

Ramona Falls—A beautiful walk from late July through October is to Ramona Falls on the Upper Sandy River on the western side of Mt. Hood. Take U.S. 26 heading east to the town of Zigzag and travel north on the Lolo Pass Road which you'll find opposite the Zigzag Ranger Station. Travel Lolo Pass Road north more than 4 miles to Road S 25. Turn east and drive for another 4 miles to the Sandy River Trail, #770. Cross the Sandy River and turn right at the Portage Trail junction and proceed east until reaching the Timberline Trail junction. (Timberline Trail is a 36-mile path which circles Mt. Hood at about the 6,000-foot level.) Continue on the Sandy River Trail to the Upper Sandy Guard Station and to Ramona Falls, where you'll find a pleasant forest camp and the 100-foot falls.

Salmon River—To reach your departure point, travel east on U.S. 26 and, just before reaching Zigzag, turn south on the Salmon River Road, #S38. Travel for 5 miles past the Green Canyon Guard Station to the north end of the Salmon River Bridge, where you'll find parking. The trail, #742, is marked. The first 1¾ miles make an easy family hike along and above the Salmon River.

Recommended short hikes in some other areas are:

Clackamas River Trail—This hike is on a beautiful reach of the Upper Clackamas River near the Ripplebrook Ranger Station. Take Oregon 224 east through Estacada. About 25 miles southeast of Estacada is the ranger station. Drive east and then south less than a mile to Rainbow Campground. Trail #723 heads south along the Clackamas River.

Silver Creek Falls State Park—You can pick your own hike in this inspiring spot 26 miles east of Salem on Oregon 214. The park contains 14 waterfalls and many trails. It is a sightseeing favorite and usually crowded on fair weather weekends.

Saddle Mountain—One of Oregon's most attainable and beautiful mountain tops—especially rewarding for the novice hiker—is up Saddle Mountain, 3,283 feet above the Oregon coast near Seaside. Departure point is Saddle Mountain State Park 2 miles off U.S. 26, 14 miles east of Seaside. The trail is well marked at the parking lot and is usually climbable from March to December. The hike is 6 miles round trip; elevation gain, 1,663 feet. Coast moisture keeps Saddle Mountain ever green. Wildflowers there are spectacular in the spring.

Hiking Postscript—For most hikes, allow 25 minutes per mile.

Horseback Riding

If you've just moved to town and want to enroll your daughter in a riding class, the best places to call are:

Horsemanship West, 19713 S. Molalla, Oregon City (656-9113), for western riding instruction.

Lake Oswego Hunt, 2725 SW Iron Mountain Blvd., Lake Oswego (636-9143), for eastern instruction.

Sunset Farms and Stables, 5000 NW 242nd, Hillsboro (648-6782), also for eastern instruction.

Sunwood Farms, Rt. 1, Box 439, Scholls Ferry Rd., Beaverton (649-3930), for show jumping and riding instruction.

For pleasure riding, Tryon Creek State Park has beautiful bridle paths, but you have to bring your own horse.

Though it's not in Portland, **Donna Gill's Rock Springs Guest Ranch**, a few miles west of Bend, deserves special mention in any section on horsemanship. Donna has combined her widely respected expertise in riding with her talents as an innkeeper at this beautiful family ranch where riding is the primary activity, but tennis, swimming, and fishing follow closely behind. Donna enhances her regular "dude" ranch riding program with annual horsemanship clinics which attract riders from all over the state. Address is 64201 Tyler Rd., Bend, 97701.

Hunting

Information about hunting seasons and regulations is available from the Oregon Dept. of Fish and Wildlife (229-5403). Tom McAllister's annual *Oregon Journal Hunting Calendar*, a handy billfold-size folder, is available in September at the *Oregon Journal*, 1320 SW Broadway, or at sporting goods stores and other outlets throughout the state.

In the Portland area, the only public hunting grounds are at the well-managed Sauvie Island Wildlife Management Area. You can hunt there during the three-month waterfowl season. Reservations are required to hunt the east side of the area. On the west side, it's first-come, first-served. Make reservations by mail or phone. Mailing address is 1634 SW Alder St., Portland, 97208.

Hunter safety training programs sponsored by the National Rifle Assn. are conducted annually. Watch the newspapers for announcements or call the state agency number.

Trap and skeet shooters are welcome at the Portland Gun Club, 4711 SE 174th (665-9977).

Ice Skating

Ice skating rinks in the Portland area where competitive figure skating is supported are:

Silver Skate Ice Rink, 1210 NE 102nd (255-4644), home of the Portland Ice Skating Club.

Valley Ice Arena, 9300 SW Beaverton-Hillsdale Hwy. (292-6631), headquarters for the Carousel Figure Skating Club.

Jantzen Beach Ice Center, 1800 Jantzen Beach Center (285-6601), which the Jantzen Beach Figure Skating Club calls home.

The same three rinks host teams of the Portland Amateur Hockey Assn., a thriving program in which about 800 9- and 10-year-old boys take part. Businesses support the various teams in the same fashion as Little League baseball. Play starts in the fall and continues into February and March. A Junior Buckaroo program for high schoolers and an adult program round out the amateur hockey scene in Portland. Call any of the three rinks for additional information.

If competition isn't your bag, you can still skate for fun at any of the above rinks or try what is probably the best-known rink in town at the Lloyd Center (288-6073), where hundreds of shoppers pause to watch pleasure skating there night and day.

Ice skaters transplanted in Portland from the east and midwest will find little here in the way of outdoor pond skating, but on those few occasions when the weather is cold enough to freeze a pond, or when the ice age returns, try the Westmoreland casting pond, the lake at Laurelhurst Park, or Smith Lake, northwest of West Delta Park Golf Course.

Jogging and Track

Back in the days when jogging wasn't a universal activity, a friend in the Chicago area commented, "No matter where you go in Portland, you see somebody jogging." That's even more true now.

Crowning Portland's jogging terrain is its 2-mile exercise and jogging trail, maintained by the Park Bureau. It starts on Terwilliger Blvd., about ¼ mile north of the Hillvilla Restaurant at 5700 SW Terwilliger. The track takes you north toward downtown. Twenty exercise "stops" provide diversion and a real workout. Few trails, if any, exist like it elsewhere. Start and finish are well marked.

Many joggers visit hilly, woodsy Washington Park where you can choose four-, six- and 10-mile treks. Some Park Bureau programs offer regular jogging schedules.

Portland State University sponsors "Run for Your Life," a jogging program conducted Mon., Wed., and Fri. from 5 to 6 p.m. Call the PSU health and physical education department (229-4401) for more information.

Also worth noting:

• Portland Track Club (244-4765), an Amateur Athletic Union Club, sponsors track programs for boys and girls.

• The Oregon Road Runners Club, which sponsors 25 or 30 road runs a year.

• The All-Comers Track and Field Meets for children all ages. Call the Park Bureau (248-4325) for more information.

Lawn Bowling

Westmoreland Park has lawn bowling facilities.

Model Airplanes and Boats

Model plane flying is allowed at Delta East Park; model boat sailing, at Westmoreland Park.

Motorsports

Portland International Raceway, 1940 N. Victory Blvd., at West Delta Park (285-6635) offers a full schedule of motorsports events throughout the year. In addition, the raceway is available for recreational riding at certain times. A sample of the activities sponsored at the raceway, which is a focal point of activity for cycling and driving in the northwest, includes Porsche Club Autocross, Yamaha Dirt Days, Columbia Corvette Club Autocross, motorcycle road races, and motocrosses.

Auto and motorcycle repair and maintenance courses are offered by Portland Community College's Community Education Divison (244-6111).

Oriental Martial Arts

Judo, karate, kung-fu, and other forms of self-defense training are offered both publicly, through Park Bureau and Community College programs, and commercially. Instruction for both men and women is also available at the YMCA and YWCA.

Roller Skating

The Park Bureau operates one public rink at the Mt. Scott Community Center, 5530 SE 72nd (774-2215), Wed. through Fri. from 1-9 p.m.; Sat. from 9 a.m.-5 p.m.; Sun. for hockey from 9 a.m.-noon, and for public skating from noon-5 p.m. Skating is free, and skates rent for 10¢/hour—a real bargain.

Scuba Diving

Classes in scuba diving are offered by Portland Community College (244-6111).

Skateboarding

The hills of Portland provide irresistable skateboarding terrain. With the new flexible boards and urethane wheels, the sport is more popular here than ever. Hospital emergency rooms, where the injuries are being treated, will testify to this. THE place for skateboards and skateboard problems is The Surfer, 2840 SE Powell (235-7983). Don't be fooled by the greying proprietress. She knows all there is to know about skateboards and surfboards; can apply a mean socket wrench and runs Mrs. A's Typing Service on the side. All this goes on in a tiny area behind the counter where Mrs. A's typewriter shares space with everything from ball bearings to "Cadillac" wheels.

Skiing

Snow depths measured in the hundreds of inches on nearby Mt. Hood make Portland a skiing center in the Pacific Northwest.

At Government Camp, 58 miles from Portland, are two ski areas, Multorpor-Ski Bowl and Summit Ski Area (for beginners), both at about the 4,000-foot elevation. At the 6,000-foot level are Timberline, at the end of a spur road six miles from Government Camp, and Mt. Hood Meadows, a few miles north of Government Camp on Oregon 35.

While the Multorpor-Ski Bowl Area offers some of the most challenging skiing on Mt. Hood, its elevation is not quite high enough to assure the very early and late season skiing enjoyed at Timberline and Mt. Hood Meadows.

At Timberline, snow is so plentiful that during the past 20 years, the ski season has opened three times before Halloween and practically every year by Thanksgiving. In 1973-74, Timberline recorded 310 inches of snow by March and had 200 inches left by June. The U.S. Ski Team holds its summer training camp every June at Mt. Hood Meadows.

Some skiers refer to Mt. Hood's heavy, moisture-laden snows as "Mt. Hood cement," but they still flock to the mountain. Those seeking lighter, drier snow and sunnier weather will drive the extra 125 miles to Mt. Bachelor, considered to be Oregon's best ski area, in the central part of the state near Bend. With its varied open terrain for the packed slope skiers and its forested slopes holding virgin powder for the deep snow skiers, Bachelor is a favorite weekend and vacation area for Portlanders as well as Californians and Washingtonians.

The larger Oregon ski areas with their day lodges and ski shops are open weekdays as well as weekends during the ski season, are well patrolled for accidents, provide ski instruction, and illuminate slopes for night skiing.

Following is a list of ski areas according to location. Lift prices are for the 1975-76 season.

Multorpor-Ski Bowl—Mt. Hood's oldest ski area and the closest to Portland at Government Camp. Here are some of the steepest ski slopes of any area on Mt. Hood. Slopes suitable for intermediates and beginners as well. Night skiing. Open Tues.-Sun. and all holidays. Equipped with 4 chairs, 7 rope tows, one ski jump. Two day lodges, ski shop, rentals, instruction. Overnight accommodations in Government Camp or nearby Rhododendron. Lift rates: All day, $8 weekends, $7 midweek; aft./night, $7; night, $5; under 12, $5 (night, $4). Rope tow: Adults, $4; under 12, $2.50.

Summit Ski Area—Located at Government Camp, this area is for beginning skiers. Day lodge and ski shop.

Rates for its T-bar, 4 rope tows, and one rope are $3.50, $3.50, and $1, respectively.

Timberline—Home of the first chairlift in the U.S., Timberline boasts a lodge that is a northwest showplace. Facilities in addition to the big lodge are a ski shop, ski school, and lights for night skiing. Runs are generally intermediate. On a clear day, the famed Magic Mile run is spectacular; in a white-out, you can't tell up from down. Late-season skiing at Timberline is one of its best features. Two snow cats haul skiers above the regular ski runs to the higher elevations for good spring skiing. Facilities also include 3 chair lifts and 2 rope tows. Accommodations in the dormitory start at $18 and in the lodge at $30 for a double room. Lift rates: All day, $8 weekends, $7 midweek; day/night, $9 weekends, $8 midweek; aft./night, $7; half day, $5.50; children under 12 and adults over 60, half-price. Rope tow: $3; under 12, $1.25.

Mt. Hood Meadows—Newest ski area on Mt. Hood, located on the southeast slopes of the mountain with terrain for all levels of skiing. Open seven days and five nights weekly (Wed.-Sun.); season normally continues through June. Spacious day lodge. Five chair lifts, three rope tows. Rentals, ski shop, ski repair, ski school, including cross country instruction. Lift rates: All day, $8.50 weekends, $7.50 midweek; half day, $6 weekends, $5 midweek; aft./night, $7.50 weekends, $6 midweek; night, $4.50. Children under 12, $5.50. Rope tow, $3.50.

Cooper Spur—Take either I-80N east or U.S. 26 to get to this small but pleasant intermediate ski area, which is about halfway between Hood River and Government Camp on Oregon 35. At the 4,000-foot elevation, this area has one T-bar, a rope tow, a day lodge, ski shop, school, and night skiing. Lift rates: $3.50 for the T-bar; $1.50, rope tow.

Mt. Bachelor—About 180 miles from Portland, 20 miles west of Bend on the Century Drive. At a base elevation of 6,500 feet, Mt. Bachelor offers Oregon's most varied skiing terrain. Six chair lifts, one rope tow, 3 day lodges, 2 ski shops, rentals, and a ski school. No lights. Overnight accommodations at nearby Bend, at resorts on the Century Drive, or at Sunriver Resort, south of Bend. High-season lift rates (mid-Dec.-April): All day, $8 weekends, $7 midweek; half day, $5 weekends, $4 midweek; under 12, all day, $6 weekends, $5 midweek; half day,

$4 weekends, $3 midweek. Low-season rates (Nov.-mid-Dec. and April-June): All day, $6; half day, $4; under 12, all day, $4.50; half day, $2.50.

Hoodoo Ski Bowl—About 75 miles east of Salem off U.S. 20 at 4,800 feet. Three chairlifts, 3 rope tows, lodge, ski shop, and lights. Lift rates: Chair, $7; rope tow, $3.

Snow Reports

For local and regional ski conditions dial:
Mt. Hood Meadows (292-9933)
Mountain Shop (281-8886)
Northwest Ski Report (222-9128), areas outside Oregon
Oregon Ski Report (222-9951)

For the state police road and weather report, call 238-8400.

Ski Organizations

Oregon Nordic Club, P.O. Box 426, Portland, 97207.
Cascade Ski Club, P.O. Box 721, Portland, 97207, which sponsors a full junior racing program and has a lodge on Mt. Hood.
Mt. Hood Meadows Ski Club (1-337-2222), organized for racing.
Bergfreunde Ski Club (that's German for friend of the mountain), P.O. Box 321, Portland, 97213. Members must be over 21.

Two other clubs, Schnee Voegli and Skiyenti Women's Ski Club, are invitational groups; both sponsor some races. Schnee Voegli sponsors an annual buy-and-sell sale at the Mountain Shop, 628 NE Broadway, the first 3 week in October. It's the place to go to recycle your children's ski gear and replace it with larger sizes.

Ski Touring

Ski touring (Nordic skiing) is attracting more and more downhill skiers away from long lift lines and turning former nonskiers into new ski enthusiasts. Mt. Hood's late spring snow pack makes the sport particularly attractive.

One of the largest ski touring programs is offered at Mt. Hood Meadows Ski Area. The Meadows operates a rental shop well-equipped with ski touring equipment. At midweek it conducts women's classes in the Nordic sport. Beginners learn about equipment, dress, and basic touring. Those who are ready to try out their skis are taken on ski tours of Badger Lake, Umbrella Falls, Elk Meadows, Barlow Pass, and other scenic spots. Cross country rentals and equipment are also available in Government Camp and Portland.

Ski Tours

Summit Meadows—For an easy ski tour on open terrain, try the Summit Meadows tour southeast of Government Camp in the Mt. Hood National Forest. Park adjacent to the State Highway Dept. station at Timberline Junction and walk to Still Creek Road. Ski on snowbound road to meadows and return.

White River Canyon—Popular cross-country terrain for all types of skiers is the White River Canyon, accessible from Oregon 35, 4½ miles east of the junction of U.S. 26 and Oregon 35. Park at the turnouts near the bridge or in a nearby parking lot. On clear days this tour, over two miles of open flat land, provides striking views of Mt. Hood.

Skiing Postscript

• Some skiers consider the ultimate in spring recreation to be skiing the corn snow on Mt. Hood in the morning and winding up at Bowman's Resort for a round of golf in the afternoon. Bowman's, offering excellent food and accommodations, is 14 miles west of Government Camp at Welches.

• For detailed information about ski touring, get a copy of *Oregon Ski Tours* by Doug Newman and Sally Sharrard (Touchstone).

Sky Diving

Sky divers do their thing at Hutchinson Airport in Molalla and at Donald, where the Pacific Parachute Center has a private strip.

Sled Dog Racing

While not in the league with soccer or basketball, sled dog racing is a growing organized sport in Oregon, with meets usually occurring in central and southern Oregon and in adjoining western states. Where there is no snow for workouts, the dogs pull sleds on wheels. For additional information, contact the Cascade Sled Dog Club or call the Jefferson Yukon Kennel, Rt. 1, Box 82, Jefferson, 97352 (1-362-3368).

Snowmobiling

If you've moved to town with your snowmobile and want to try it out, check with the U.S. Forest Service in the area where you're headed to learn on which roads snowmobiling is permitted. Two good areas to start with are Frog Lake, southeast of Government Camp off U.S. 26, and the Larch Mountain Road, accessible from the Columbia River Gorge Scenic Highway. If you're interested in purchasing a snowmobile, one dealer who will give you a free demonstration on Larch Mountain is Moen Machinery Co., 268 NE Hogan Rd., Gresham (665-9159). Some snowmobilers belong to the Mt. Hood Snowmobile Club, 13880 SE Rustway, Boring, 97009.

Soccer

As in other areas, soccer is the "in" sport in Portland, especially since the Portland *Timbers* adopted the city. At many parks, you can see kids bouncing the ball off each others' heads and knees either in informal play or scheduled matches. A grade school soccer program is sponsored in the fall by the Parks Bureau for children from grades 3 through 8. Occasional clinics are held as well. Columbia Boys' Club (289-7253) in North Portland also sponsors a soccer program. The Oregon Soccer Assn. sponsors an adult program in the fall and spring. For additional information, call Park Bureau (248-4325).

Swimming

Pools

Three indoor pools and 10 outdoor pools are operated by the Park Bureau, all free of charge. Pool hours vary. Outdoor schedules, with the exception of a port-a-pool, are Mon.-Fri., 10 a.m.-8 p.m., and Sat. and Sun., noon-8 p.m., but check with each pool or the Park Bureau for public swim times. Other activities are often scheduled in the pools.

Indoor pools, open year-round, are:
Buckman, 320 SE 16th (235-0704)
Couch, 2033 NW Glisan (227-6075)
Columbia, 7600 N. Chautauqua (283-9302)

Outdoor pools, open summer months only, are:
Creston, SE 44th & Powell (774-9113)
Dishman, 77 NE Knott (282-1460)
Grant, 2300 NE 33rd (249-9992)
Montavilla, 8219 NE Glisan (254-4101)
Mt. Scott, 5530 SE 72nd (774-9215)
Peninsula, 6400 N. Albina (285-4222)
Pier, foot of N. Seneca, St. Johns (286-9943)
Sellwood, SE 7th & Miller (238-9216)
Wilson, 1151 SW Vernon (no phone)

A port-a-pool at Woodlawn Park, NE 11th and Dekum, is open Mon.-Fri. from 10 a.m.-6 p.m.

Swim Instruction

Many excellent swim instruction programs are available for adults and children in the Portland area.

The Park Bureau sponsors a "Learn to Swim" campaign at local public pools in June and a city-wide swim-athon in August.

Swimming instruction of various kinds is offered at two YMCA centers—the John R. Leach, 6036 SE Foster (775-4396) and the Northeast, 1630 NE 38th (281-1169); and at the YWCA, 1111 SW 10th (223-6281).

Portland State University (229-4401), Reed College (771-1112), Lewis and Clark College (244-6161), and Marylhurst Education Center (636-8141) offer swim lessons for children. Call for more information.

Recreational Swimming

Portland Community College (244-6111) opens its pool at the Sylvania Campus, 12000 SW 49th, for public swimming Tues. & Thurs. from 6-8 p.m.; Wed., 8-9:30 p.m.; Fri. 6-9:30 p.m.; Sat., 1-9:30 p.m.; Sun., 1-4:45 p.m. Fee is 75¢, over 16, and 50¢ under 16. If under 16, swimmer must be accompanied by an adult. Bring towel.

Lewis and Clark College's outdoor pool is open for recreational swimming in the summer. Fee is 50¢.

Retired persons 60 and over may swim free at the YWCA Wed. & Fri.

Several close-in parks mentioned elsewhere in this book offer good lake and river swimming.

Tennis

Portland is fortunate to have a municipally owned and operated indoor tennis center which tennis players agree is first rate.

In addition to the 4 indoor courts, the Park Bureau maintains 87 outdoor tennis courts throughout the city, 52 are lighted for night play. Lighted courts may be used until the midnight curfew hour.

Unlike the indoor center, which operates under a reservations system, most of the outdoor courts are available on a first-come, first-serve basis, although some at Washington Park and Mt. Tabor Park may be reserved by calling 248-4325.

At the *Portland Tennis Center*, 324 NE 12th (233-5959) at Buckman Park, hours of operation are 9 a.m.-10 p.m. from July 1 to Sept. 30 and 7 a.m.-11 p.m., Oct. 1 to June 30. Court times are one hour in length beginning on the hour. Reservations must be made and there is a fee. Fees from Oct. 1-June 30 (1975-76 fee schedule, effective until Oct. 1, 1976) are: Adult singles, $3.25 each, from 7 a.m.-5 p.m. weekdays (nonprime time), and $4, weekday evenings after 5 and all day Sat. & Sun. (prime time); adult doubles, $2 each, nonprime time, and $2.50 each, prime time; junior singles (20 and under), $2.25, and doubles, $1.50 each (nonprime time only). During prime time, juniors are charged adult fees.

Court fees from July 1 to Sept. 30 are: Adult singles, $2, and doubles, $1 each; junior singles, $1, doubles, 50¢.

Reservations may be made one day in advance by calling 233-5959 or 233-5950. Anyone wishing to reserve a court more than a day ahead (and up to seven days) is charged $1 extra. You may purchase one court time per week for the same day of the week and the same time on a quarterly basis. Costs during the rainy seasons are $104 for nonprime time and $130 for prime time. From July 1 to Sept. 30, cost is $52.

The center rents ball machines and offers private and group lessons. The facility also includes a players' lounge with full view of the tennis courts; a pro shop; dressing rooms and showers for men and women, with lockers and towels available; and a balcony with seating capacity for 300.

Across the Columbia River in Vancouver, Wash., is the *Vancouver Tennis Center*, a municipal facility like Portland's.

Following is a list of the outdoor public courts in Portland, with the total number indicated first; lights (L), if any, second; and practice backboard (PB), if any, last:

West

Burlingame Park, SW 12th & Falcon—1
Gabriel Park, SW 45th & Vermont—4 (L), PB
Hamilton Park, SW 45th & Hamilton—2
Jackson High School, 10625 SW 35th—2
Lair Hill Park, SW 2nd & Woods—1 (L), PB
Portland Heights, SW Patton & Old Orchard—2 (L), PB
Washington Park, SW Kingston Ave.—6 (L)
Wilson High School, 1151 SW Vermont—2

Southeast

Berkeley Park, SE 39th & Cooper—2 (L)
Clinton Park, SE 55th & Division—4 (2-L)
Creston Park, SE 44th & Powell—2, PB
Essex Park, SE 79th & Center—2
Glenwood Park, SE 87th & Claybourne—2 (L)
Kenilworth Park, SE 34th & Holgate—2
Laurelhurst Park, SE 37th & Stark—2
Lents Park, SE 92th Steele—2 (L), PB
Marshall High School, 3905 SE 91st—2
Mt. Scott Park, SE 72nd & Harold—2
Mt. Tabor Park, SE Salmon, between 60th & 69th—2, E. side; 3 (L), W. side
Sellwood Park, SE 7th & Miller—4
Westmoreland Park, SE 22nd & Bybee—2 (L)
Woodstock Park, SE 47th & Steele—2, PB

Northeast

Alberta Park, NE 19th & Killingsworth—2
Buckman Field, NE 12th & Everett—8 (6-L), PB
Fernhill Park, NE 38th & Simpson—2
Glenhaven Park, NE 79th & Siskiyou—4
Irving Park, NE 7th & Fremont—4 (L), PB
Montavilla Park, NE 82nd & Glisan—2, PB
Rose City Park, NE 62nd & Tillamook—2 (L)
U.S. Grant Park, NE 33rd & Thompson—6 (L)

North

Columbia Park, N. Lombard & Woolsey—2 (L), PB
Jefferson High School, 5210 N. Kerby—3
North Gate Park, N. Geneva & Fessenden—2 (L)
Peninsula Park, N. Portland Blvd. & Albina—2 (L), PB
Pier Park, N. Seneca & St. Johns—2

Fish ladders at Bonneville Dam permit salmon and other migratory fish to reach spawning grounds upstream.

PARKS

Portland Play Areas, Community Centers

FROM 3,700-ACRE FOREST PARK to tiny mini-parks in the central city, Portland's system of 127 public parks (not including some parkways and circles) has much to offer citizens and visitors.

For example, you can reserve a park for your wedding, play tennis, picnic in the rain under shelter, swim free, hike, bike, watch your child in a Little League game, swing, slide, or read a best seller under a Douglas fir tree. You can sniff roses, ogle huge rhododendrons, or feed ducks.

For complete information or to arrange for permits for park use by groups of 50 or more, call the Park Bureau (248-4315). Tennis and swimming facilities are listed separately under sports.

Community Recreation Programs

Summer, fall, winter or spring, public use of Portland's 11 community centers and 13 swimming pools (10 outdoor) is free, so get your tax dollar's worth by visiting the center nearest you.

Each center offers its own program with recreation specialists. Some have gyms, others craft facilities such as looms and kilns. One even has a roller rink. All offer a full schedule of classes, some of which carry fees.

A guide to the city's recreation programs is published quarterly by the Park Bureau. Phone 248-4315 to get on the mailing list.

In addition to the community centers and pools (listed under Sports), the Park Bureau operates an indoor tennis center, a motor raceway, seven after-school centers at public schools, and several cultural centers.

Regular programs of the Park Bureau are expanded in summer to more than 50 locations around the city, including many city parks and playgrounds not used in the spring, fall, and winter months.

Sports Fitness Camps provide a full morning or afternoon of rapid-fire athletics for boys and girls ages 9-13 at both east- and west-side locations. Three 3-week sessions are scheduled each summer. A fee is charged.

The 11 community centers are:

Fulton, 68 SW Miles (244-8449); Hillside, 653 NW Culpepper (223-8992); Matt Dishman, 77 NE Knott (282-1460); Montavilla, 8219 NE Glisan (254-4101); Mt. Scott Center and Roller Rink, 5530 SE 72nd (774-8156 and 774-2215, rink); Overlook House, 3839 N. Melrose (282-2053); Peninsula, 6400 N. Albina (285-4222); Sellwood, 1436 SE Spokane (236-4022); St. Johns, 8427 N. Central (286-1551); University, 9009 N. Foss (289-2414); Woodstock, 5905 SE 43rd (771-0784).

After-school centers are located at:

Beaumont, 4043 NE Fremont; Bridlemile, 4300 SW 47th Dr.; Clark, 1231 SE 92nd; Kelly, 9030 SE Cooper; Markham, 10531 SW Capitol Hwy.; Scott, 6700 NE Prescott; Sunnyside, 3421 SE Salmon.

Elaborate schedules are planned for both children and adults at these city-wide cultural recreation facilities:

Ballet Workshop, 6433 NE Tillamook (248-4315); Children's Museum, 3037 SW 2nd (227-1505); Civic Contemporary Dance Theater, 1436 SW Montgomery (248-4738); Community Music Center, 3350 SE Francis (235-8222); Firehouse Theater, 1436 SW Montgomery (248-4737); Little Loom House, 8427 N. Central (286-1551); Portland Parks Art Center, 2909 SW 2nd (228-4911); Multnomah Community Design Center, 7780 SW Capitol Hwy. (246-2706); Theater Workshops at Laurelhurst Park, 3854 SE Oak, and Irvington School, 7320 NE Brazee (235-4551 for both).

In addition, a specialized recreation program for mentally and physically handicapped individuals of all ages is offered at 6525 SW Capitol Hill Rd. (248-4328).

Structured classes carry a minimum $2 registration fee, but in summer more free activities are offered than at other times of year.

ART

Galleries and Art in Public Places

OWNING SCULPTURE or a painting by a well-known local artist carries plenty of status in Portland where regional "names" enjoy the patronage of art collectors. Mention your Tom Hardy, Amanda Snyder, Carl Morris, and, above all, your C.S. Price,¶ and you're launched— without the help of any New York galleries.

Fortunately for the buyers and artists, Portland has experienced a proliferation of small, intimate art galleries during the past 15 years. Some are commercial, some non-profit. Several, including the largest, are located in the Old Town section of the city, a convenience for tourists who want to "do" a group of galleries all in one day. Virtually all the galleries show regional or local work, some of it inspired by Oregon's coast and mountain scenery; much of it abstract; less of it objective.

The Portland Art Museum's long-established Rental Sales Gallery¶ has helped to stimulate interest in local art by making it possible to rent a painting and apply the rental fee toward purchase if you decide to buy.

Three excellent college and university galleries are included in the list below, which contains, we believe, the most tenacious outlets on the gallery scene. Schedules change so it's best to call before you go.

Galleries

Arts and Crafts Society of Portland—616 NW 18th (228-4741). In the Julia E. Hoffman gallery, rotating exhibits show work by contemporary artists and craftsmen as well as arts and crafts of folk and primitive cultures. Gallery talks arranged on request. In the gift gallery, books, prints, sculpture, ceramics for sale. Nonprofit society has been operating since 1906. Hours: Mon.-Thurs., 8 a.m.-10 p.m.; Fri., 8 a.m.-4 p.m.; Sat., 8 a.m.-4 p.m. (Summer schedule varies.)

Attic Gallery—2478 SW Sherwood Dr. (228-7830). Paintings, sculpture, drawings, ceramics take their turn in rotating shows at this small gallery in a residence on Portland Heights. Hours: Sun., Tues., Wed., Thurs., 2-5 p.m.

Camerawork—Lobby, Good Samaritan Medical Center Nursing Education Building, 2255 NW Northrup (no gallery phone). Rotating exhibits, primarily by local and regional photographers. Physician-photographer reviews portfolios of would-be exhibitors.

Contemporary Crafts Gallery—3934 SW Corbett (223-2654). Ceramics, sculpture, wood, jewelry, weaving, and other handcrafts. Rotating exhibits. Long-established. Noncommercial. Hours: Mon.-Fri., 11 a.m.-5 p.m.; Sat., 11 a.m.-4 p.m.; Sun., 1-4 p.m.

Fountain Gallery—115 SW 4th (228-8476). Leading artists of the Pacific Northwest, such as Carl Morris, Louis Bunce, Mike Russo, and Horiuchi, are represented by Portland's largest private gallery featuring contemporary sculpture, paintings, prints, and drawings. Exhibitions include one-man shows and continuing exhibits by the gallery's group of artists. Hours: Mon.-Sat., 11 a.m.-5 p.m.

Gallery West—4836 SW Scholls Ferry Rd. (292-6262). Sculpture, watercolors, original prints, oil paintings, weavings, batiks, ceramics, representing 60 professional Northwest artists. Wide range of styles. Hours: Tues.-Sat., 11 a.m.-4 p.m.; Sun., 1-4 p.m. Call for directions because gallery is difficult to find for first-time visitors.

Anne Hughes Gallery—224 SW 1st (223-9441). Contemporary west coast paintings, sculpture, prints, and drawings. Hours: Tues.-Sat., noon-5:30 p.m.

Oregon Society of Artists—2185 SW Park Pl. (228-0706). Regular exhibitions of generally traditional work are presented by society, made up of retired professionals, art hobbyists, and others. Hours: Weekdays, Sat., Sun., 1-4 p.m.

Portland Art Museum Rental Sales Gallery —SW Park & Madison (226-2811). Hours: Tues. & Thurs., noon-5 p.m.; Sun., 2-4 p.m.

Portland Center for Visual Arts—117 NW 5th (222-7107). Nothing like it on the west coast, it's said. PCVA shows contemporary art in all media; also a center for theater, dance, music. Noncommercial. Hours: Tues.-Sun., noon-6 p.m.; Fri., noon-9 p.m.

Portland Community College's North View Gallery—in the Communications-Technology Building. Sylvania Campus, 12000 SW 49th (244-6111). Hours: Mon.-Fri., 8 a.m.-5 p.m. Closed weekends.

Portland State University's White Gallery—Smith Memorial Center (229-4463). Hours: Mon.-Fri., 8 a.m.-10 p.m.; Sat., 9 a.m.-5 p.m.

Reed College Faculty Office Bldg. Gallery—3203 SE Woodstock (771-1112). Hours: Mon.-Fri., 9 a.m.-5 p.m.; Sat.-Sun., 10 a.m.-5 p.m.

The Camera's Eye—1307 SW Broadway (227-7828). Photography, sometimes trendy, experimental. Hours: Tues.-Sat., noon-5 p.m.

The Fibres Gallery—205 NW 2nd (222-4837). Hand-loomed hangings, other works. Mon.-Sat., 10 a.m.-6 p.m.

Art in Public Places

As much as they might have liked it, the Skidmore Fountain "sisters" have never poured beer in the 88 years they have been holding their font above the horse trough in the historic Old Town area.

They almost did, however, in 1888, and the story is indicative of the spirit with which Portland claims her art treasures. Portlanders got pretty excited that year over their new fountain—a rival to New York's best—and to celebrate its completion, Henry Weinhard, a local brewer, offered to pump beer through it—if a hose could be stretched from his brewery 11 blocks away.

Because the fountain was a watering trough, the city fathers, fearing what would happen if the city's horse-drawn transit system became tipsy, declined the offer. The lovely maidens are still spraying pure water in the heart of Old Town and symbolize Portland's long romance with art and artists.

Once art is in place in Portland it's likely to remain there.

The Elk Fountain, honoring a former mayor, still occupies the middle of downtown Main Street despite attempts to remove it as a traffic hazard.

And while the Portland International Airport undergoes a major overhaul, its Louis Bunce mural, "Communication," and the wall it's glued to remain untouched.

The Skidmore maidens have stayed home and done their bit to inspire renovation of the neighborhood surrounding them.

Four C.S. Price canvases commissioned in 1936 by the PTA for the Beach School auditorium were almost relocated by the school district administration some 30 years later but saved for Beach when the irate PTA secured a lawyer and produced proof of ownership.

A tour of the city's public art collection turns up several treasures which were completed for the Lewis and Clark Exposition in 1905. "They seemed to be quite busy at that time trying to make it look like something was here," one observer of the art scene commented. In the last 15 years, new buildings have brought much new art to Portland, i.e., the Halprin fountains and considerable sculpture.

At the Evan H. Roberts Memorial Sculpture Mall, adjoining the Portland Art Museum, a range of styles may be viewed, from Renoir to Hepworth.

Controversial or ridiculed works are in Portland, too.

Georgia Pacific Co.'s marble nudes on SW 5th downtown have been dubbed "Three Groins in the Fountain" or "Men's Night at the 'YW,'" but admirers point to the 190-ton piece of white marble from which they're carved with pride. The five figures are supposed to symbolize growth and awakening.

Decide for yourself about two controversial paintings hanging in the Civic Auditorium's first balcony foyer. They were commissioned for the building when it was completely remodeled in 1968, but some of the town fathers were so outraged when they saw the works that city hall relegated them to a back room. Time passed and the art community seethed. Finally, persistence from artists and a fearless female commissioner combined to get the work out of hiding and up. Jack McLarty's "Sunburst of Non-Discrimination," a sectional allegorical painting which "performs" both in opened and closed positions, is considered the most controversial, although now few remember there was a controversy.

Downtown

Bank of California—407 SW Broadway—Mushroom-shaped bronze fountain, 10 feet in diameter, in enclosed courtyard visible from main lobby, Robert Woodward; untitled bronze fountain, reminiscent of rocks and leaves, Aristides Demetrios.

Central Library—SW 10th and Taylor—Two paintings by C.S. Price, "Indians" and "Pioneers;" also a study sculpture of horses by Tom Hardy; all on third floor.

Chapman and Lownsdale Squares—between SW 3rd & 4th, Salmon & Madison—Bronze Elk Fountain dividing the two squares, and, incidentally, the street between them, Roland H. Perry, animal sculptor, and H.G. Wright, architect, 1900; in Lownsdale Square, the northern of the two parks, the Second Oregon Volunteers Memorial (Spanish American War), featuring a bayonet-charging soldier, Douglas Tilden, 1904.

Civic Auditorium—SW 3rd between Clay & Market—Forecourt Fountain (across the street facing the building), Lawrence Halprin, 1970. Inside, orchestra level: "Sculpture No. 1," Bruce West; "Memory From the Shore," painting, James McClintock; first balcony level: "Sunburst of Non-Discrimination," painting, Jack McLarty; "The Magician's Screens," painting, George Johanson; "Mistral #3," sculpture, Frederick Littman; "In Reflection," painting, Sally Haley; bronze bust of William VanHoogstraten, first conductor of local symphony, Marie Louise Feldenheimer; second balcony level: "Monument," 83-inch high welded steel modern sculpture, Manuel Izquierdo; "Love Rug," painting, Frank Elliott.

Equitable Center—1300 SW 6th—Paintings, main floor, Shirley Gittelsohn and LaVerne Krause.

Far West Federal Savings—444 SW 5th—Pleasant fountain amidst downtown din, Bridge Beardsley, 1971.

Federal Park—between SW 3rd & 4th, Madison & Jefferson—One of a number of identical ornamental drinking fountains located throughout downtown. Designed by A.E. Doyle, original 20 were given to city by logger-philanthropist Simon Benson. Additional ones are being cast for new locations.

First National Tower—between SW 4th & 5th, Jefferson & Columbia—"Birds and Water," welded bronze sculpture, Tom Hardy.

Georgia-Pacific building—SW 5th & Taylor—"The Quest," sculptured marble fountain featuring five nude figures, Count Alexander von Svoboda, 1970; "Perpetuity," redwood surrounding bronze seedling sculpture, symbolizing growth, von Svoboda, 1970; in underground tunnel to parking garage, sculpture, 16 modules of welded steel covered with chrome, Bruce West.

Hilton Hotel—SW 6th between Salmon & Taylor—Bronze lily pond, Tom Hardy.

Lownsdale Square—See Chapman Square.

Mohawk Galleries—SW 3rd between Morrison & Yamhill—Interior courtyards display fountains and statuary in this gallery which is really an office building.

O'Bryant Square—between SW 9th & Park, Washington and Stark—Contemporary fountain, honoring first mayor of Portland, Donald W. Edmundson and Evan Kennedy, 1973.

Portland Art Museum—north of Jefferson between SW 10th & Park—Evan H. Roberts Memorial Sculpture Mall, 1970: "Dual Form," Barbara Hepworth, 1965; "Seated Woman," Henry Moore; "Split Ring," Clement Meadmore; "Standing Woman," Wilhelm Lehmbruck, 1910; "Venus Victorious," Auguste Renoir, 1914; rhododendron plaque, Marie Louise Feldenheimer. (Not necessarily a permanent exhibit.)

Portland Center—south of SW Market between 1st & 4th—Lovejoy Fountain, Lawrence Halprin; in American Plaza area, large "Druidic" sculpture of rusted monuments faced with segmented orange panels, Lee Kelly; Pettygrove Park, between SW 1st & 4th, Market & Harrison, large bronze piece, Manuel Izquierdo, to be in place by 1977; west wall of 200 Market building, on 3rd Avenue Mall between Market and Pettygrove Park, yellow folded aluminum plate sections, Douglas Senft, to be in place by fall, 1976.

Portland State University—On face of Neuberger Hall, between Hall and Harrison—Bronze panels at eye level depicting various kinds of sea life and flora of Oregon, Tom Hardy, 1962.

South Park Blocks—from SW Salmon & Park to PSU—Small plaza containing one of Benson drinking fountains; Shemanski Fountain, with its classical bronze figure of a girl, Oliver Barrett, 1927; statue of Abraham Lincoln, George Fite Waters, 1926; equestrian statue of Theodore Roosevelt, A. Phimister Proctor, 1924.

Standard Plaza—1100 SW 6th—"Ring of Time," sculpture based on the mathematical phenomenon of the Moebius Strip, Hilda Morris.

U.S. National Bank—321 SW 6th—Bronze doors depicting allegorical scenes of Oregon history, A.E. Doyle, 1917. (Can be viewed only when bank is closed.)

Old Town

Area at river end of SW Washington & Front—Not exactly art but still statuary, the foremast of the Battleship *USS Oregon*, commissioned in 1896, was obtained by the city in 1943 and subsequently planted here. The ship's smokestacks and anchor are across Burnside to the north in the parking lot of Import Plaza, a shopping bazaar.

Skidmore Fountain Plaza—SW 1st & Ankeny—Skidmore Fountain, with its two maidens and inscription "Good Citizens are the riches of a city," Olin Warner, 1888. Fountain honors Stephen Skidmore, who left a bequest for a fountain for the "horses, men, and dogs of the city." As usual, the women were left to carry the load, in this case, the font.

Southwest

Council Crest Park—Laberee Memorial Fountain, "Mother and Child," romantic bronze drinking fountain supports figures silhouetted against scenic natural backdrop, Frederic Littman, 1956.

Triangle Plaza—SW 19th & Burnside—David Campbell Memorial Fountain, a sculptural fountain and bronze plaque erected in memory of a Portland fire chief killed on duty, Avard Fairbanks, sculptor, E.F. Tucker, architect, 1928. Other Portland firemen killed on duty are named here, too.

Washington Park—"Sacajawea," bronze statue of woman Indian guide, Alice Cooper, 1905; "Coming of the White Man," bronze statuary of two natives, H.A. MacNeil, 1904; in Rose Gardens, large contemporary sculpture of burnished metal blocks, Lee Kelly.

Southeast

Duniway School—7700 SE Reed College Pl.—Metal sculpture, Lee Kelly.

Reed College—3203 SE Woodstock, at west end of campus—Abstract metal and concrete sculpture, a memorial to William Alderson, who was a professor of literature, Charles Kelly, 1974.

Northwest

ESCO Corp.—NW 25th & Vaughan—"Flogger" (foundry worker), 11-foot statue of stainless steel, Frederic Littman.

Temple Beth Israel—SW 19th & Flanders— Bronze doors for the Ark, depicting the Burning Bush, Frederic Littman.

Northeast

Intersection—NE 57th & Sandy—Bronze statue of George Washington, Pompeii Coppini, 1927.

Laurelhurst Area—axis at NE 39th & Glisan—Equestrian statue of Jeanne D'Arc, a replica of one in Paris.

Lloyd Center—"Birds in Flight," dramatic metal sculpture suspended above bridge at east end of ice skating rink, Tom Hardy, 1960; bronze fountain, west mall, George Tsutakawa, 1960.

Memorial Coliseum—Lighted memorial fountain, with pulsating cycles, honoring Multnomah County war dead, Skidmore, Owings & Merrill, 1960; in Coliseum's Georgia-Pacific Room, abstract mural, 20 feet long, with recognizable Portland symbols such as Benson drinking fountains, Skidmore and Elk Fountains, Louis Bunce.

Portland International Airport—Mural, "Communication," Louis Bunce, 1960.

North

Beach School—1710 N. Humboldt—Four canvases depicting "The Coming of the White Man West," C.S. Price, 1936. They show a family in a covered wagon, Indians, horses, and men at work in a sawmill.

Southeast

Mt. Tabor—Statue of Harvey W. Scott, celebrated editor of *The Oregonian*, Gutzon Borglum, 1933.

GETTING AWAY
FROM IT ALL

(Or Where Tri-Met Doesn't Go)

For VACATIONS and recreation some Oregonians prefer the coast. Others look to the mountains. Portland is strategically located about 1½ hours from either.

Oregon Coast

All roads to the Oregon Coast are mountainous. The most popular routes from Portland arrive at Astoria and Seaside to the north, and Lincoln City, the start of the southern beaches.

U.S. 30 follows the Columbia River to Astoria and is the most beautiful—but longer. No-nonsense U.S. 26 rolls right through Mountain Man Joe Meek's donation land claim near North Plains and then straight over the coast range to Seaside with a well-marked turnoff for Cannon Beach and points south. To reach Otis Junction and Lincoln City, take the valley route, 99W.

All Oregon beaches are public. The weather is temperamental at best, but natives will tell you when an east wind blows in Portland, the skies on the coast will be clear without fail. A temperature of 70 degrees is warm at the beach, but take a windbreaker regardless of the time of the year. For reasons obvious when you stick a toe in the water, the coastal chambers of commerce do not publicize ocean swimming. The water is cold by any standards. However, during the summer months, life guards on duty at Seaside and Cannon Beach protect the hardy.

The beach has always been a retreat for man, according to the Smithsonian Institution which sponsors architectural diggings at the edge of the Seaside Golf Course. Their findings have proven that the inland Indian spent

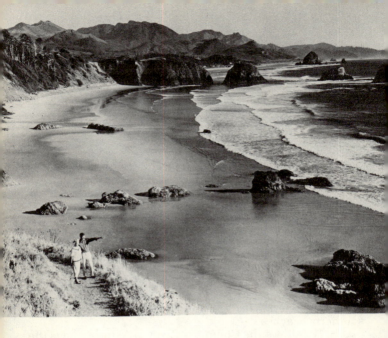

summers at the beach with his family, just as we do today.

What to Look for and Where

Astoria, to the north, is the west's first city, established in 1811 as a fur trading post by parties sent out by John Jacob Astor, German-born New York fur trader for whom the settlement is named.

From the top of the 125-foot Astoria Column on Coxcomb Hill, you'll see the mighty Columbia River join the Pacific Ocean. Unless you are 12 or under, your legs will remember the climb to the top of the tower for at least a week, but it's worth it. Astoria serves as a fishing village, and the docks and moored fishing trawlers make an interesting, if breezy walk.

The Flavel House, opened by the Clatsop County Historical Society and Museum, 441 8th St., is worth a stop. This Victorian beauty includes a "widow's walk" from which the late captain's wife watched for her husband's return. The rooms are jammed with coast memorabilia, including mint-condition remains of wrecked ships.

If shipwrecks interest you, drive quickly south to Ft. Stevens Park where the skeleton of the Peter Iredale is fast settling into the sand. At low tide you can touch some of the timbers, and part of the superstructure remains for photographs. Ft. Stevens, coastal defense installation, is due a face lifting and will be restored soon for war buffs.

South of Astoria, just off U.S. 101, is Ft. Clatsop National Monument. The National Park Service has built a replica of the fort where explorers Lewis and Clark wintered with their expedition in 1805. The children will enjoy the tight quarters and small bunk houses. Adults will wonder how the famous team ever stayed together after being confined in such a small area for an entire winter. If the day is fair, stroll down the well-marked path to the boat launching. There, children can climb into a replica of one of the Indian canoes used by the explorers.

From Astoria drive south toward *Gearhart*, where Portland's oldest families have maintained beach homes for almost a century, or to Seaside, a beach town with salt water taffy, a main street full of carnival attractions, and the renowned Harrison's Bakery. City-stranded Portlanders have been known to telephone "bus" orders

to this bakery for such delicacies as English muffin bread, prune cake, or buttery tarts filled with jam and given an unpronounceable name.

The whims of the tide turn up unusual flotsam on every Oregon beach. While the weather is always a little wild, even in August, driving storms deliver the best treasures, so take comfort in walking the sand during the foulest weather. You may have sand in your teeth, but this is when you find a glass float at your feet. Beachcomber Amos Wood has written two guidebooks for the dedicated—*Beachcombing for Japanese Glass Floats,* (Binfords & Mort, 1967) and *Beachcombing the Pacific* (Regnery, 1975).

Gearhart Beach is known for delivering a wealth of sand dollars and is excellent for razor clam digging. Shovels may be rented at stores and service stations from Gearhart to Seaside. For late risers occasional good clam tides arrive after 10 a.m. in the spring.

If you find your talents do not lie at the end of the shovel, the Bell Buoy on the highway south of Seaside will supply you with fresh clams in season; frozen the rest of the year. They also offer excellent kippered salmon (smoked as the Indians did it). Look for chowder clams frozen in pints—a good way to beat supermarket prices.

Cannon Beach also will supply you with razor clams, either at the low tide or at Malo's on Main Street. This will be your last stop for fresh clams. Farther south the emphasis is on Yaquina oysters. Most coastal communities, north and south, sell fresh Dungeness crab in season.

The beach at Cannon provides material for June sandcastle contests as well as periwinkle shells, rather like a mandarin's hat, and perfectly round black stones which are becoming quite collectable. Tide pools at Haystack Rock let the public look into the private life of small marine animals. To learn more about sea life, as well as the fine arts from writing to theater and painting, students of all ages join Portland State University's Haystack classes during the summer months. Call the school (229-4800) for additional information.

Indian Beach, just off the edge of Ecola Park, is fast gaining a reputation for surfboarding. The park is furnished with picnic facilities, including fire pits, and provides that much-photographed view of the coastline.

Look for agates farther south. **Road's End** is the best place, since the tides have quit throwing them up on the sands of **Agate Beach**. Agates and other decorative stones tend to arrive in clusters. If you have the sand to yourself, keep walking and squinting. When you see three or more people crouching unnaturally on the horizon, you can be pretty sure that they have found the agate trove for the day. Just grin and work your way into the group.

Driftwood is free for the taking on the beaches and provides excellent fires, if dried, either on the beach or back at your cottage. For some reason the pungent odor, so comforting at sea level, becomes obnoxious in the city, so don't bother to stock up except for ornamental use.

Lincoln City lies immediately to the south of Road's End and represents a consolidation of several old beach towns. The marriage has resulted in a frustrated off-spring evident in several miles of shops and enterprises which generally block the ocean front effectively. Barnacle Bill's at Lincoln City is legitimate and has a long reputation for fresh seafood on the shell. Take a crab or Pacific shrimp cocktail to go and wait while B.B. takes the backs off your Dungeness Crab. He also sells crab legs and meat by the five-pound can, pressure-packed just as it is shelled. Ask him about oysters also.

About two miles south of Lincoln City is Salishan Lodge, the widely known "destination" resort with golf, swimming, and even indoor tennis but without easily accessible beach frontage.

Depoe Bay and Newport both offer good beach town browsing with little or no beach walking. Depoe Bay, home of the Memorial Day fleet of flowers, is a little Atlantic City, only the pier is turned sideways. The Channel Book Store, one block south of the bridge (765-2352), lends an air of intelligensia to the town. Old and sometimes rare books are to be found in these cramped quarters. Paperback lovers will have a field day in the back room and save half the price on nearly new editions.

Newport's old town on the waterfront is thriving. Begin with chowder or oyster stew at Mo's and rub elbows on the oilcloth covered tables with the locals. The atmosphere is negligible and that's intentional, but the view through steamed windows of fishing boats coming and going sets the pace for the day.

The children will love the strictly-for-fun Undersea

Gardens, nearly next door, where the brave diver drags out the reluctant octopus several times a day.

Across Yaquina Bay is the Oregon State University Marine Science Laboratory where the study of sea life is more serious. The Marine Science museum is open to the public, free of charge, and includes a comprehensive and scholarly assortment of books and charts on every phase of Pacific marine life.

Mt. Hood

Most visitors to Oregon want to see its highest mountain, 11,285-foot Mt. Hood: dormant volcano; one of the nation's most climbed major peaks; rugged setting for the high-altitude baronial resort, Timberline Lodge; and site of the first skiers' chairlift in the U.S.

Some Portland visitors come and go without ever seeing Mt. Hood through the clouds, but for most a clear day comes along sooner or later and then "the" mountain dominates the Portland scene.

If you can see it from Portland and want a closer view, hurry to U.S. 30-I-80N and head east to the Wood Village-Mt. Hood exit. Get on U.S. 26 going east.

If you're touring in winter, carry tire chains and check on road conditions (238-8400). Winter or summer, carry coats.

Off the highway at Sandy, about 30 miles east of Portland, is the Oral Hull park for the blind, where carefully built trails, signs in Braille, tinkling water, and strong-scented plants combine to give the sightless an experience of Oregon's out-of-doors. Another place with special appeal to the handicapped is Wildwood Recreation Area, 39 miles southeast of Portland, where paths are paved and rest rooms have been especially designed so that they can be used by persons in wheelchairs.

Ask at Chamber of Commerce, 824 SW 5th (228-9411), for "Loop" map. Follow U.S. 26 through Douglas fir forests and past swift streams to Government Camp, so named because it was the camp of a detachment of soldiers in 1849. They were forced to abandon their government wagons, leaving them as a landmark and a name for the place.

To see the village, now a resort for skiers and climbers, take the loop through town; otherwise continue on the

main road less than a mile to the junction with the Timberline Lodge Road, a 6-mile side trip up the south slope of the mountain to the 6,000-foot level.

Timberline, so-called because it is at the elevation where trees stop growing, was built, furnished, and decorated by Works Progress Administration workers during the depression. It is a museum of sturdy mountain crafts with massive beams and inspiring interior. Among its treasures is a collection of C.S. Price paintings, executed while the famous artist was employed by the WPA.

Timberline has dining and guest facilities and a swimming pool. Timberline's Magic Mile ski lift, a much newer model than the original, runs in summer as well as winter to give scenic rides to visitors. *Sno-Cat* tours to the 10,000-foot level of the mountain are also available. Timberline is the starting point for many climbing expeditions.

Those who venture above the lodge to climb will encounter a complete mountain climbing experience. Steam heat rises from the fumaroles, the obvious indication that this is indeed a volcano. Oregonians like to say you can fry an egg on a rock on Mt. Hood.

Columbia River Gorge and Mt. Hood Loop

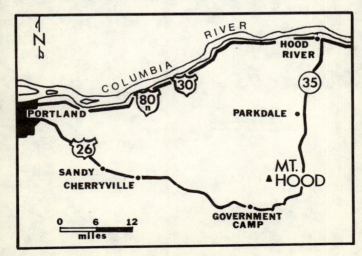

The Columbia River Gorge, carved through the Cascade Mountains by America's second largest river, dramatically blends rock formations and waterfalls. This is the wide watery highway of Northwest exploration.

An hour's travel on U.S. 30/I-80N hits the major sights, but for the full drama of the gorge turn off the freeway at Troutdale for the Columbia Gorge Scenic Route. This, by the way, is a good rainy day trip, because the gorge is most spectacular when storm clouds are at work. And, of course, during the rainy season the waterfalls work better.

Before starting to the gorge in the winter, check the road reports. Freezing east winds sometimes coat gorge roads and scenery with ice and frost.

Suggested first stop on the winding road which used to be the main route east is at *Crown Point*, with its English Tudor vista house. Here the visitor gets the full impact of the job the mighty Columbia has done. Wayside and picnic spots, waterfalls, and rest facilities abound from this point for the next 10 miles.

Don't fail to stop at *Multnomah Falls*,¶ about 8 miles east of Crown Point, where the freeway and scenic route join. This 620-foot falls is considered by many to be among the most beautiful in the United States. A short trail spans the pool between the upper and lower falls. A restaurant and visitor information center are located at the base of the falls.

About 2 miles east of Multnomah Falls (scenic route), look for *Oneonta Gorge*,¶ a narrow cleft in a basalt bluff. A bit beyond Oneonta you'll see appropriately named *Horsetail Falls*. Oneonta and Horsetail are visible from the freeway but reachable only by the scenic route.

Near *Ainsworth State Park* the scenic route merges with the freeway and you're on your way to Bonneville Dam, one of many great dams which provide the Pacific Northwest with the larger part of its electric power supply as well as with benefits for navigation, irrigation, flood control, and recreation. For the visitor who is not interested in the engineering spectacle of a dam, there are the fishways.

Sometimes called fish ladders, the fishways, wide stair-steps carrying rapid flowing water, allow passage of salmon and steelhead to spawning grounds above the dam and of fingerlings from spawning grounds to the ocean.

Stop at the new Bradford Island Visitors Center for underwater viewing of migrating fish. Best time for fish viewing is between late March and the end of September. The very best, according to guides at the center, is around Sept. 1.

Regular tours of the dam are scheduled daily every half hour from June to September. In off-season months tours can be arranged on request by calling 777-4441 and asking for Bonneville Dam.

Bradford Island Visitors Center is open from 8 a.m.- 5 p.m. in the winter and 8 a.m.-9 p.m. in the summer.

When leaving the dam site, you'll have a chance to drive into the Bonneville Fish Hatchery area. This is worth a stop if only to see the primeval-looking 9-foot sturgeon who inhabits a nearby pond with some of his fellows.

Four miles east of Bonneville is Cascade Locks National Historic Site. The "Oregon Pony," a little locomotive under a shelter in the park near the locks, hauled the narrow gauge railroad train which portaged goods between steamboat landings above and below the Cascade's rapids before the locks were built.

At this point, you may return to Portland or continue on the "Mt. Hood Loop Drive," which returns to the city via Mt. Hood.

At *Hood River* look for the junction with State Highway 35. Pears and apples, the wealth of the Hood River Valley, can be found in many forms—from the real thing to tiny earrings—at the Fruit Tree, part of a large restaurant-motel complex near the junction.

Take Highway 35 south through pear and apple orchard country—blossom time is May—toward Mt. Hood. About 14 miles from Hood River you'll pass through the community of *Mt. Hood.* Consider a stop at the Mt. Hood Country Store, built before Timberline Lodge, where you can mail a card or letter that will bear the unique postmark, "Mt. Hood, OR."

Less than 10 miles south at the Cooper Spur Inn, a turn-off to the right offers a worthwhile fair weather side trip to *Cloud Cap*, 10.5 dusty and bumpy miles up the north side of Mt. Hood. (The road is closed in winter.) On the parking lot at the end of the road are two historic log structures. The larger one, closer to the mountain, is Cloud Cap Inn, erected as a hotel in 1889 and now operated as a climbing base by the Hood River Crag Rats, a mountaineering club.

The smaller building was erected in 1910 and still is owned by the Snow Shoe Club, a private group, mostly Portlanders.

Rest rooms and tent camping facilities can be found at the U.S. Forest Service's nearby Cloud Cap Saddle and Tilly Jane Forest Camps.

On a clear day Cloud Cap offers a breathtaking view of the north side of Mt Hood—more rugged and spectacular than the more frequently visited south side. To the north also can be seen the Hood River Valley and the great Washington snow peaks—Mt. St. Helens, Mt. Rainier, and Mt. Adams.

From Cooper Spur Inn, a small public restaurant, Highway 35 continues around the east side of Mt. Hood to Government Camp. From there the traveler may complete the Mt. Hood Loop, returning to Portland on U.S. 26.

Willamette Valley

For those who travel to Portland from far places, especially carrying children, a day in the Willamette Valley can bring peace to a family too long cooped up in the confines of a city, even one as nice as Portland.

Oregon's I-5, a total freeway system, running from the northern border to the California crossing, can put you in touch with many small communities. From slow-cured bacon to selected antiques, there is reason to travel and get off I-5 from time to time.

Heading south from downtown Portland, the freeway splits the rolling hills which begin what we call "the valley."

Champoeg is hallowed ground to Oregonians. It was under these old trees that Joe Meek, U.S. marshal and mountain man, called upon the men to cross his line for the United States. Home of the French voyageurs retired from Ft. Vancouver, the property is maintained by the State of Oregon. In addition to excellent picnicking and ball playing facilities as well as wooded glimpses of the Willamette River, the park includes three museums which are open most of the year.

The home of Dr. Robert Newell is all that remains of the vast settlement of McLoughlin's former employees.

Doc Newell's house became the refuge for the community during the great flood of 1861 which demolished the area.

The Champoeg Pioneer Museum is open any time the park is open. The curator is on duty from June through Labor Day, although the park admits the curious year around, extreme weather permitting. The Daughters of the American Revolution Pioneer Mothers' Home (678-5365) is open from Feb. 1 to Nov. 30 as is the Newell House (678-5537). These two charge a small admission fee.

Champoeg is a remnant of many historical firsts: it was the site of the largest village of the Calapooya tribe before the arrival of the white man, a trading post for the Hudson Bay Company in 1828, and the first land purchased for any Oregon park (1906).

Don't miss the turnoff marked Canby-Hubbard, for it is at *Hubbard* that you find fine slow-cured ham and bacon.

Drive into town (don't plan a lunch stop here) and turn right at the old, white church for Voget's Meats. Behind that sterile exterior wafts some of the most mouth-watering scents in the state. Sides of bacon, thick with ribbons of lean meat, can be cut into one pound pieces and double-wrapped on the spot to be dropped into your freezer. Voget's chipped beef is close to proscuitto (maybe better), and you should take along a pepper stick to munch on in the car.

A little farther down and to the east is *Aurora*. Keep in mind that all colonists were not without humor and enjoy a visit to the Aurora Ox Barn Museum. The museum is open afternoons, Wed.-Sun. with admission at 75 cents for adults, 50 cents for students, and 25 cents for children. The charge includes a well-guided tour.

Dr. William Keil, leader of the Aurora Colony, marched across the United States with a brass band preceding his oldest son, Willie, whom he had promised could lead the trek to Oregon country. Unfortunately Willie died shortly before the departure of the wagon train, so Dr. Keil preserved him in a coffin filled with Golden Rule whiskey. Between the band and the stops to let interested Indians observe the corpse, no one disturbed this gathering as they headed west.

Once there they developed a reputation as furniture craftsmen for early settlers. Much of that furniture remains in Oregon families and is made of ash, maple, and other native hardwoods.

The museum contains a wide variety of the furniture-making equipment, musical instruments from the very band, and gaily colored clothing worn by the colonists. Behind the Ox Barn is an excellent replica of an early settler's cabin and next door is a later home of Aurora.

Aurora today is peppered with antique shops. Naturally, anything of great value is to be found in the museum, but a clever eye may spot some remnant of Oregon history on the shops' shelves.

Meanwhile, back on the freeway, this time prepare for an exit at *Woodburn* to reach *Mt. Angel* and *Silverton*. Mt. Angel Abbey, run by the Benedictine order, sits atop a cliff just like the movie version, with its own farmlands spreading out below. Any time of the year, its library is worth a visit by bibliophiles, but two times are special in Mt. Angel. One is the Oktoberfest, held every autumn when the entire town goes rural Germany with great kegs of beer, homemade sausage and sauerkraut, and dancing in the streets. A more sober occasion, but equally worth the trip, is Easter sunrise at the Abbey.

Beyond Mt. Angel lies Silverton, the start of a do-it-yourself covered bridge tour, which follows this section.

The freeway rushes by and the legislature comes and goes, but *Salem* remains a small town. Residents keep it that way by not advertising some of its finest features: excellent restaurants and exciting shopping.

The Oak Pit, 159 High St. SE, is an old Salem standby for lunches and early dinners. Homemade bread and cream pies lie at either end of the cafeteria style counter and in between great haunches of beef, ham, and pork are drawn juicy and steaming from brick ovens to be cut to order. The atmosphere hasn't changed in more than 25 years, the prices only slightly.

The closest thing to "home cooking" for dinner only (possibly better than yours) is the Colonial House, 5005 Commercial SE (364-2235). Fried chicken is the specialty of the house; homemade biscuits, chilled green salads, and fresh soups grace every meal. If he doesn't like it, owner Reuben Worcester won't serve it, but moves as far afield as scampi tossed in herb butter, prime steaks, and Dungeness crab. And it will be Dungeness or you won't get it at his house. Petite oysters are fresh and icy cold. If there is an extra chair at your table, don't worry, it will certainly be filled by your host at some time during your meal.

A visit to the white marble state capitol building and the governor's office will supply you with enough free literature on the state to keep you in reading material for a week and in Oregon for a lifetime.

The capitol grounds back onto the campus of Willamette University, the state's oldest college. During pleasant weather it is fun to walk the paths and photograph the statuary and the squirrels.

Five commodities mark Salem a must for the intrepid shopper: art, antiques, women's clothing, old doors, and mushrooms.

Yes, mushrooms. If you plan your trip for a week day don't miss the West Mushroom Farm, 255 50th NE (581-2471) east of the city. Try touring the mushroom caverns in a lighted miners helmet. The outlet store sells freshly picked mushrooms.

Worth a stop weekdays is E.S. Ritter and Co., just south of Kale Street on 99E. The Ritter brothers' warehouse is stacked with old doors (some beautiful), screen doors with years of squeak left in them and other Victorian has-beens. It is not unusual to find a whole porch—pillars, scroll-work and all—for a reasonable price. Even if you don't find one, one of the brothers will tell you with a twinkle in his eye, "We had just what you were looking for last week."

Peg Fry is the "little woman" who stands 5 foot 8 in her stocking feet behind her Lemon Tree Boutique (581-2471), and she is as charged with style as with energy. Her specialty shop for women is at 345 Owens St. SE (399-1010); her stock is different from any chain store in the state. It takes a while to work your way through her reconverted house, but you may find yourself with a good cup of coffee in your hand to tide you through two floors of everything from sportswear to formal dress.

Antique shops grow as abundantly as the crops in the Willamette Valley, and two of the best are within Salem city limits. Don't miss Cynthia Day's "Et Cetera," 442 Church NE (next to the Greyhound Bus Depot) for a fine assortment of small pieces including jewelry, china, and rare Willamette Valley Indian baskets. The Assistance League of Salem's Thrift Shop is at 533 Commercial St. SE.

Open Mon.-Sat., this late Victorian home is jammed with consignment and donation pieces, some of them very nice, all of them collectable to someone.

Covered Bridges

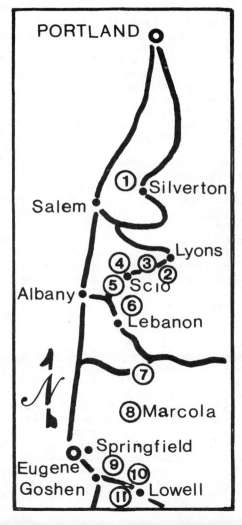

Graft, corruption, and an occasional murder built Oregon's covered bridges, but perseverance has kept them up across rivers in the state much to the delight of photographers and Sunday drivers.

Not long ago, the Oregon Historical Society's 3-day historic bridges outing drew so much interest that Director Thomas Vaughan released the map for others. The actual tour takes eight hours, allowing ample stopping time for photography and musing.

There are more than 60 covered bridges in the state, most of them usable—all of them worth the viewing. But the Silverton-Cottage Grove tour includes 11 of the best.

The Gallon House Bridge at Silverton is a brown wooden reminder of local option days when the bridge was heavily traveled by residents of "dry" Silverton who drove out to a tavern to buy liquor by the gallon. The tavern burned down during prohibition while the bridge remains 84 feet high across Abiqua Creek. Its original cost was $1310.

Thomas Creek, out of Lyon, was once nearly covered by bridges. The creek still flows beneath two wooden structures known as the Jordan Bridges. The longer one was built in 1936; the shorter, in 1937.

Fourth on the tour is the Shimanek Bridge near Scio. It is the latest to be built and was dedicated in 1966. Linn County engineers replaced a storm-damaged covered bridge with a replica since there was no money in the county budget for a steel structure. It is the only red covered bridge in Oregon.

Right in the middle of the farm country, north of Crabtree, is the gothic-style Hoffman Bridge, crossing Crabtree Creek and built in 1936.

Larwood Bridge, near the Roaring River Fish Hatchery, sits calmly amid local controversy. Residents insist that this is the only place in the United States where a river flows into a creek, and no one has disputed them.

Off highway 212 is the Crawfordville Bridge, built over the Calapooya River in 1932. It was bypassed in 1963 but has been maintained and is a variation of the county's open truss sides with a narrow, continuous slit window.

The Mohawk River at Marcola introduces the first Lane County bridge. Lane County has been a leader in bridge restoration and has 21 covered crossings in excellent condition.

In 1904 the Pengra Bridge measured 192 feet in span. The newer bridge, built alongside the original in 1938, is shorter but was necessary since the original began to slide into Fall Creek. This bridge holds the record for the longest single chords running the entire length and measuring 126 feet. Since the 18-in. thick chords were too large to be run through a mill, they were rough hewn in the woods, hauled to the bridge site, and resurfaced there.

Unity Bridge, across Big Fall Creek, is 90 feet long with daylight windows to allow drivers to see traffic around a very sharp bend in the road.

For the grand finale, the society picked the Lowell Bridge. The original bridge at this site, 210 feet long, was built in 1907 to replace the Hyland Ferry across the middle fork of the Willamette River.

Lane County began to rebuild the bridge in 1945 when they saw that dam control would take out the original. The water began rising in 1955 until the bridge now spreads out much like a giant water lily on the lake. This bridge alone is worth the tour.

Recreational Facilities near Portland

Blue Lake Park—Off I-80N, 15 miles east of Portland. A large open Multnomah County park where you can swim, fish, or picnic at one of 900 tables.

Dabney State Park—On the Columbia River Scenic Route, 19 miles east of Portland. A wooded riverside park—the Sandy, not the Columbia—where the river is pleasant for swimming.

Lewis and Clark State Park—Off I-80N, 16 miles east of Portland. Another Sandy River site near the spot where the Sandy joins the Columbia. This is especially pleasant for small children; the water is shallow, the bottom sandy.

Oxbow Park—Off U.S. 26, 20 miles s.e. of Portland. Oxbow has 42 campsites and 44 trailer sites along the swift Sandy River. Facilities include a boat ramp, but swimming is not suggested—and no flush toilets here.

Rooster Rock State Park—On I-80N, 22 miles east of Portland. A popular Columbia River park for swimming, picnicking, and boating. Towering Rooster Rock, a landmark of the Gorge, is nearby.

Scoggins Valley Park—Off Oregon Route 47, 6 miles

s.w. of Forest Grove. This Washington County Park on Henry Hagg Lake, created by the Scoggins Dam, offers boating, biking, and swimming. User fees are charged. Call the Washington County Park department (640-3553) for per-car and car-boat rates.

Fishing is "advertised" at all these facilities, but you're not guaranteed a catch.

Heceta Head Lighthouse just off U.S. 101, named for Bruno Heceta, an early Spanish sea captain.

BITS AND ODDMENTS

A Potpourri of Miscellany

Annual Events

IN ADDITION to the first crocus, the first tomato, and the two-week winter cold, Portland and the rest of the state host other memorable annual events.

For more detailed information and activities as well as exact dates, good sources for information by the day, week, or month are:

Travel Information, Oregon State Highway Division, Salem, Oregon, 97310 and the Portland Chamber of Commerce for activities planned well in advance. Information by the week is available in the "Northwest" magazine section of the Sunday *Oregonian*, or by the day through the "What's Doing" section of the *Oregon Journal*. *Willamette Week* runs a week at a glance in its newspaper also. Dick Klinger and Robin Chapman, hosts for KGW-TV's channel 8, keep an up to the minute eye on new events sprightly and nightly at 7 p.m.

January

Boat Show, Memorial Coliseum
Horse racing at Portland Meadows opens to run into May ❧

February

Storm Festival at Reedsport
Southern Oregon Dog Sled Races, Diamond Lake
Beachcombers Festival, Civic Convention Center, Seaside
Shakespearean Festival, Stage II, opens in Ashland to run through April. Tickets are available in Portland.
Portland Roadster Show, Coliseum
Auto Show, Multnomah Exposition Center, Portland

181

International Airlines Ski Championships, Mt. Hood ski
  areas, Government Camp

March

Shrine Circus, Coliseum
All-Northwest Barbershop Contest and Gay 90's Festival,
  Forest Grove
Oregon Ceramic Show, Multnomah Exposition Center
Home and Garden Show, Multnomah Exposition Center
Dog Show: Willamette Valley Kennel Club, State Fair-
  grounds, Salem
Old Time Fiddlers Show, Fairgrounds, Eugene
Spring salmon run begins in Columbia-Willamette rivers ¶
Arts and Crafts Show, Portland Community College,
  Sylvania Campus
Recreational Vehicle Show, Coliseum

April

Root Festival, Warm Springs
Festival of the Arts, George Fox College, Newberg
Cherry Festival, The Dalles
Tidal Treasure Days, Lincoln City
Blossom Festival, Hood River
Hobby Show, Memorial Coliseum
Ice Follies, Memorial Coliseum
Trout season opens ¶

May

Tour, John Day Dam, through Sept. 30
Tours, The Dalles Dam, through Sept. 10
Chemawa College Indian Rodeo, State Fairgrounds,
  Salem
Music in May, Pacific University, Forest Grove
Pea Festival, Milton-Freewater
Pacific Northwest Championship All-Indian Rodeo, Tygh
  Valley
Saturday Market, Old Town in Portland open through
  December ¶
Dog Racing: Multnomah Kennel Club, Portland, opens
  to run through August ¶
Fleet of Flowers Memorial Service, Depoe Bay

June

Strawberry Festival, Lebanon

Portland Rose Festival, Portland, including:
  Queen's coronation
  Night Parade
  River Carnival
  Rose Society Show
  Festival of Bands
  Junior parade
  Grade Floral parade
  Rose Cup races
Lamb Show, State Fairgrounds, Salem
Oregon Shakespearean Festival opens in Ashland, tickets available in Portland
Phil Sheridan Days, Sheridan
Scandinavian Festival, Astoria
Gem and Mineral Show, Douglas County Fairgrounds, Roseburg
Art Festival, Lake Oswego
Pow Wow and Treaty Days, Warm Springs
Sand Castle Building Contest, Cannon Beach ¶
National Rooster Crowing Contest, Rogue River

July

Music by Moonlight begins at Washington Park, Portland ¶
Annual Rotary Club, Concours d'Elegance, Forest Grove
Happy Days Celebration, Hillsboro
Molalla Buckeroo, Molalla
World Championship Timber Carnival, Albany
St. Paul Rodeo, St. Paul
Miss Oregon Pageant, Seaside
Turkey-Rama, McMinnville
Silver Smelt Fry, Yachats
Crooked River Round-Up, Prineville
Wallowa County Rodeo, Enterprise
Arts Festival, Nehalem
Oregon Broiler Festival, Springfield
Fort Dalles Days and Rodeo, The Dalles
Bohemia Mining Days, Cottage Grove
Santiam Bean Festival, Stayton
Chief Joseph Days, Joseph
Abbey Bach Festival, Mt. Angel Abbey
Highland Games, Parkrose High School, Portland
Antique Powerland Farm Fair, Brooks
Fourth of July Pageant, Alpenrose Dairy, Portland

Fourth of July Fireworks, Oaks Park, Portland
Fall Chinook-Steelhead run begins in the Columbia and
  Willamette rivers

August

Music by Moonlight, Washington Park, Portland♪
Mary's Peak Trek, Corvallis
Astoria Regatta, Astoria
Multnomah County Fair, Portland
Polk County Fair, Rickreall♪
Clackamas County Fair, Canby
Washington County Fair, Hillsboro
Peter Britt Music and Arts Festival, Jacksonville
Threshing Bee and Draft Horse Show, Dufur
Great Oregon Rally, Vintage Autos, Forest Grove
Huckleberry Feast, Warm Springs
Football: Oregon North-South Shrine All-Star Game,
  Civic Stadium, Portland
Oregon State Fair, Salem

September

Far West Nursery and Garden Show, Memorial Coliseum
Indian Style Salmon Bake, Depoe Bay
Pendleton Round-Up, Pendleton
Oktoberfest, Mt. Angel♪
LPGA Portland Classic, women's professional golf tour-
  nament, Portland
Ringling Bros. Circus, Memorial Coliseum

October

Pacific International Livestock Exposition, Multnomah
  County Exposition Grounds, Portland
Portland Zoo train ride through "haunted forest"♪

November

OMSI♪ Auction, Memorial Coliseum
Verboort Sausage and Kraut Dinner, Verboort
Lucia Bride Festival and the First Light of Christmas
  Festival, the Lloyd Center, Portland

December

Rickreall Christmas Pageant, Rickreall
Basketball: Far West Classic, Memorial Coliseum, Port-
  land♪

Medieval Christmas Faire, Portland Park Blocks and
   participating buildings
Ice Capades, Coliseum
Singing Christmas Tree, Civic Auditorium
Storybook Lane, Alpenrose Dairy, Lloyd Center
Pittock Mansion, open house for Christmas

Name Dropping
(or Living With the Willamette Valley Twang)

"Welcome to Oregon"

You probably read that on the sign as you crossed the
border or saw it posted prominently at the airport.

It's a sincere, simple phrase with a devilish twist to it,
and the natives delight in challenging a foreign dialect
by listening for those who fumble and grasp for the
proper pronunciation of a local name.

The very name, "Oregon," (make that Ore-y-gun) is apt
to send otherwise solemn matriarchs into unsophisticated
snickers when dropped from the untutored tongue of a
Bostonian. (Here, it is pronounced Boss-tun.)

Early trappers and traders carried a dictionary, the
intertribal Indian language, to speak to our first natives.
Oregonians today enjoy living by the word and watching
outsiders flounder upon it.

Most Oregon names come easily if you will remember
to sit heavily upon the middle syllable or lean firmly upon
the last. However, there are many exceptions where you
must tramp on the first syllable, sliding down the rest.
Oregonians also love to be inconsistant as they turn
proper names into "insider" jargon.

In spite of the French Canadians who left Ft. Vancouver to settle land further south and who might have lent
a little class to the state with their accents, Oregon has
managed to squash any fancy ideas until everything rolls
out with the same determined twang. The French made
an initial run at upgrading the language by christening
La Creole Creek, a beautiful name for a sparkling run
of clear water in the Willamette Valley.

Oregonians, even then, snorted unless it was flattened
into "Lack-ree-all" (sit on the lack) and finally heeled
under any chance of Parisian participation by creating
the Willamette Valley version which to this day remains:
Rickreall. There isn't a French dictionary which would

touch that one with a badly burned crepe (or as most Oregonians say "crape".)

Which is not to downgrade Oregonian speech patterns. They are as much a part of the state as Mt. Hood, the Rose Festival, or the annual rodeos (make that: *row-dee-ohs*).

Take this test: pronounce the name of the Eastern Oregon river, the Deschutes.

Unless you said "da-*shoots*" (there is no multiple choice), you are in trouble.

To talk to the natives without their breaking into sporadic guffaws, we have compiled a list of Oregon names to start your Willamette Valley twang to vibrating. In addition are some names which may be universal in pronunciation, but which bear a special part in Oregon history.

If you are inclined to make an occupation out of this game, we recommend reading *Oregon Geographic Names* by Lewis A. and Lewis L. McArthur.

Albina (Al-bine-a)—Now a section of North Portland, was named for Albina Page, daughter of the first mayor of that small community which was laid out in 1872.

Astoria (Ass-tore-ia)—named for John Jacob Astor of New York City, who organized the Pacific Fur Company in 1810. Astoria was the first American settlement on the Pacific Coast.

Aurora (Uh-roar-uh)—is the town founded by Dr. William Keil and named for his daughter. Keil was born in Prussia in 1811 and came to Oregon in 1855.

Calapooya (Cala-poo-ya)—the Indian tribe which lived where Oregon City stands today.

Cannon Beach—as in the armament. Named for a cannon washed up on the beach after the wreck of the schooner Shark in 1846. The cannon is still there.

Champoeg (Sham-poo-eek)—possibly pure Indian, meaning a root or weed. Others believe it could be a combination of the French (champ: field) and the Indian (pooich: root).

Chinook (Shin-ook) soften the oo—a coastal Indian tribe. Also the universal tribal language as in: ik-poo-ie la-pote (shut the door).

Clackamas (Klak-a-mus)—Indian tribe, part of the Chinooks. Clackamas County was one of the first four districts of early Oregon.

Clatsop (Klat-sup)—An Oregon Indian tribe; original spellings given as Tlatsap or Tschlahtsoptchs. The tribe was part of the Chinook family.

Couch (Kooch)—Capt. John Couch was one of the founders of Portland who built his home upon Couch Lake, a shallow pond which covered approximately 22 city blocks where Union Station stands today.

Dallas (Dallus)—a valley town west of Salem, formerly named Cynthia Ann, but citizens figured the name to be too flighty. Under the administration of President Polk, the county seat of Dallas changed its name to match that of the vice president of the United States. This town is not to be confused with:

The Dalles (Dals)—in Wasco County which comes from the French word "dalle" meaning flagstone. The word, "dalles," as used by the French voyaguers, applied to the Columbia River rapids flowing through a narrow channel over flat rocks.

Douglas Fir—as any Oregon school child learns, is named for the Scotch botanical collector, David Douglas, and should not be confused by name with:

Douglas County—which is named for Stephen Arnold Douglas, an American politician and Democratic candidate for the presidency in 1860.

Glisan (Gliss-an)—the most often mispronounced street name in the city of Portland. Rodney L. Glisan was born in Portland, April 3, 1869, so the pronunciation of his name may not seem important to many of the young. Glisan was an attorney, a member of the Portland city council, and the Oregon legislature as well as a very active citizen. He would be pleased to have his name pronounced correctly.

Kinnikinnick (Kinny-key-nik)—also known as bear-berry, this low evergreen plant is thought to have been used by the coast Indians as a tobacco. It is pronounced just as it is spelled, with difficulty.

Molalla (Mole-al-uh)—the name of the tribe of Indians which lived in Clackamas and Marion counties and were the only horse Indians in the northern Pacific segment of the state.

Multnomah (Mult-know-muh)—Lewis and Clark first used this word in their journals to describe the river now called the Willamette. The Mulknomans, as they called them, lived on what now is Sauvie Island. All died, except for two men, during a smallpox epidemic while John McLoughlin was at Ft. Vancouver.

Multorpor (<u>Mult</u>-or-pour)—Originally a name for a Republican club in Portland, the word was coined by combining the first syllables of Multnomah, Oregon, and Portland.

Oneonta (On-ee-<u>onta</u>)—Said to mean "place of peace," this name was probably taken from New York State. A steamboat, built in the tradition of the Mississippi River side-wheelers, was built at Cascades in 1863 and given this name. Possibly the name was transferred to the spot in the gorge.

Oregon (<u>Ore</u>-y-gun)—The history of this name is the most twisted and clouded of any in the state. It is possible that the name originated with Major Robert Rogers (see Kenneth Roberts' *Northwest Passage*), an English army officer who tried to find the fabled Northwest Passage. He used the term Ouragon or Ourigan in a petition for an exploring expedition into the country west of the Great Lakes. The name Oregon was not known to Vancouver or to Gray or referred to by Lewis and Clark.

Oswego (Oss-<u>wee</u>-go)—named by A. A. Durham who operated a sawmill on Sucker Creek (later called Oswego Creek). Durham called his Oregon settlement after Oswego, New York. The Indians called the lake, Waluga, meaning wild swan. Local real estate dealers upgraded the name of the artificial lake on the creek to Oswego lake, and the town later took the name Lake Oswego.

Sacajawea (Sack-a-ja-wee-a)—the Shoshone Indian woman who guided the Lewis and Clark Party west.

St. Johns—James John came to Oregon in 1843, first settling in Linnton and then moving to the community which bears his name. Efforts to change the name to the singular have been turned down. However, John was a pioneer; there is no record that he was ever canonized.

Salishan (<u>Sal</u>-ish-ann)—family of Indians who built houses of planks and beams and lived on salmon. This name has been given to a contemporary plank and beam resort on the Oregon coast.

Sauvie (<u>So</u>-vee)—Lewis and Clark called this island Wapato, the Indian name for a wild potato. The present name is that of the French-Canadian who ran the dairy farm on the island for Ft. Vancouver. Although at one time it was, in fact, Sauvie's Island, perfectionists say that pronouncing it as a possessive puts you in the same class with those who insist the district on lower Burnside is "skid row."

Tenino (Ten-<u>ine</u>-o)—a part of a tribe found in the Columbia and Deschutes valleys, the Tenino Indians are now classed with the Warm Springs Indians. The name means a river channel where the water is held by steep rock walls.

Tualitan (<u>Twall</u>-it-an)—is an Indian word meaning lazy or sluggish. Another meaning is "a land without trees."

Willamette (Will-<u>am</u>-et)—derived from the Indian word "Wal-lamt," which marked a spot on the Willamette River near Oregon City on the west bank.

Children

One mother of many devised the perfect children's dining room. The tile floor leads to a central drain and above all will be a gigantic sprinkling system. After mealtime the water will be turned on and everything, children and all, will be rinsed squeaky clean. Her idea has merit, but she is not the only one giving original thought to children.

The Portland area offers several restaurants where it is better to be chaperoned by the Little League set, as well as many places of special interest to the young.

Two Portland publications devote themselves exclusively to entertaining children—*Discovering Portland With Children* by Claudia Lauinger and Arlene Haan and *Now Where?* by Joyce Tuggle and Nancy Martin McCarthy. Both books, naturally, are available at the Children's Book Store in Lake Oswego and other outlets.

Restaurants which help you to relax with children include: Farrell's Ice Cream Parlours, the Organ Grinder, the Carnival, the Old Fashioned Ice Cream Parlour, the Old Spaghetti Factory, and The Trees at the Hilton Hotel. All are listed under Restaurants.

Travels with Children

Alphabetically correct or not, all children's lists should start with the zoo.

Portland's *Zoo*❡ is part of a large complex at 4001 SW Canyon Rd., which flows into the Oregon Museum of Science and Industry (OMSI)❡ and the Forestry Center❡. Between the three major enterprises, open year around, there should be enough to keep any family busy for more than a week.

Of interest to children from the fourth through sixth grades is a special metric tour. Call the zoo in advance (226-1561). Young ecologists will enjoy the new solar house being built by Pacific Power and Light Co. for OMSI and everyone can see the danger of a forest fire in action at the Forestry Center.

Tired parents may wish to book a "sit down" at the Planetarium at OMSI. Once the lights go off and the chairs tilt back, no one will know you are restoring strength unless you snore. Tickets are available to see the stars at OMSI.

Alpenrose Dairy, 6149 SW Shattuck Rd. (244-1133) offers a day at the farm for all those urban dwellers. Stroll through the barn and smell the warm hay while young sheep, goats, and horses nuzzle salty young fingers. Take a picnic lunch to eat on the grassy meadows and visit Story Book Lane as well as a western village. Call ahead for special attractions including an Easter Egg hunt and a Fourth of July party. Admission is free.

American Rhododendron Test Gardens, SE 28th just off Woodstock, has wide paved paths, perfect for a baby stroller. Visit here anytime, but the spring is the best since the rhododendrons are in bloom and the baby ducks are hatching. Take plenty of stale bread. The birds will come up the path to meet you and expect to be fed.

Ride one of the last of the cable-drawn *ferries* in the state at Canby. Take 99E and follow the signs out of Oregon City to cross the Willamette River on this free ferry, which is in operation all but the coldest months of the year. As you await your turn to cross the river, look upstream for the blue heron which inhabit the river banks.

Chief Lelooska is awaiting you at his lodge at Ariel, Washington, and just as soon as you've taken your seat in the longhouse the potlatch will begin. Easterners who long to see the American Indian will delight in this two hour session of Indian tales and dances complete with intricate wooden masks. And Oregonians will enjoy having their children see a part of the coast heritage—albeit Alaskan in tradition. Ariel is less than an hour's drive from Portland. Call Dorothy Mason at 248-5937 (OMSI) to schedule a visit with the chief. Potlatches are scheduled for every third Saturday Mar.-June and Sept.-Nov., and special meetings of the "tribe" are often called. A seat on the bench is $1.25 a person.

The *Children's Museum,* 3037 SW 2nd (227-1505) is especially geared for the young with two floors of exhibits. Classes are offered in the basement in pottery, painting, and drawing. For group tours or classes, call the museum in advance.

Ducks are plentiful at several spots around the city. Take all your bread and visit:

Alpenrose Dairy, 6149 SW Shattuck Rd.

American Rhododendron Test Garden, SE 28th off Woodstock

Laurelhurst Park, SE 39th & Stark

Ledding Library, 820 21st, Milwaukie

Westmoreland Park, 7700 SE 22nd

Another time take I-5 heading south past the last Salem turnoff for the *Enchanted Forest*, which is commercial but not as bad as it sounds. Children, and adults with strong backs, can go down the rabbit hole just as Alice did, as well as meet many nurseryland characters peeping through the undergrowth. The latest addition is a haunted mansion patterned after the Disneyland favorite. The forest is open May 1-Oct. 1 and includes room for picnicking and a refreshment stand. Admission is charged.

All county fairs pipe the kind of music which draws the young, but the *Polk County Fair* at Rickreall is special. Drive into Salem and take the bridge to Dallas. Rickreall is about 10 minutes west of the state capitol. The entire family is admitted to this last of the small-town fairs for the price of a 50 cent parking ticket. The entire area is about six city blocks square, all in the open, so parents can find a warm bench while children visit the midway. All concessions are run by local philanthropic organizations, no hucksters here, and the prices are low. The few carnival rides available are for the very young, and the Dairy Association runs the milkshake stand. Check with Tourist Information in Salem for the week, but the fair is always held in August.

The National Park Service is building a precise replica of Dr. John McLoughlin's fort at *Fort Vancouver*, just across the Interstate Bridge in Washington. For children who find the written word hard to believe, a trip to the fort may well be worth a thousand volumes. The fort is open year around.

Halloween is the time to plan a good shiver, and the weeks that precede this night should include a call to the Portland Zoo to book tickets on the Spook Special, a train ride through the darkest corners of Washington Park. For ticket arrangements and departure times (starting after dusk) call 226-1561.

Students in the Portland public schools form a fine *Junior Symphony*, which performs at the Portland Civic Auditorium, 222 SW Clay St. (226-2876).

Parents with budding musicians appreciate the *Community Music Center*, 3350 SE Francis (235-8222), which begins with the 5- and 6-year-old early learner, carrying him on to Junior Symphony level.

The *Ladybug Theatre* has built a sound reputation among the young set for such presentations as "Aladdin and His Wonderful Lamp" and other remarkable tales. The players hold an open sort of theater which encourages even the youngest to listen with good audience manners so that they may contribute at the right time. Productions are held Sat. and Sun. throughout the year, adjacent to the Children's Zoo, 4001 SW Canyon Rd. (228-5648). It is not necessary to visit the zoo to attend the plays for which a small admission fee is charged.

Oaks Amusement Park, at the foot of SE Spokane, just off the Sellwood Bridge on the east side of the Willamette River (236-5722), offers roller skating all year and amusement rides during the warmer months. The park is responsible for a gigantic Fourth of July fireworks display and offers picnic facilities along the river. Many of the rides are geared for the preschool set.

At the *Oregon Historical Society*, 1230 SW Park (222-1741) young groups may experience the problems of the pioneer in prearranged programs Monday through Friday, by carding wool and handling artifacts which provide a direct touching point with the past. Call the society to reserve a time for your group.

Just across the street at the *Portland Art Museum* (226-2811), the young will be enchanted with the Northwest Indian artifact room which includes a tour, if pre-arranged, and the opportunity to press small fingers to a great box of "touchables" used by the earliest dwellers of the Oregon country.

Mothers who frequently trip over miles of unconnected tracks in the kitchen will be relieved to take junior engineers to a magnificent collection of five miles of track (all connected) by the **Columbia Gorge Model Railroad Club** at 3405 N. Montana (281-8591). The club is open for inspection during November.

Dig a few worms and tie some leader to a pole before heading for **Sauvie Island** where the catfishing is still good. The wide sandy beaches provide a good place for children to release a little energy, and they might even bring home dinner.

There comes a time for all children when they prefer to argue that black is white. That is the day to take them, map in hand, to visit the **Willamette Stone**, NW Skyline Blvd., just west of Mt. Calvary Cemetery. The stone marks the meridian line and the 00 base line for surveying all Northwest boundary lines. The Oregon Historical Society will provide you with additional information on the stone and mapping, so stop there first.

Child Care

Babysitting cooperatives thrive in Portland. Members of neighborhood organizations take turns caring for each others' children. Ask in your neighborhood about a cooperative. If there is none and you can't make an informal arrangement with a neighbor, try one of the following:

One private baby sitting agency in Portland is **Wee-Ba-Bee Attendants** (244-8835). You might call Wee-Ba-Bee if you're planning a vacation or if you're visiting in a motel and want to do the town—without children. Rates are: $8.25 for the four-hour minimum and $1.25 each hour after until midnight. After midnight, the price goes up to $1.75 per hour. For 24-hour care, rates vary according to number of children: $17 a day for two, $19 for four, and so on.

If you're a working mother and need help finding day care, call the **Metropolitan Community Coordinated Child Care Council** (226-7638) for help in finding someone. There's no charge for this referral service.

Senior Citizens

If you're 65 or older and want to know the services and programs available to you in Portland, a central information and referral office for problems of the elderly is as close as your telephone. The number is: 222-5555. The Tri-County Community Council in cooperation with the city's agency on aging provides the service.

Community-based support services are also available. Depending on where you live, call these numbers:

Northeast (288-8303)   North (286-8228)
Southeast (233-5426)   Downtown (227-5605)
Northwest (224-2640)   Model Cities (288-8338)
Southwest (226-3251)   East County (665-7189)

Following are some programs available to elderly persons in Portland:

Congregate Dining and Meals-on-Wheels—These programs are managed in Portland by Loaves and Fishes Corp. Call 222-5555 for the dining center nearest you or to be referred for the meals for the home-bound program.

Discounts—Senior Citizen discounts are given at some movie theaters, certain businesses, and drug stores and for certain personal services. For additional information call the number listed above for your area.

Food Buying Clubs—Providing groceries at lower costs, the Seniors North Food Buying Club sells food at 20-30 percent below the retail price at the Peninsula Senior Center, 7508 N. Hereford, from 9 a.m.-4 p.m. weekdays. It also takes its traveling store to these places where the elderly live or congregate:

Northwest Center, 1956 NW Everett, Thurs., 2-4 p.m.
Schrunk Towers, 8832 N. Syracuse, Wed. & Fri., 1:30-4 p.m.
University Park Methodist Church, N. Lombard and Fiske, Wed. & Fri., noon-1 p.m.

Free Tuition—Any person 65 or older may attend any course free at Portland State University if not taking it for credit and if space is available. For more information call 229-4739.

Homemaker Service—Older persons who need part-time help in the home may be eligible for it under the city program or directly through the agency which provides it, Metropolitan Family Service (228-7238).

Hub-Cap Tours—Sponsored by a coalition of churches, day trips leave at 1:30 the last Fri. of each month from the NW 20th Pl. entrance of the Fred Meyer Stadium store on W. Burnside. No reservations necessary. Trips are to local parks or sights.

Telephone Reassurance—To be placed on a telephone list for a phone check or a friendly visit, call 222-5555 or Metropolitan Family Service (228-7238).

Transportation—Tri-Met issues "honored citizen" cards to persons over 65 to qualify for 10¢ fares during weekday nonrush hours and free rides on weekends and evenings after 7. Special transportation is also provided when needed. Call 222-5555 for more information.

Other Counties—For senior citizen information in other counties call these numbers:

Clackamas (655-8578)
Clark County, Wash. (1-206-694-3091)
Columbia (1-397-4000)
Washington (640-3489)

Schools

Portland supports an excellent public school system, which is holding its own against the problems of urban transiency and suburban flight. Voters have approved two money requests for schools in recent years, and aging buildings are being remodeled as a result.

Newcomers with children enrolled in the public schools might be interested to know that the special natural environment of the area provides the setting for a superior public school program for all sixth graders in Portland and many in the suburbs—a program known as Outdoor School. This is a week-long nature camp experience which the children share with their classroom teachers and with nature specialists. For many a student, Outdoor School is the most memorable public school experience of all.

Community Schools

The Portland School District also sponsors the following Community Schools which offer adult education, usually in the evenings, designed by and for the neighborhoods

where the schools are located:
Alameda—2732 NE Fremont (288-6036)
Fernwood—3255 NE Hancock (281-0089)
Portsmouth—5103 N. Willis (285-5609)
Sabin—4013 NE 18th (288-6538)
Woodmere—6540 SE 78th (777-2527)

Colleges and Universities

Columbia Christian College—200 NE 91st (255-7060)
Lewis and Clark College—615 SW Palatine Hill Rd. (244-6161)
Marylhurst Education Center—Marylhurst (south of Lake Oswego) (636-8141)
Portland State University—724 SW Harrison (229-3000)
Reed College—3203 SE Woodstock Blvd. (771-1112)
University of Oregon Health Sciences Center—3181 SW Sam Jackson Park Rd. (225-8252); School of Dentistry (225-8220); School of Medicine (225-8220); School of Nursing (225-8220)
University of Portland—5000 N. Willamette Blvd. (283-7911)
Warner Pacific College—2219 SE 68th (775-4368)
Western States Chiropractic College—2900 NE 132nd (256-3180)

Community Colleges

Clackamas Community College—19600 S. Molalla, Oregon City (656-2631)
Mt. Hood Community College—26000 SE Stark, Gresham (667-1561)
Portland Community College—12000 SW 49th (244-6111). Operates centers in southwest, north, southeast, downtown Portland, St. Helens, and Forest Grove.

Other Schools

Museum Art School, Portland Art Museum—1219 SW Park (226-4391). Grants bachelor fine arts degree, for a four-year course and offers classes for adults and children.
School of the Arts and Crafts, Arts and Crafts Society—616 NW 18th (228-4741). Offers wide variety of daytime, evening, and Saturday classes for adults and young people.
Center for Urban Education—0245 SW Bancroft (221-

0984). An agency of the Ecumenical Ministries of Oregon which offers seminars and workshops at various locations on social problems, concerns, and strategy.

Oregon Museum of Science and Industry—4015 SW Canyon (248-5900). Science enrichment classes from kindergarten through high school.

Publications

If it's in print and recent, the chances are excellent you will find it at Rich's Cigar Store, 734 SW Alder (228-1700), a combination smoke shop and periodical store which caters to everyone. From the *London Times* (one day old) to the most expensive French magazines and those special interest, Jesse Rich stocks them all and the print mingles well with the aroma of special tobacco blends. Rich's is as much a part of Portland as that proverbial rose by any other name.

The city itself publishes a wide variety of newspapers and magazines. Here is a list of the major periodicals.

The Oregonian—1320 SW Broadway (221-8327). Just celebrated its 125th anniversary in the city; obviously here to stay as a morning newspaper.

The Oregon Journal—1320 SW Broadway (221-8275). The afternoon daily (except Sunday) paper for the state. While both are part of the S.I. Newhouse chain, the papers are in direct opposition to one another frequently, and the reporting staffs remain aggressively separated.

Willamette Week—320 SW Stark (243-2122). A smart weekly newcomer on the city streets which leans toward in-depth studies of Portland.

Daily Journal of Commerce—2014 NW 24th (226-1311). Handles the business news of the community.

Daily Shipping News—1221 SW Alder (227-6543).

Labor Press—Portland Labor Center (222-1791). Draws a regular readership but particularly at election time when endorsements can mean a vote.

Old Portland Today—125 W. Burnside (227-6550). Monthly publication which dwells upon the importance of Old Town. It can be picked up at many of the businesses in the area.

One Dollar—919 SW Taylor (223-1748). Local magazine which sells for 50 cents. The editorial outlook is as unique as the theory behind the name.

Oregon Grange Bulletin—1313 SE 12th (234-7577).

Oregon Historical Quarterly—1230 SW Park (222-1741). Recently celebrated its 75th year of continuous publication, which is unique among historical societies. The *Oregon Quarterly* is available with a membership or by individual copies which may be purchased at the Oregon Historical Society.

Oregon Times—1000 SW 3rd (223-0304). Alternates between a weekly and a monthly. This paper changes hands frequently; raises establishment eyebrows just as often.

The Portland Guide—4475 SW Scholls Ferry Rd. (297-3050) serves as a tourist information guide to coming attractions in the city.

Senior Citizen News—1019 SW 10th (226-1245).

Times Publications—11725 SW Canyon Rd. (643-1531) publishes six regional neighborhood newspapers.

Weather

There is one way to tell a Portlander born and bred, but, it takes patience.

If he says it is too hot when the thermometer on the back porch reaches 85 degrees, he's probably the real thing. If he complains when the temperature drops below 35 degrees, he may belong here. If he owns no umbrella and looks upward as the drizzle comes down to meet him, its fairly certain he's genuine. If, in March, on a 50-degree day, he takes off his jacket and puts the top down on his convertible because it certainly will be raining by June for the Rose Festival and this is the time to get a head start on a sun tan, you've met a native son.

If the woman, standing at the bus stop, her back braced against a fierce east wind whipping down the Gorge says brightly, "Today I'll set out the pansies, I smell spring in the air," you've spoken with the native daughter.

Weather is a serious topic for Portland.

Like strange Aunt Minnie, Portlanders can talk about it amongst themselves, but should an outsider of say 50 years or less residency in the city dare to criticize the smallest puddle, the retort is likely to imply that he move back home.

Climatic Average in Portland
Monthly Averages

	Jan.-Mar.	Apr.-June	July-Sept.	Oct.-Dec.	Annual Aver.
Precipitation (inches)	5.35	2.17	1.0	5.57	42.32
Temperature (degrees)	43.2	57.6	65.8	47.9	53.7
Snowfall (inches)	2.5	Trace	0.0	.4	9.3
No. days 1/100" or more precip.	17.0	12.0	5.0	16.0	152.0

No. of days in growing season: 251

(Data from Travel Info. Section, Oregon State Highway Div., in *Oregon Climates* folder)

Historic Landmarks

Men and the women stood silently as tears streamed unashamed down their faces the day the old Portland Hotel came down. Even now the mention of that turreted building where the city spent its most gracious years (and President Taft was stuck in the bathtub) brings a lump to the throats of those who know its gravestone is a two-tiered parking lot.

Mention of the New Market Theatre, also a parking lot, stirs excitement among residents who hear that it may be transported back into its original glory.

From the greatest building to the smallest surviving cobblestone, Portland has learned the hard way to count its blessings in the form of Historic Landmarks, and most of the credit is due to the Portland Historical Landmarks Commission which annually puts its protective arm around a growing list of moments from the city's past. Many of the landmark buildings and their history are described in the Oregon Historical Society's excellent book *Portland, A Historical Sketch and Guide,* by Terence O'Donnell and Thomas Vaughan.

Those sites and buildings designated to date, include, by area:

Area 1—Skidmore Fountain Area

New Market Theatre, 50 SW 2nd (1872)
233 Front Street, 233 SW Front (1883-84)
No. 71 Oak St., 71 Oak (1865)
Packer-Scott, 28 NW 1st (1890)
New Market Annex, 58 SW 2nd (1889)
Poppleton Building, 83 SW 1st (1873)
Smith's Block, 10 SW Ash & 111, 117 SW Front (1872)
Bickel Building, 213 SW Ash & 208 SW Ankeny (1885)
Chown Electric Co., 112 SW 2nd (1889)
Oregon Marine Supply, 235 SW 1st (1886)
Haseltine Building, 133 SW 2nd (1893)
Two-story C.I. and masonry, 224 SW 1st (1889)
Spaghetti Factory, 126 SW 2nd (1886)
Skidmore Fountain, SW 1st & Ankeny (1887-88)

Area 2—South River Front

Bishop's House, 219 & 233 SW Stark (1879)
Concord Building, 208 SW Stark (1891)
Pacific Stationery, 415 SW 2nd (1886 and 1894)
The Leland, 421-29 SW 2nd (1886)
Hamilton Building, 529 SW 3rd (1893)
Dekum Building, 519 SW 3rd (1892)
Willamette Block, 722-738 SW 2nd (1880)
Strowbridge Building, 101 SW Yamhill (?)
Three-story C.I. and masonry, 728 SW 1st (1878)
Two story masonry, 730 SW 1st (1878)
Northrup-Blossom-Fitch Building, 737 SW Front (1858)
71-73 SW Yamhill, same address, (1878)
Four-story C.I. and masonry, 124 SW Yamhill (1885)
Mikado Block, 837 SW 1st (1880)
818 First, same address (1875)
Flynn Office Supply, 814 SW 1st (1875)
"Auditorium" Building (New Haven Hotel), 920, 924, 926, 928 SW 3rd (1875)
Harker Building, 824 SW 1st (1878)
Reingold Clock, 504 SW 4th (1900)

Area 3—Downtown Portland

Pioneer Post Office, 520 SW Morrison (1869-75)
First Presbyterian Church, 1200 SW Alder (1886-90)
First Congregational Church, 1126 SW Park (1889-90)
Calvary Presbyterian Church ("Old Church"), 1422 SW 11th (1882)
Plaza Blocks, bound by SW Salmon & Madison between 3rd & 4th, (1852)
Portland City Hall, 1220 SW 5th (1895)
Multnomah County Courthouse, 1021 SW 4th
University Club, 1225 SW 6th (1913)
Fruit and Flower Nursery, 1609 SW 12th (1928)
Equitable Building (Commonwealth Bldg.), 421 SW 6th (1948)
Visitor's Information Center, 1021 SW Front (1949)
First Baptist Church, 909 SW 11th (1894)
Central Library, 801 SW 10th (1913)
Portland Art Museum, SW Park & Madison (1932)
Sherlock Building, 309 SW 3rd (1894)
U.S. National Bank, 321 SW 6th (1916 and 1925)
Old Bank of California, SW 6th & Stark (1924)
Ladd Carriage House, 715 SW Columbia (1883)
Elks Temple, 614 SW 11th (1920)
Zion Lutheran Church, 1015 SW 18th (1950)
Masonic Temple, 1119 SW Park (1924)
Old First National Bank, 409 SW 5th (1915)
Olds and Kings Store (Exchange Building), 514 SW 6th (1903)
Benson Hotel, 309 SW Broadway (1913)
Church of St. Michael the Archangel, 1701 SW 4th (1901)
Paramount Theater, 1037 SW Broadway (1927)
First Unitarian Church, 1011 SW 12th (1924)
Farrell's Sycamore, NW corner of SW Main & SW Park intersection
Robert S. Howard residence, 1632 SW 12th (1893)
Burrell's Elm, 1111 SW 10th (1820's)
Zales Clock, 529 SW Broadway (1900)

Area 4—Southwest Portland, Residential

Morris Marks residence, 1501 SW Harrison (1882)
Governor Curry residence, 1020 SW Cheltenham Ct. (1865)
Milton W. Smith res., 305 SW Curry (1891-92)

Judge Wallace McCamant res., 1040 SW King (1899)
Nicholas-Lang res., 2030 SW Vista (1884-45)
Maegly res., 226 SW Kingston (1914)
A.R. Watzek res., 1061 SW Skyline Blvd. (1937)
Wilcox res., 931 SW King (1892)
Edwin J. Burke res., 1707 SW Hawthorne Terr. (1926)
Jennings Sutor res., 1100 SW Skyline Blvd. (1938)
Town Club, 2115 SW Salmon (1930)
L. Allen Lewis res., 2164 SW Park Pl. (1900)
Piggott's Castle, 2591 SW Buckingham Terr. (1892)
Thomas Mostyn res., 2660 SW Vista (1924)
Ascension Episcopal Chapel, 1823 SW Spring (1889)
The Diocesan Library, 2428 SW 19th (1911)
Cable House, 1903 SW Cable (1886)

Area 5—Northwest Portland

Blagen Block, 78 NW Couch (1888)
Merchants Hotel, 200 NW Davis (1885)
Gann Building, 1410 NW Johnson (1909)
U.S. Custom House, 220 NW 8th (1901)
Townhouses, 1705-19 NW Irving (1893)
Union Station, end of NW 6th (1890)
Blitz-Weinhard Brewery, 1133 W Burnside; Ice House
    (1906), Brew House (1907)
Cor-Berry Press, 1201 NW 17th (1906)
Temple Beth Israel, 1931 NW Flanders (1927)
I. Leeser Cohen res., 2343 NW Irving (1892)
Isom White res., 311 NW 20th (1905)
MacKenzie res., 615 NW 20th (1892)
Mills res., 733 NW 20th (1908-09)
W.B. Ayer res., 811 NW 19th (1904)
John F. Shea res., 1809 NW Johnson (1892)
Koehler res., 732 NW 19th (1905)
Pittock House, end of NW Monte Vista Terr. (1914)
St. Patrick's Church, 1639 NW 19th (1889)
T.B. Treviett house, 2347 NW Flanders (1891)
Bates-Seller House, 2381 NW Flanders (1891)
George F. Heusner res., 333 NW 20th (1897)
Ashley res., 2847 NW Westover Rd. (1913)
St. Mark's Episcopal Church, 1035 NW 21st (1925)
Three-story building, 105 NW 3rd (1883)

Area 6—North Portland

St. Johns City Hall, 7214 N. Philadelphia (1907)

West Hall, Portland University, 5000 N. Willamette Blvd. (1891)
St. Johns Bridge, N. Syracuse & Philadelphia (1931)
Mock res., 4333 N. Willamette Blvd. (1894)
David Cole res., 1411 N. McClellan (1885)
Town Hall, 3425 N. Montana (1907)
Interstate Firehouse, 5340 N. Interstate (1910)

Area 7—Northeast Portland

Freiwald res., 1810 NE 15th (1906)
Central Lutheran Church, 2104 NE Hancock (1950)
Yee res., 202 NE Graham (1894)
Sauter res., 4314 NE Mississippi (1898)
Union Pacific Smokestack, U.P. Railroad yards at N. Interstate (1887)
Peninsula Park, 6400 N. Albina & N. Portland Blvd. (1913)

An example of French Renaissance architecture, the Pittock Mansion with its fine marbles, cast bronze, hardwoods, and classic plaster work is owned by the City of Portland, the centerpiece of Pittock Acres Park.

Area 8—Southeast Portland

St. Johns Episcopal Church, 8039 SE Grand
Buehner res., 5511 SE Hawthorne Blvd. (1905-06)
Reed College, 3203 SE Woodstock Blvd.; Eliot Hall (1912),
   Old Dorm Block (1912)
Third Church Christ Scientist, 1722 SE Madison (1926)
Kendall Homestead, 3908 SE Taggart (1894)
W.F. Burrell house, 2610 SE Hawthorne Blvd. (1902)
Robert D. Inman res., 3040 SE Grand (1890)
Portland Community Music Center, 3350 SE Francis
   (1912)
Judge W.D. Fenton res., 626 SE 16th (1892)
Johnson Clock, 6680 SE Milwaukie Blvd. (1880)

Recycling

Portland Recycling Team, Inc., accepts bottles, cans, bundled newspapers, scrap paper, and aluminum at these locations seven days a week around the clock:
Southwest—1207 SW Montgomery (228-6760) and Lewis
   and Clark College on Huddleston Road.
Southeast—2209 SE Hawthorne Blvd. (235-1218)
North—2003 N. Portland Blvd. (289-7925)
A center in northwest Portland at 1801 NW Irving (228-5375) is open from 8:30 a.m.-5 p.m. daily.

Stairs of Portland

Climbing stairs is good exercise and Portlanders thrive on exercise. If climbing stairs is your idea of keeping in shape, Portland has plenty of steps and not all in the stairwells of tall buildings.

The latest inventory lists 152 outdoor stairways maintained by the City of Portland. Built to take pedestrians, like mountain goats, up or down from one street to another, the stairways range from the old wooden ones to brand new concrete flights.

One, at SW Spring and Vista, is broad, terraced and landscaped and is more like a park than a staircase.

Probably the longest is a series of stairs, with connecting walkways, from SW Kelly at Custer down to SW Taylors Ferry Rd. (almost to Macadam).

One of the most picturesque and steepest starts at the

foot of SW Broadway Dr. and rises to SW Hoffman. To those who know it, it's the "SW Elevator Street" stairway and if Portland were San Francisco, it would no doubt be a street.

One of the newest and nicest connects N. Greeley with N. Going, which is beneath it. This stairway is most likely to serve bus passengers going from one street to the other.

Singles

Parents Without Partners, 7011 SE Wilshire, Milwaukie (235-9317)
Servetus-For Single Adults, 5314 NE Irving (282-2221). Dances, card parties, cocktail parties, lectures, camping.

Private Clubs

In addition to many fraternal clubs and other affiliates of national organizations, these private clubs, some of them having reciprocal guest arrangements with other clubs across the country, are probably Portland's most established:
Aero Club of Oregon, 804 SW Taylor (227-7400). Social, athletic.
Arlington Club, 811 SW Salmon (223-4141). Exclusive, men.
Multnomah Athletic Club, 1849 SW Salmon (223-6251).
Racquet Club, 1853 SW Highland Rd. (223-5460).
The Town Club, 2115 SW Salmon (226-4084). Exclusive, women.
University Club, 1225 SW 6th (223-6237).

Emergency Stops

A good clean restroom can be a blessing. Portland has several, scattered in sometimes unmarked spots around the city. In addition to large department stores and restaurants, there are other emergency stops in the downtown area. Try:
The Oregon Historical Society (use the Broadway entrance, the extremely well-kept facilities are on the basement level just inside the door).

The Main Branch, Multnomah County Library (this is an excellent place to brush your teeth before visiting any one of the many dentists who practice in the Medical-Dental Building just across the street on SW 11th).

City Hall (use the 5th Ave. level entrance; restrooms are located to the left of the council chambers).

County Courthouse

Lownsdale Square (for the men's restroom)

Chapman Square (for the women's facilities)

SW 6th & Yamhill is marked with a green iron cage affair. Although it may seem spooky to descend below the city streets, these city-maintained restrooms are clean and well-kept.

Couch Street Galleries, Old Town, has nonsexist restroom which is clean.

TELEPHONE NUMBERS

A Handy Guide to Services

AAA (American Automobile Assn.) 227-7777
Abandoned Vehicles, 248-4478
Air Pollution Control, 229-5359
Alcoholics Anonymous, 223-8569
Alcohol-Drug Abuse Counseling, 248-3653
Animal Bites, 666-3711
Animals (dead and injured), 666-3711
Animal Emergency Center, 666-4565
Attorney (city), 248-4047
Attorney General, 229-5725
Auto Impound, 248-5670
Auto and Driver's Licenses
East, 238-8201
North, 283-5716

Better Business Bureau, 226-3981
Birth & Death Certificates, 229-5710
Burning Permits, 232-1383

Career Training Program, 248-4141

Carpool, 227-7665
Chamber of Commerce, 228-9411
City Club of Portland, 228-7231
City Hall, 248-3511
City
Council Agendas, 248-4085
Hearing Notifications, 248-4082
Civic Auditorium, 226-2876
Civic Stadium, 248-4345
Civil Service Board, 248-4352
Community Use of School Bldgs. (to reserve a room), 234-3392
Congressmen
Robert B. Duncan, 221-2123
Les AuCoin, 221-2901
Consumer Product Safety Commission, 221-3056
Consumer Protection, 229-5522
County Courthouse, 248-3511
Crime Prevention Bureau, 248-4126

Defensive Driving Course, 248-4360

Dental Health Info., 248-3711

DEQ, 229-5696

Detoxification Center, 248-3770

Dial-A-Daily Bible Reading 24 hours, 283-3020

Dial-A-Devotion, 235-2233

Dial-A-Diet Lunch, 232-1311 or 233-5743

Dial-A-Meditation, 284-8555

Dial-A-Miracle, 234-1443

Dial-A-Prayer, 234-7436

Dial-A-Story, 246-2010

Dial For Courage, 224-1143

Dog Licenses, 666-3711

Draft Board, 234-3361

Draft & Military Counseling Center, 224-9307

Drug Enforcement Adm., 221-3371

Education & School Superintendent, 255-1841

Environmental Quality (Dept. of), 229-5696

Environmental Protection, 221-3250

Environmental Sanitation, 248-3400

Environmental Services, 248-5000

Exposition Center & Fair, 285-7756

FBI, 224-4181

FCC, 221-3097

Federal Information Center, 221-2222

Fire Department Info., 232-8135

Fire Hydrant Damage, 248-4874

Fire Alarms, 232-2111

Fish & Wildlife Info., 229-5403

Food & Drug Adm., 221-2031

Food Stamps, 238-8424

Forest Service, 221-2877

Gray Line Tours, 226-6755

Highway Travel Info., 285-1631

Historical Society of Oregon, 222-1741

Immigration Office, 221-2271

Indian Affairs, 234-3361

Information Desk (Portland), 248-4583

Internal Revenue, 221-3960

Land Management, 234-3361

Lawyer Referral Service, 229-5788

Legal Aid, 224-4086

Library—Multnomah Co., 223-7201

Marriage Licenses, 248-3027

Mayor's Office, 248-4120

Medical Services Info., 248-3816

Medicare, 221-3381

Methadone Treatment, 229-5089

Memorial Coliseum, 235-8771

Mental Health Adm., 248-5002

Metropolitan Arts Com., 248-4569

Metropolitan Human Relations Com., 248-4187

Motor Vehicles Inspection (DEQ), 229-6235

Multnomah Kennel Club Track, 665-2191

National Park Service, 234-3361

Neighborhood Assns.:
Northwest, 223-3331
North, 248-4524
Northeast, 248-4575
Southeast Uplift, 233-6236
Southwest, 248-4592

Noise Complaints, 248-4465

Nuisance, 248-4458

Older Worker Manpower System, 248-4752

Ordinances, 248-4082

Oregon State Bar Assn., 229-5788

Oregon Symphony Orchestra, 228-1353

Outside-In, 223-4121

Park Bureau
General Info., 248-3580
Recreational Programs, 248-4315

Parking Patrol, 248-4134

Parking Tickets, 248-3809

Passport Info., 248-3800

Peace Corps, 221-2411

Physician Referral, 222-9977

Pittock Mansion, 248-4469

Police
Chief's Office, 248-5600
Emergency, 760-6911
General Info., 248-5730

Population Research & Census, 229-3922

Port of Portland, 233-8331

Portland Beautification Assn., 244-0055

Portland International Raceway, 285-6635

Portland Opera Assn., 248-4741

Public Defender, 248-3880

Rape Relief Hotline, 235-5333

Recreation (Specialized), 248-4328

Recycling Switchboard, 229-5555

Secret Service, 221-2162

Senators
Mark O. Hatfield, 221-3386
Bob Packwood, 233-4471

Senior Citizen Programs, 248-4752

Sewers (back-up), 248-4109

Sheriff's Dept., 248-3265

Sidewalk Repair, 248-4111

Sierra Club, 222-1963

Small Business Adm., 221-3441

Small Claims Info., 248-3022

Social Security, 221-3381

Social Services-Tri County, 222-5555

Sport Fishing Info., 229-5403

State Patrol, 653-3132

State Division of Continuing Education, 229-4800

Streets
Lighting, 248-4403

Repair & cleaning, 248-4109

Tax Information
Federal, 221-3960
State, 229-5833
Property (Mult. Co.), 248-3326
Taxicabs
Broadway, 227-1234
Radio, 227-1212
Rose City, 282-7707
Tel-Med, 248-9855
Time, 229-1212
Traffic Tickets, 248-3233
Traffic Signs (248-4295)
Travel Info. (Salem), 1-378-6309
Tri-Met
Route schedule 233-3511
Lost and found, 238-4855
Urban Indian Program, 248-4562

VD Clinic, 248-3414
VD Info., 248-3700
Veterans Adm., 221-2431
Veterans Hospital, 222-9221
Vital Statistics, 248-3745
Volunteer Bureau, 222-1355
Voters Registration, 248-3720

Water Repair, 248-4874
Weather, 255-6660
Weeds & debris, 248-4458

Youth Opportunity, 229-6972
Youth Services, 248-4356

Zoning & Planning, 248-4250
Zoo, 226-1561

INDEX

Airlines, 88
Airplane rides, 32, 146
Airports, 32, 87-8, 146
Amusement parks, 192
Annual events, 181-5
Antiques, 59-60, 67, 74, 176
Archery, 113
Art exhibits, 21, 101, 155-62
Aurora, 174, 186
Auto racing, 112, 141, 181

Babysitting, 193
Bakeries, 39, 61-2, 80, 165
Ballet, 154
Banks, 17, 24, 35, 40, 159
Baseball, 111-13
Basketball, 111-14, 184
Benjamin Franklin Plaza and Museum, 17, 104
Benson drinking fountains, 159
Bicycling, 100, 114-18
Billiards, 122
Bird watching, 8, 114
Blue Lake Park, 115-16, 179
Boating, 118-22, 181
Bonneville Dam, 119, 137, 171
Book stores, 20, 60-1, 63, 74, 77, 156, 167
Bowling, 122, 141
Boxing, 122
Bridge, 122-3
Bridges (see also by name)
    Portland, 1, 24, 102, 114
    covered, 177-9
Broadway Bridge, 1, 114
Burnside Bridge, 1, 106, 114

Busses
    airport, 88
    inter-city, 93
    local: see Tri-Met
Bybee-Howell House, 26

Calligraphy, 62, 63
Camassia Natural Area, 11
Camping, 98-9, 100, 120, 173, 179
Canoeing, 120-2
Canned goods, 80
Champoeg, 173-4, 186
Chapman Square, 104, 159
Chess, 123
Children's activities, 153-4, 189-93
Children's Museum, 18, 154, 191
Chinatown, 24, 108-9
Churches and synagogues, 105, 162, 201-4
City Hall (Portland), 17-18, 104-5, 201
Civic Auditorium, 16, 51, 53, 103-4, 158, 159
Civic Stadium, 111, 207
Clackamas River, 11, 120, 123, 125, 138, 186
Clackamette Park, 11
Clothing, furnishings
    children, 62, 74-6
    men, 68, 74-6
    women, 71, 74-5, 176
    resale and used, 74-5, 77-9
Clubs, social, 129-32, 201, 202, 205
Coast, 99, 100, 124-5, 130-1, 138, 163-8

Colleges and universities *(see also by name)*, 52, 54-5, 122, 176, 196
Columbia River, 2, 10, 25, 42, 49, 98, 117-22, 163-4, 182, 184
    Gorge, 116, 133-7, 170-2, 179
Community centers *(see also individual sports)*, 153-4
Cooking supplies, 62
Copying service, 62
Council Crest Park, 4, 116, 161
Courthouse, Multnomah County, 18, 104, 201
Courts, 18, 22
Crafts, 63, 154-7
Curling, 123

Dabney State Park, 121, 179
Dairies, 39, 190
Dance, 154, 157
David Campbell Memorial Fountain, 161
Delta Park, 113, 128, 141
Department stores, 72, 78, 104
Dog racing, 112, 182
Dolls, 66, 68

Eastmoreland Park, 10, 127
Electric supplies, 77
Elk Fountain, 104, 158, 159, 162
Exposition Center, 208

Fabrics, 64, 79
Fairs, 184, 191, 208
Fareless Square, 89-91, 105
Federal Park, 104, 159
Fire Bureau, 39
    alarms, 208
First National Bank (and Tower), 17, 35, 104, 160
Fish and Wildlife Dept., Oregon, 113, 114, 126
Fish markets, 64, 166, 167
Fishing
    salmon, 28, 117, 118, 182, 184
    trout, 99, 100, 123, 125-6, 139, 180
    ocean, 124-5
    warm water, 120, 123, 179, 193
    shellfish, 126
Florists, 64-5, 85
Football, 127, 184
Forecourt Fountain, 16, 103, 159
Forest Park, 3, 8, 134-5
Ft. Vancouver, 24-5, 27, 192

Fountains *(see also by name)*, 16, 24, 103, 104, 108, 157-62
Fremont Bridge, 1

Gardens, 5-10, 68-9, 85, 114, 190
General merchandise, 77-9
Georgia-Pacific Building, 17, 19, 104, 158, 160
Gift shops, 65-6
Golf, 4, 12, 100, 127-32, 146, 184
Gourmet shops, 66
Grotto, The, 10
Gymnastics, 132

Handball, 132
Handicapped, services for, 154, 168, 194-5
Hawthorne Bridge, 1, 102, 114
Hiking, 132-8
Horse racing, 112, 181
Horseback riding, 100, 138-9
Hotels *(see also Resorts)*, 95-7
Houseboats, 25, 26, 119
Hoyt Arboretum, 8, 12, 134-5
Hunting, 113, 139

Ice hockey, 111, 140
Ice skating, 73, 139-40
Imports, 67, 108

Jantzen Beach Center, 73, 111, 140
Japanese Garden, 5, 7
Jewelry, 67-8, 156, 176
Jogging, 103, 140
John's Landing, 26

Kelley Point Park, 10
Kennels, 67

Ladybug Theatre, 192
Lake Oswego, 1, 26-7, 129, 188
Landmarks, historic, 199-204
Laurelhurst Park, 10, 140, 150, 154
Lawn bowling, 141
Leather goods, 79
Lee Kelly Sculpture Park, 103, 160
Lewis and Clark College, 54-5, 122, 148-9, 196
Lewis and Clark Column, 5
Lewis and Clark Exposition, 5, 14, 158
Lewis and Clark State Park, 179
Libraries, 20, 21-2, 102-3, 159, 175
Library, Multnomah County, 21-2, 52, 102-3, 159, 201

Limousines, 93
Lloyd Center, 36, 73, 140, 162
Lovejoy Fountain, 16, 103, 160
Lownsdale Square, 104, 159

Macleay Park, 8, 134-5
Macramé, 63
Maps, 30, 90, 102, 107, 120, 122, 134, 168, 170, 177, 178
Marquam Bridge, 1, 122
Martial arts, 141
Mary S. Young State Park, 117, 121
Marylhurst Education Center, 148, 196
Masonic Temple, 103, 201
McLoughlin House, 28
Meat markets, 174
Medical services, 208, 209
Memorial Coliseum, 37, 111-12, 162
Milwaukie, 1, 121
Miniatures, 68
Mobile home parks, 98-9
Mocks Crest, 5
Models
    airplanes, 10, 141
    boats, 10, 141
    trains, 193
Mohawk Galleries, 104, 160
Morrison Bridge, 1, 102, 114
Motorcycles, 141
Motion pictures, 21, 52-3
Mt. Bachelor, 100, 143-4
Mt. Hood, 3, 133, 137, 142-7, 168-73
Mt. Scott, 4
Mt. Tabor Park, 4, 117, 149, 150, 162
Mountains (see also by name), 3, 100, 132-4, 137-8, 142-7, 168-73
Multnomah Falls, 116, 135, 171
Multnomah Kennel Club, 112, 182, 209
Museum Art School, 21, 196
Museums (see also by name), 12-17, 19-21, 24-6, 28, 154, 168, 173-4, 190, 191
Music
    classical, 53-4, 154, 157, 182, 183, 192
    popular, 54-8, 183
    recorded, 79, 103

Names, geographic, 185-9
Neighborhoods, 29, 30
New Oregon Singers, 54
Newspapers (see also by name), 38, 41, 181, 197-8

Night clubs, lounges, 56, 96-8
Northwest Film Study Center, 21, 52
Nurseries (plants), 68-9
Nuts, 82

OMSI, see Oregon Museum of Science and Industry
O'Bryant Square, 160
Old Church, The, 19, 75, 103, 201
Old Town, 23-4, 72, 90, 105-9, 155, 157, 161
Oneonta Gorge, 135-7, 171, 188
Oregon (name), 188
Oregon, Battleship, 106, 108, 161
Oregon City, 1, 26-8, 119, 121
Oregon Historical Society (and Center), 19-20, 26, 74, 192
Oregon Humane Society, 37
Oregon Journal, 38, 41, 118, 126, 139, 181, 197
Oregon Junior Symphony, 54
Oregon Museum of Science and Industry (OMSI), 12-13, 123, 184, 190, 197
Oregon Symphony Orchestra, 16, 53,
Oregon Times, 41, 198
Oregon Trail, 87
Oregonian, 38, 56, 123, 126, 162, 181, 197
Oswego Lake, 27, 188
Oxbow Park, 98-9, 121

Painting, 21, 154-62
Parking, 88, 96, 98, 105-8
Parks (see also by name)
    city, 3-16, 54, 101-4, 113-22, 127-9, 134-5, 147-62
    county, 98, 115-16, 179
    state, 27, 99, 117, 135-8, 171, 173, 179
    Vancouver, Wash., 109
Parks and Recreation, Bureau of (see also activities and parks by name), 54, 153-4, 209
Pharmacies, 69, 78, 194
Photography, 156-7
Pioneer Courthouse (and post office), 22-3, 102, 104, 201
Pittock Acres Park, 3, 15, 134
Pittock Mansion, 3, 8, 15-16, 185, 202
Pittock Wildlife Sanctuary, 8, 114
Planetarium, 13

Plumbing supplies, 77
Police, 24, 105
    emergency, 209
Police Museum, 24, 108
Port of Portland, 29-32, 87, 209
Portland (city)
    population, 2
    history, 2, 105, 157
Portland Air Base, 38
Portland Art Museum, 21-2, 52, 102, 155, 158, 160, 192, 201
Portland Center, 16, 101-3, 160
Portland Chamber of Commerce, 104, 120, 181
Portland Chamber Orchestra, 55
Portland Civic Theatre, 51
Portland Community College, 119, 141, 142, 148, 157, 182, 196
Portland Heights, 4, 116
Portland International Airport, 32, 87, 97, 116, 158, 162
Portland Junior Symphony, 192
Portland Mall, 89
Portland Meadows, 112, 129
Portland Opera Association, 16, 53, 209
Portland Speedway, 112
Portland Sports Arena, 112
Portland State University, 9, 55, 101-4, 141, 148, 157, 160, 166, 194, 196
Portland Symphonic Choir, 55
Ports O'Call Village, 32, 73
Post offices, 22, 39
Produce, 80-5, 176
Publications, 197-8

Racquetball, 132
Radio stations, 36, 58
Railroads, 87, 89, 100
Records, phonograph, 79, 103
Recycling, 204
Reed College, 9, 55, 122, 148, 157, 162, 196, 204
Resorts, 99-100, 139, 144, 165-70
Restrooms, 104, 109, 205
Restaurants
    Portland area, 17, 36, 41-50, 95-8, 101, 103, 105-8, 116, 128
    non-Portland, 100, 166-7, 175
    children's, 37, 189
Rhododendron Test Gardens, 9, 114, 190
Rocky Butte, 4
Rodeos, 182-4

Roller skating, 142, 192
Rose Festival, 6, 117, 183
Rose Test Gardens, International, 3, 5, 6, 161
Ross Island Bridge, 1
Rowing, 122
Rummage sales, 74

Sacajawea, 5, 161, 188
St. John's Bridge, 1, 114, 115, 121, 203
St. John's Episcopal Church, 19, 204
Sailing, 120
Salem, 2, 131-2, 138, 175-7, 191
Sandy River, 120-1, 123, 137, 179
Saturday Market, 106-8, 182
Sauvie Island, 20, 25-6, 114, 117-21, 123-4, 139, 187-9, 193
Schools (see also by name), 195-7
Scoggins Valley Park, 179-80
Scuba diving, 142
Sculpture, 5, 6, 21, 24, 101, 103, 104, 154-62
Sculpture Mall, 21, 103, 158
Sellwood Bridge, 1, 114, 121
Senior citizens, 78, 91, 117, 149, 194-5, 198, 209
Shemanski Fountain, 103, 161
Shoes, 74-7
Shopping, 32, 36, 59-85, 104-9, 133-4, 142, 145, 197
Shopping centers, 71-3
Sightseeing, 1-40, 101-9, 115-17, 120-2
Silversmiths, 103
Singles, 205
Skateboarding, 142
Skidmore Fountain, 24, 106, 157, 161, 162
Skiing, 100, 142-6, 182
Sky diving, 146
Sled dog racing, 146, 181
Snowmobiling, 147
Soccer, 111-12, 147
Softball, 113
South Park Blocks, 9, 101-4, 160-1
Spinning, 63-4
Sporting goods, 69, 77-8, 133-4, 142-5
Squash, 132
Stairways, 204-5
Standard Plaza, 105, 161
Stationery, 70
Steel Bridge, 1, 114

Surfboarding, 166
Surplus stores, 77-9
Swan Island, 5, 31
Swimming
    Portland area, 96-8, 116, 147-9
    153, 179-80
    non-Portland, 99-100, 139, 163

Tailors, 70
Taverns, 56-8
Taxicabs, 93, 210
Television stations, 36, 58, 181
Tennis, 97, 99-100, 139, 149-51
Terminals (port), 31
Theater, 51-3, 101, 106, 154, 157,
    181, 183, 192
Thrift shops, 74-5, 80, 145, 176
Timberline Lodge, 100, 142-4, 170
Tourist information, 104, 181, 210
Tours
    airplane, 32
    auto, 29, 163-79
    bicycle, 115-18
    bird watching, 114
    boat, 118-22
    bus, 32-33
    coast, 163-8
    fishing, 124, 126
    guided, 29-40
    hiking and climbing, 132-8
    industrial, 34-40
    rail, 100
    senior citizen, 195
    ski, 146
    walking, 33, 101-9
Toys, 70, 77, 106
Track and field, 112, 140-1
Trailer parks, 98
Transportation, 32, 87-93, 195
Trap and skeet shooting, 139
Tri-Met, 29, 89-93, 105, 210
Tryon Creek State Park, 11, 27, 117,
    139
Tualatin (Valley and River), 4, 121,
    189

Union Station, 89, 187, 202
U.S. National Bank, 24, 40, 161, 201
University of Oregon Health Sci-
    ences Center, 116, 196
University of Portland, 5, 55, 196

Vancouver, Wash., 24-5, 27, 93, 109,
    150
Viewpoints, 3-5
Visitors Information Center, 104,
    120, 201

Wallpaper, 77
Washington Park, 3, 5-7, 14, 54,
    113, 141, 149, 150, 161
Washington Square, 73, 98
Water skiing, 120
Water Tower, The, 26, 73
Weather, 198-9, 210
Weaving, 63-4, 154, 156-7
West Linn, 27-8, 121
Western Forestry Center, 12, 14-15,
    129, 190
Westmoreland Park, 10, 126, 140,
    141, 150
Willamette Falls, 28, 119
Willamette National Cemetery, 4
Willamette River, 1, 5, 10, 11, 26, 28,
    29-32, 49, 105, 117-23, 182, 184,
    189
Willamette Stone, 193
Willamette University, 176
Willamette Valley, 173-9
Willamette Week, 41, 113, 181, 197
Wine, 66
Wrestling, 112, 122

YMCA, 132, 142, 148
YWCA, 103, 142, 148, 149

Zoo, 12, 13-14, 129, 190
Zoo Railway, 5, 7, 14, 184

Downtown Location Guide

1. Portland State University
2. Oregon Historical Center
3. Portland Art Museum
4. Old Church
5. First Congregational Church
6. First Unitarian Church
7. First Baptist Church
8. Central Library
9. First Presbyterian Church
10. O'Bryant Square
11. Benson Hotel
12. U.S. Customs House
13. Import Plaza
14. Portland Police Museum
15. Skidmore Fountain
16. Central Police Station
17. Battleship Oregon Mast
18. Meier & Frank
19. Pioneer Courthouse
20. Tri-Met Customer Service
21. Chamber of Commerce
22. Central Bus Depot
23. Hilton Hotel
24. Trailways Bus Depot
25. Multnomah County Courthouse
26. Lownsdale Square
27. Chapman Square
28. City Hall Annex
29. City Hall
30. Federal Courthouse
31. Federal Plaza
32. Civic Auditorium
33. Forecourt Fountain